From Plaintiff

to

Defendant

By: Peter Kirisits and Jo Anne Gleason

Copyright © 2016 Peter Kirisits and Jo Anne Gleason

Published by: Dolittle&Seymore

All rights reserved. In accordance with U.S. Copyright Act of 1976, the scanning, uploading, and electronic sharing of any part of this book without permission of the publisher constitute unlawful piracy and theft of the author's intellectual property. No part of this book may be reproduced in any form by any electronic or mechanical means (including photocopying, recording or information storage and retrieval) without permission in writing from the author or publisher. Thank you for your support of the author's rights.

ISBN: 0692779493
ISBN-13: 9780692779491

DISCLAIMER

This book is designed to provide information on court cases in Buffalo, New York. This information is provided and sold with the knowledge that the publisher and author do not offer any legal or medical advice. In the case of a need for any such expertise, consult with the appropriate professional. This book does not contain all information available on the subject. This book has not been created to be specific to any individual's or organization's situation or needs. Every effort has been made to make this book as accurate as possible. However, there may be typographical and/or content errors. Therefore, this book should serve only as a general guide and not as the ultimate source of subject information. This book contains information that might be dated and is intended only to educate and entertain. The author and publisher shall have no liability or responsibility to any person or entity regarding any loss or damage incurred, or alleged to have incurred, directly or indirectly, by the information contained in this book. You hereby agree to be bound by this disclaimer or you may return this book within the guarantee time period for a full refund. In the interest of full disclosure, this book contains affiliate links that might pay the author or publisher a commission upon any purchase from the company. While the author and publisher take no responsibility for the business practices of these companies and or the performance of any product or service, the author or publisher has used the product or service and makes a recommendation in good faith based on that experience.

TABLE OF CONTENTS

DISCLAIMER iii
STATEMENT OF CLIENT RIGHTS viii
INTRODUCTION 10
CAST OF CHARACTERS 12
THE RULES OF ENDING THE CHESS GAME 15
PART I 16
CHAPTER 1: YEARNING FOR A GOOD CHESS GAME 17
CHAPTER 2: THE MOVES 21
CHAPTER 3: PAWNING AROUND 23
CHAPTER 4: CONNECT THE ROOKS 32
CHAPTER 5: THE CHESSMEN RULE THE DAY AFTER 43
CHAPTER 6: SEPTEMBER 30, 2000 51
CHAPTER 7: THE CHESS GAME BEGINS 53
CHAPTER 8: WOW, CHECKMATE 63
CHAPTER 9: WHAT IS A DEPOSITION? 65
PART II 74
CHAPTER 10: THAT DAY IN SEPTEMBER 2001 77
CHAPTER 11: THE ROOK MAKES A MOVE 79
CHAPTER 12: THE SECOND ROOK MAKES A MOVE 80
CHAPTER 13: CONTROL YOUR CENTER 85
CHAPTER 14: THE CHESS GAME HAS BEGUN 88
CHAPTER 15: EN PASSANT CAPTURE YOUR PAWN 93
CHAPTER 16: KEEP YOUR KING CLOSE AND YOUR QUEEN CLOSER 95
CHAPTER 17: THE JUDGE FROM THE LABOR FINE 101

CHAPTER 18: THE BISHOP	116
CHAPTER 19: TWO KINGS	122
CHAPTER 20: 202 WEEKS	126
CHAPTER 21: 341 HEARING	131
CHAPTER 22: PROMOTION	134
PART III	137
CHAPTER 23: BYE BYE BUFFALO	138
CHAPTER 24: A SALE	142
CHAPTER 25: WELCOME HOME TO FLORIDA	146
CHAPTER 26: THE SIXTH ADMENDMENT	149
CHAPTER 27: BUT WAIT HERE COMES 2008	151
CHAPTER 28: CHESS GAME STALLS	156
CHAPTER 29: CASTLING THE ROOK AND THE KING	165
CHAPTER 30: CHESS CHEAT - MAKE SURE YOU HAVE THE SUN IN YOUR OPPONENTS EYES AT ALL TIMES	172
CHAPTER 31: CHESS MIDDLEGAME	176
CHAPTER 32: CLASH OF THE KINGS	182
CHAPTER 33: THE CHESS MEETING - AN INVITE-ONLY EVENT	188
CHAPTER 34: A DEAL IS CUT TO ELEMIATE THE ROOKS ON THE CHESSBOARD	205
CHAPTER 35: INVISIBLE CHESS MOVES	216
CHAPTER 36: CHANGES IN THE LEADERSHIP OF THE GAME	223
CHAPTER 37: 3 QUEENS TRICK	225
CHAPTER 38: HERE COMES ONE OF THE CHEATS	245
CHAPTER 39: BAD CONDUCT OF THE PLAYERS IN THE CHESSGAME	248
PART IV	254
CHAPTER 40: 937 WEEKS	255

CHAPTER 41: HOW MANY PIECES ARE ON THE CHESS BOARD? 262

CHAPTER 42: CHESS GAME TIME CLOCK 278

CHAPTER 43: 5,028 DAYS. 291

CHAPTER 44: CHESS CHEATS AMONG FRIENDS 333

CHAPTER 45: THE QUEEN 339

ABOUT THE AUTHORS 358

STATEMENT OF CLIENT RIGHTS

1.   You are entitled to be treated with courtesy by your attorney, other attorneys, and their staff.

2.   You are entitled to have your attorney handle your matter competently and diligently in accordance with the highest standards of the profession. If you do not feel he or she is handling your case competently, you have the right to fire the attorney, although you may need a court approval.

3.   You are entitled to expect your attorney uses professional judgment and loyalty, and is uncompromised by conflicts of interest.

4.   You are entitled to be charged reasonable fees and expenses by your attorney and to have your attorney explain within a reasonable time how the funds are spent. If you do not agree with how the funds were spent, you have the right contest them and to go to arbitration. You are entitled to request and receive a written itemized bill from your attorney at reasonable intervals.

5.   You are entitled to have your questions and concerns answered promptly by your attorney.

6.   You are entitled to be kept informed about the status of your case, and have your attorney promptly respond to your reasonable requests, including your requests for copies of paperwork regarding the matter.

7.   You are entitled to have your legitimate objectives respected by your attorney. The decision to settle a case is your decision, not your attorneys. Your attorney should tell the truth to the court and the judge.

8.   You have the right to privacy in your communications with your attorney. Your communications with your attorney are confidential and he or she may not discuss the case with anyone, except in limited circumstances, without your approval.

9. You have the right to have your attorney conduct him or herself ethically and in accordance with his or her state's Rules of Professional Conduct.

10. You may not be refused representation on the basis of race, creed, color, religion, sex, sexual orientation, age, national origin, or disability.

In other words, your attorney should use good manners, be professional and Do No Harm.

INTRODUCTION

Before we start this book, Peter and I would like to make this written statement: this is not a story about all attorneys by any means. We disagree with the well-known analogy that all attorneys are slovenly, speak with forked tongues, and slide away from the issue at hand, looking out for themselves first versus their client.

We have met great attorneys along this trek who have been forthright and honest. Unfortunately, they were not familiar with the corporation or insurance laws that pertained to our case. They did, however, encourage us to get the truth out to the public. As one attorney told us: "its guys like this that make it bad for the rest of us."

Ours is a different story. Documented by many years of hard work, it includes paperwork pulled from attorney's files and documents pulled from Supreme Court and Federal Court in New York State. This is a true chain of events that happened to us in Buffalo, New York, involving narcissistic personalities of not only our insurance company, by also by their attorneys, law clerks, judges, and even our own attorneys.

You see, we had a fire at our business. This book is an accounting from August 28, 2000, until September 3, 2014. We started out as plaintiffs suing an insurance company with very deep pockets, and we ended up being defendants.

What had started as a reluctant diary turned into a full-fledged true story, fueled by massive amounts of paperwork - including court transcripts collected from the court system in New York State, plaintiff's and defendant's attorney's letters to each other, and an accounting of meetings with our insurance company.

This was a case in black and white that ended up in a murky mess. It was a case of immense greed, jealousy, and hate. Our lives were stolen from us while the insurance company and their attorneys held us in a vice that would squeeze us tighter and tighter as the years went by, through the greed of a few.

We endured sickness, sudden loss of the vitality of life, the loss of two businesses, the loss of our home, the loss of self-esteem, and fourteen years of our lives.

What the insurance company wanted was for us to go away, to not fight back. We did fight back and we did it to prove to everyone who may follow in our path that something is very wrong in this country. We did it with the inspiration of those that had come before us in the courtrooms in this country, who had given up the battle for lack of what else to do. We are here to explain to you what to look for, to pay attention to your instincts, and to stop, look, and listen. If you feel the chill, something is probably happening and you better be prepared.

CAST OF CHARACTERS

It is suggested that the reader use the following list as a reference while reading this book. Peter and I made this list make this as easy as possible for the reader to keep track of the individuals in our passage of time over our fourteen years involvement with our lawsuit.

New York Unified Court System (also called E-Court) - A way of tracking a case filed in New York State by using the internet.

New York State Labor Department (also referred to as the Labor Department) - Determines what a company can or cannot do according to the business laws in New York State. In our case, they levied a fine for our business not having a time clock, even though we did have it installed in the entrance to the building.

Mary Coleman - Worked for the New York State Labor Department.

United States Department of Labor (also referred to as Department of Labor) - Administers federal labor laws and levied the labor fine against us.

Michael Fitzgerald - Assistant Director for Federal Department of Labor.

Ginger Schroder - Attorney who represented us for the labor fine.

Peerless Insurance Company (also referred to as Peerless Insurance) - A subsidiary of Liberty Mutual Insurance Company and registered as a foreign company in New York State. They are located in Keene, New Hampshire.

Michael Christenson - CEO of Peerless Insurance.

Gary Gable Fire Adjusters - Comprised of Gary Gable and John Shera, the fire adjusters for Peerless Insurance.

National Fire Adjusters - Hired by Evans Services to determine damage from the fire.

Meserendino & Celiker - Michael Drumm, attorney for the firm, represented us and filed suit against Peerless Insurance.

Brown & Chiari - Michael Drumm's second law firm.

<u>Demarie & Schoenborn</u> - Daniel Schoenborn was the attorney who replaced Michael Drumm in representing us in the suit against Peerless Insurance.

<u>Brown & Lustig</u> - Law firm for Peerless Insurances, including attorneys Maurice Sykes, David Lustig, and Katherine Fijal.

<u>Hurwitz & Fine</u> - Law firm, including attorney Katherine Fijal, which represented Peerless Insurance.

<u>New York State Grievance Board (also called the Grievance Board)</u> - A board made of other attorneys that hears grievances filed against an attorney.

<u>John Elmore</u> - Attorney for Brown & Chiari, who sits on the Grievance Board.

<u>New York State Bar Association</u> - An association of and for attorneys licensed to practice in New York.

<u>Thomas Burton</u> - The attorney Michael Drumm contacted about our case without our knowledge. Apparently Michael Drumm was looking for a new attorney after eight years to take our case over for him.

<u>Honorable Magistrate Hugh Scott</u> - Federal Court judge who presided over the case involving our labor fine.

<u>Honorable John Curtin</u> - Federal Court judge who presided over the case involving our labor fine.

<u>Honorable Joseph Glownia</u> - New York State Supreme Court judge.

<u>Kurt Sajda</u> - Judge Glownia's law clerk.

<u>Dennis Gaughan</u> - Bankruptcy attorney.

<u>Goldstein, Bulan, & Chiari</u> - Law firm where attorney Harold Bulan worked, who was the Trustee for the bankruptcy.

<u>Honorable Deborah Chimes</u> - New York State Supreme Court judge.

<u>Jill Toholski</u> - Law Clerk for Judge Chimes.

<u>Honorable James Dillon</u> - New York State Supreme Court judge.

Keybank, MBNA, Citibank - Companies who held the loans for our businesses tools of trade.

Honorable Michael Kaplan - Federal judge who presided over Jo Anne Gleason's personal bankruptcy.

Honorable Carl Bucki - Federal judge who presided over Peter's personal bankruptcy.

Morris Horwitz - Bankruptcy attorney who represented Harold Bulan.

Shawna Hunt - Massage Therapist.

Lisa Plaster - Massage Therapist.

Pamela Ashmall - Massage Therapist.

Plaintiff to Defendant

THE RULES OF ENDING THE CHESS GAME

The game of chess is perhaps 23,000 years old. In the 15th century, it became popular in Europe as a game of intellect. The game can last for hours, and even days. Occasionally, the game does not end with a winner, but a draw.

The five reasons for a game ending in a draw are:

1. A player reaches a stalemate: his king is not in check and he does not have another legal move.

2. The players agree to the draw.

3. There are not enough pieces on the board.

4. A player declares a draw if the exact position is repeated three times.

5. Fifty consecutive moves have been played where neither player has moved a pawn or captured a piece.

The game is over if the opponent cheats, lies, or uses other unethical behavior including collusion, manipulation, or deceit. While some of the unethical moves may be judged as acceptable, to it is considered cheating. Unethical behavior should be reported to the proper people involved in the chess game. This in itself, however, can be a problem if the people you are to report to are the same ones that are behaving unethically.

PART I

CHAPTER 1: YEARNING FOR A GOOD CHESS GAME

It all started as the winter of '99 was slipping and sliding to an end in Buffalo, New York. The area is known for its brutal winters, massive amounts of snow, low temperatures, and cold dark days. Buffalo experienced less than the normal snowfall (about seventy inches) and had been blessed with less than a foot of snow over the last four months.

Looking forward to spring, we knew we would possibly get a few more inches of snow coming from the Western Plains or a Nor'easter, as we liked to call them. Lake Erie was still frozen, so we were not out of the woods yet. It was still cold with below freezing temperatures but we, my partner Peter and I, were ecstatic - the sun appeared to be staying out longer and we were excited about moving our new business in a month to a new location. We owned two businesses: Evans Services Industries, or Evans Services for short, a company that Peter would continue to run for me, and Advanced Massage Therapy, with offices in Orchard Park and Williamsville, New York.

Evans Services consisted of outsourcing for the major automobile companies, including Ford, General Motors, Chrysler, and Chevrolet. We also outsourced to Moldtec, Kodak, and numerous other firms all contracted through American National Rubber, which is also located in Buffalo. The work consisted of working with rubber and foam, punching out parts from long sheets of material. It was messy at times, but it was light manual labor.

Most of the employees were moms who wanted to work while their kids were in school, and needed flexible hours so they could work around their family's schedule. Often they would take portable small jobs home after they left for the day, and bring it back the following workday.

Whether the work was done on Evans Services' property or at home, every job would involve time studies to make sure a fair wage was being paid to each worker after the hourly rate. To do this, two individuals would take a particular part and put it on their own table. A stopwatch would be used to determine how long it would take each person to complete the job. This was the study, and in essence, the employee's hourly rate was paid plus whatever the time the specific job required.

As winter turned into spring, a woman dressed in a muted plaid skirt and coordinated jacket came into Peter's soon to be vacated office in Angola. When he looked up from his desk he greeted her with surprise, wondering if she was lost and had stopped for directions. She identified herself as Mary Coleman, a representative from the New York State Labor Department. Overpowering the small office, she stated she wanted to see all the work records and time cards of all the people who worked on the property. Peter told her we were in the process of moving to a newly bought building and all the records she was looking for were on a computer at Advanced Massage Therapy in Orchard Park.

As the conversation continued, Ms. Coleman appeared to be angry and apparently wanted to know about the business. As the work was explained to her She was told the employees made their own hours, working as subcontractors. Ms. Coleman stated the business needed time worksheets or a time clock. Peter said he would inform the workforce immediately that they would be moving to a time clock system, and that Ms. Coleman could go to Advanced Massage Therapy in Orchard Park to check out anything she wanted. She was told that all of the records for Evans Services were on the computer, with the hard copies in the filing cabinet there.

Half turning, then coming back to look at Peter, Ms. Coleman stated, "You need a work at home permit for the people that want to assemble product but, I'm not going to let you have one!"
Peter, aghast at the behavior of Ms. Coleman, asked her, "Why not?"

Ignoring him, Ms. Coleman stalked out of the building got in her car and drove away.

A few days later Ms. Coleman, identifying herself by her name only, dressed in the same type of attire, came into Advanced Massage Therapy. She appeared disgruntled, angry at the whole situation. I received her in the front office and led her to the back room where the computer for Evans Services was located, waiting for its new home. It seemed like something was bothering her. It didn't help that she had to dodge between pieces of massage equipment, since Advanced Massage Therapy had also recently obtained a new space and would be expanding soon into the center of Orchard Park, New York

After looking at the computer, Ms. Coleman turned to me and indicated for us to go into my massage room. In my mind, I questioned her attitude and wondered what she was looking for. Whatever she wanted to know I was ready and willing to answer. As we sat down, we used a massage table as a desk. She started to ask me about Advanced Massage Therapy. Looking at her somewhat amused, not because of her attitude but also because of her mission, I answered, "Are you here to look at the computer and hard copy paperwork for Evans or to ask me about Advanced Massage Therapy?"

Without waiting for an answer, I offered her the information about the massage business and about myself in particular. I assured her that Advanced Massage Therapy was not an employee based business.

I told her, "I have one person that works the front desk, I pay everything I'm required by the state and federal government to pay that employee, and the rest is a sub-contractor business. It is a business by appointment, the massage therapist gets paid by the service."

She exclaimed "This is serious business!"

I looked at her in confusion, wondering what her true motive was thinking she might be looking to collect her pension and retire. I stated to her, "You need a massage you are a wreck." Continuing I said "If you want to go back to the room to look through the computer feel free to do so."

Getting up from the chairs surrounding the massage table and leaving the room, I turned left to go to the computer to show her where everything was located. Ms. Coleman turned right and stalked out through the front office and out the front door, never bothering to look at any paperwork, I never saw her again.

Ms. Coleman wasn't done with us. Despite never making an appointment with Peter, me, or any of the worker's, she started showing up at the worker's homes unannounced. In a panic one of the workers called Peter, stating: "She followed me to my house and chased me from my driveway to the door! She asked me if my kids helped me at home with my work, she wrote something down on a piece of paper and left!"

Peter told the worker that everything was alright and to calm down. After hanging up the phone he proceeded to tell me what happened. I replied, "Are you kidding? When I worked for L'eggs my kids helped me all the time. Once a week they would help me count the inventory or watch me work to make everything perfect in case there was an audit for the company. I never had an 'at home' work permit, neither did L'eggs. I would have known if it was against the law, trust me."

Oddly, it was all quiet from then on, with no more unannounced appearances from Ms. Coleman. She was finished with her assignment.

CHAPTER 2: THE MOVES

As winter faded away, new clean air became noticeable. Spring was bouncing into full view, the tulips along with the daffodils beginning to arrive along the entranceway of the Orchard Park Country Club. Soon, I, as well as Peter, would be moving into a new space within the four corners of quaint Orchard Park.

We had a lot of moves in the past year, having bought a new house, a building for Evans Services, and a new renovated location for Advanced Massage Therapy. The long negotiations had been completed for Evans Services. Peter had then taken charge of the renovations to make the interior of the building brand new. It now had a formal receiving area for new customers, a lunch room, conference room, Peter's office and 3,000 feet of working area A time clock replaced the work sheets and was placed in the hallway next to the entrance of the building.

The move for Evans Service had been a considerable feat with all of the heavy equipment used for the outsourcing business. Desks, tables, benches, lunchroom necessities, computers, along with the usual paperwork to be used for the new building was also be moved.

We were grateful for a forklift to move the heavier items. The staff appeared delighted with the new ample space, now they were able to spread out and work comfortably.

A sense of accomplishment came over us. Not only had we renovated Evans Service but also Advanced Massage Therapy during the same period of the winter and spring of '99. We felt we would be doing some amazing things in the future: growing the two businesses, providing a workplace, and contributing to the community. We were happy, with no intention of going south fo owing the ever growing exodus out of

Buffalo.

April 2, 1999, was the day scheduled for the move of Advanced Massage Therapy. We would do the move over the weekend and be open for business the following Monday. Working throughout the weekend, we moved into the newly renovated space with a waiting room and a half wall with a shelf to comply with the new HIPAA law. Three massage rooms, two storage areas, and another very small massage room in case of overflow. We finished both Evans Service's and Advanced Massage Therapy's moves without missing any work from the respective companies. It was an accomplishment we were proud of and we looked forward to the new lives we had created for ourselves.

The following Monday, Peter received a letter from the United States Department of Labor addressed to Evans Services. He opened the letter to read a written statement instructing him to appear before the United States Department of Labor in Buffalo to answer questions. Peter did not seem to upset with the notice and informed me that he was well within his rights regarding the employment issues mentioned during his meeting with Ms. Coleman.

A few weeks later, on a somewhat rainy day, Peter arriving at the federal building located at Huron and Delaware Avenue in Buffalo. He parked the car and headed to the entrance of the building. As he proceeded through security, he checked the signage indicating the correct area for the Department of Labor. He then headed to the elevator for his meeting at the designated floor.

Arriving at the main reception area, the personnel directed him along a narrow hallway to a small room. He was instructed to make himself comfortable and was told someone would be in soon. Sitting down, he waited for the moment when he would find out what this was all about.

CHAPTER 3: PAWNING AROUND

Michael Fitzgerald, a small man with brown hair and an air of importance, swaggered into the small room accompanied by two women. They joined Peter at the conference table.

With no pleasantries, Fitzpatrick demanded, "Explain to us what you do and how you keep your records."

Recognizing the nature of the questioning, Peter thought that Ms. Coleman from the New York State Labor Board had informed the Federal Department of Labor whatever findings she had observed while talking to Peter or me. Peter proceeded to tell Mr. Fitzgerald the nature of Evan's Services, how the records were kept, payroll, workman's compensation, and taxes Fitzgerald stated, "You should have listened to the State. You are probably in violation of the United States wage and hourly labor law, give me $240,000 and I will go away!"

Amazed of the threat, without anyone having gone through the paperwork on the computer, the hard copies, or the time-clock that had been installed, Peter said, "You have just put me out of business, I don't have $240,000."

Mr. Fitzgerald replied, "It isn't our intention to put anyone out of business so this will be settled in court!"

Continuing with his chest filled with self-admiration, he spoke of a famous case, where the celebrities involved had paid over a million dollars in fines.

Without letting anyone else to get in a sentence, his chest continued to puff as if he were going to let his plumage of feathers burst through the room. "They want me in Washington, but I won't go," he stated, rising to his full stature, adding, "you better get a lawyer, this meeting is over!"

Peter stood up and looked down at him astounded. Mr. Fitzgerald turned with his entourage intact to leave the room. It was clear this was not a meeting to gather information but more of a one ended conversation.

As Peter drove back to the Orchard Park, he called me to discuss what had just happened. I asked, "Did anyone ever go over the records after you moved the computer and file cabinets to your new building?" Peter replied with a resounding "No."

I was shocked at the unprofessional behavior of Mary Coleman and. Fitzgerald. Clearly, they were not in favor of free enterprise of the small businessman. There was one statement of his I did agree with, which was that Peter needed to get an attorney and a good one. That afternoon Peter called his long standing attorney and made an appointment for the next day.

The following day, Peter went to see his attorney and friend, Michael Drumm. Peter had been one of Michael's first clients shortly after he had passed his bar exam. Knowing he was new at the law game, Peter had hired him for various undertakings over the years. Michael is an extremely neat man of average build, with a somewhat pointy, almost bird-like nose. Peter and Michael made small talk for a few minutes, after which Michael explained he was not versed in labor law and referred Peter to attorney Andy Fleming who was located in Hamburg, New York, a suburb of Buffalo.

That night at home, Peter and I discussed the state of our affairs including his meeting with Michael. I asked Peter, "Did he have any paperwork on his desk when you saw him?"

Looking at me, frustrated with the situation, Peter answered, "No, why?"

I replied saying, "I don't know. I have never seen such a neat attorney. When I was with you a couple of years ago and met him for the first time, everything in his office was so neat, so orderly, maybe he keeps his files in another room."

Peter responded, "He won a case for me before, also I referred a case to him and he won a couple of hundred thousand dollars."

I said, "Every attorney I have ever dealt with had paperwork and files everywhere! He has no visible paperwork or files where does he keep them?"

Peter, ignoring the question, responded, "Mike gave me the name of an attorney in Hamburg, you can go with me and meet him to see what your opinion is."

Within a few days we found ourselves in the offices of Attorney Andy Fleming, a tall, lean, affable man possibly in his early forties. Paperwork lined the wall of the room, telling me he was busy. Peter explained the meeting with Michael Fitzgerald at the Department of Labor. We agreed that Mr. Fleming would call Michael Fitzgerald and schedule a meeting to educate himself about the case. Peter felt cautious relief that the mess would end soon and everyone, including the employees, could move on with their lives.

A few days later, Mr. Fleming called Peter, telling him Michael Fitzgerald had refused to schedule a meeting for him to go over the paperwork. Mr. Fleming added, "This is not a warm and cozy case." Mr. Fitzgerald had told Mr. Fleming that Peter needed a more experienced attorney and strongly suggested the law firm Buchanan & Ingersoll, and specifically Attorney Ginger Schroder, who was the head of the Buffalo office.

Several days after this, Peter found himself in another attorney's office. Located in the downtown area of Buffalo, Peter once more rode the elevator to a well-appointed office. Sitting in the front greeting room, he waited for Ginger Schroder to enter the reception area. As she appeared through the doorway from her office, Peter notice she was of average height with reddish blonde hair. She was waving her hands in the air, brashly telling Peter that she, and she alone, was responsible for the success of this law office in Buffalo. Dumbfounded by the coarseness of all the boasting, Peter chose to bite the bullet and accept it. This was the third attorney within as many weeks.

Peter and Ms. Schroder discussed the issues involving the Department of Labor. Peter told her that a time clock had been installed after Ms. Coleman came to the business and that he had the hard copies of the time sheets. He also told her that no one had audited his records or seen his computer files, hard copy records, or inspected the presence of the time clock. Ms. Schroder informed Peter she would put a phone call into the office of Mr. Fitzgerald to discuss the problem without going to court.

As they stood up from the meeting, Ms. Schroder told Peter, "You need to bring me a cashier's check for $15,000 and bring Jo Anne Gleason when you bring it in."

When he got home after the meeting, Peter told me, "She wants you there when I bring the check in to her."

When I asked why, he told me, "Because you own the business remember?"

Once again things were not quite matching up. I said, "I think there is more going on than we are aware of. Let's just get this over with and continue to operate our business without too much more aggravation. Something smells peculiar, like a decomposed animal."

On April 22, 1999, a letter arrived from Ms. Schroder to Peter indicating she was pleased to offer her quality services at a reasonable rate. As mentioned at the previous meeting, the charge would be $15,000 up front and $200.00 per hour after that. We found this interesting since we had never been accused of anything other than the vague comments by Michael Fitzgerald.

On April 27, 1999, Peter had a meeting with Ms. Schroder to hand over the cashier's check. As ordered, I was also going. After canceling my afternoon massage appointments, we walked from Advanced Massage Therapy to Peter's car. Sitting down in the driver's seat, Peter handed me the check from our savings to be turned over to Ms. Schroder. Shoving it into my purse, we discussed the cold weather coming in from the west. The frigid air and the blowing wind, with the snow still that would remain on the ground until it got warmer, what had been a winter of little snow turned into one with cold air that lingering well into April.

Plaintiff to Defendant

Arriving at the offices of Buchannan & Ingersoll, we headed up the elevator. My shoulders felt cold from the relentless wind and torrid air. Soon I would be able to sit and press my back into the spindles of a chair to warm up.

As we entered the office, Ms. Schroder bounded out of her office and immediately converging on me as if on a mission. Exclaiming with disgust as she looked at me from head to toe, "You're wearing leather boots!" Oddly it did not stop there.

"You should be wearing boots like this!" she said. Taking this as a hint to look down, I looked down to see elastic or spandex cutting into the calves of both of Ms. Schroder's legs. Inwardly I smiled to myself, thinking "now that is not material you can wear socks with, and it looks cold and uncomfortable, especially in Buffalo."

Tilting her head, her somewhat red hair falling to the side, she peered at me, asking, "Do you have the check?"

I pulled the check out of my purse handing it to her. Without as much as a thank you she rushed into her office behind a large panel of doors.

Still standing in the large outer office, Peter and I sat down, and I implanted my spine along the back of a nearby chair. We looked at each other with amazement, wondering what the next move would be. A few minutes later, Ms. Schroder came back to the outer office with the following information: She would make a phone call to Mr. Fitzgerald, explain the issues, we were assured this matter would be taken care of without going to court.

She added that Michael Fitzgerald was a good friend and that they went out to dinner a couple of times a week.

We found this very odd since clearly they were on the opposite sides ... or were they? It was too late, the check had been given the deal had been made. All we could hope for would be fair representation.

As the days turned into weeks, Mr. Fitzgerald discovered we did not have $240,000. He had obviously gotten the wrong information about Peter's wealth. Mr. Fitzgerald then turned to American National Rubber, the supplier for Evans Services, for funds for his coffers.

Mr. Fitzgerald made an appointment to see Patrick Walsh, the Superintendent of the Buffalo division, in Cheektowaga, New York. Within a week, Peter received a call from Mr. Walsh. Mr. Fitzgerald had appeared early for his appointment with Mr. Walsh, pushed his way past the reception area, through the doors of the inner office of Mr. Walsh, with the same boorish narcissism he had exhibited with Peter.

Mr. Fitzgerald had taken over the room, declaring American National Rubber had violated the labor law over the wage and hour issue, and would be getting a $500,000 fine.

It looked like Mr. Fitzgerald had eyed bigger pockets than Peter's.

The scenario was getting crazier and loonier and had to be stopped. Michael Fitzgerald continued over the next few months, running all over Buffalo making threats to the local small businesses.

Days were now turning into weeks, then months of 1999, and nothing changed. If Mr. Fitzgerald's intent was to avoid putting businesses out of commission, he was failing miserably. All work had stopped, we were now dependent on our savings and Advanced Massage Therapy to fill the gap.

During the summer of '99, there were meetings scheduled by Michael Fitzgerald, included with Ms. Schroder, Peter, and Mr. Walsh. When the season turned into early fall, Michael Fitzgerald called another meeting for American National Rubber and Evans Services at the Department of Labor. Michael Fitzgerald sat at the head of the conference table, surrounded by the executives of National Rubber. Mr. Walsh attended with two attorneys for American National Rubber. Peter was there with Ms. Schroder representing Evans Services. The meeting started with the executives of American National Rubber and Peter explaining how their initial contact was made, the distributions of the various parts to Evans Services, the invoices, and the pay schedule.

As the meeting progressed through the afternoon, it became apparent to the parties present that Michael Fitzgerald was on a "seek and destroy mission."

He stated if the two companies did not pay him the money he wanted in fines, he would declare all cars that were using parts from American

Plaintiff to Defendant

National Rubber "Hot Items." They would then be taken off the highways throughout the country and then a trial will be scheduled!

One of the attorneys casually looked up from his paperwork located on the table and slowly interjected, "I love to go to trials." It must have clicked, Michael Fitzgerald that he had met his match. During an awkward suspension of time, all eyes were on Michael Fitzgerald for his next move. Perhaps feeling the pressure, Michael Fitzgerald stated he wanted another meeting, this time with the owner Thomas Maxwell American National Rubber present. That meeting never took place.

Late that fall, Peter received a phone call from Ms. Ginger Schroder stating the labor fine had been reduced to $50,000. It was to be paid at the rate of $500.00 a month, with an tag on of $5000.00 every six months until the fine was paid off. The document was being sent with a message from Michael Fitzgerald. "Tell those two to sign the documents or I will have them splashed all over the media for violation of child labor laws."

Apparently he was referring to Mary Coleman's habit of going on people's property and asking them if their children helped them do work at home. It did not take a whole lot of thought to figure out the New York State Labor Department, and likely Ms. Coleman, had informed the Department of Labor about locally owned companies operated by smal business owners.

We signed the document, agreed to the fine, and no longer had an income from American National Rubber.

It seemed odd, so soon after expanding Evans Services, putting renovations into both businesses, that one business was put to death. Once again it appeared too personal, and it had a rank smell.

American National Rubber paid their fine, and they closed their 63-year-old business putting close to 350 people out of work. Peter did not fare any better. Mr. Fitzgerald made Peter close his business down, putting another 60 people out of work in the already depressed area of Buffalo.

A small blip made the local newspaper about American National Rubber closing their doors. Nothing about Evans Services. It had been easy money for Michael Fitzgerald. Every dime he collected from fines stayed in the Western New York district for him to put in his war chest. Once again the community suffered, and people were starting to move out of the area for a better life.

Later that same week, Peter and I met up with some friends at a local event. It was good to see everyone and return to as less stressful atmosphere. One of our friends, a union organizer and his wife, walked up to us with the usual pleasantries. It was wonderful to see them until he stated, "You know if you were union none of this would have happened to you." It appeared to be said with knowledge of something we were not in the know about. His wife whacked his arm as we looked at him with bewilderment, followed by an uncomfortable silence between the four of us. We left the event soon after.

Getting into the car, I had questions for Peter. "Why can't you be a non-union business in this town? You used to be a union representative, what is the big deal with unions and whether to belong to one or not?"

Peter looked at me, shrugging his shoulders, "I don't know what any of this is really about." It was starting to get creepy and would get much worse.

Christmas of '99 was stressful but we managed to get through it with family and close friends without too much of a problem. The house was decorated, presents bought, and family came over to enjoy the warm glow of the fireplace. The grandchildren, now tired from the festivities, were moving a little slower than the previous few days. We enjoyed the time, having a delicious dinner. As early evening approached, my grandchildren became sleepier and ready for their own beds. A lot of preparation by everyone was over too soon.

The next day we knew it was time for reflection on the past year. We weighed the pros and cons. Should we stay in Buffalo or follow the exodus of people leaving for other parts of the country? We decided to stay, building the business without American National Rubber.

Peter also had many contacts throughout the community and he was well liked by his allies. Advanced Massage Therapy was doing well, but it was still new and it did not make enough to pay our mortgage, taxes, utilities, food, and the labor fine.

What we had in our favor was great customers. Peter also had a business idea. The prospects were bright and we had the energy to overcome this problem of the distressing labor fine.

As 1999 faded into 2000, the Department of Labor, under Michael Fitzgerald's helm, issued a swath of labor fines across his district. He won more than he lost. However, a few companies and a country club shoved him back. That year he also proudly made a statement that made the local newspaper. His statement made the media. Over six million dollars in labor fines had been collected throughout the United States. Out of the six million, four million of that had been made in his district of New York. It appeared lopsided in Buffalo, but as usual no one questioned him or his cronies until one local company sued him, and his henchmen, in the Western New York District. They won over one million dollars.

We applauded the bravery of this company from afar, too hesitant ourselves to say anything. We had to stay mum. I hadn't gotten over the union official who had said to me his fist in the air, "I'll get you if it's the last thing I do." Known as a bully with a self-absorbing attitude in the community, I laughed back then but, there seemed to be an undercurrent of evil going on in the area, that I had not seen in years.

Michael Fitzgerald ordered Evans Services to be closed and the building to be sold. We put it up for sale but didn't have much luck. It appeared to be harder to sell that empty building then what we were expecting. We were paying the mortgage on the building when we could, in addition paying the fine at $500 a month. It was a ridiculous assumption by Mr. Fitzgerald. How were you supposed to pay a fine if you did not have a business or job to go too? It was silly and stupid at the same time.

CHAPTER 4: CONNECT THE ROOKS

The year 2000 came to be much ado about nothing. It had been predicted that on New Year's Eve computers would fail, the stock market would go belly up, and doomsday would happen with the turning to a new century. We stayed home on New Year's Eve to enjoy some relaxation. As the evening commenced, Peter stated he was going to reopen Evans Service despite what Michael Fitzgerald said. He even had a new name. It would be called Pro-Pak.

The New Year rang in with new meaning - of growth, prosperity, and success. Michael Fitzgerald had refused to allow Evans Service continue as a clean and pack industry, so Peter started off the year by making sales calls to market a new business of outsourcing. It was basically the same business, but with a slight twist. It would involve more machinery to handle the jobs that were expected to come our way. The birth of Pro-Pak had begun.

In January of 2000, Peter made a sales call to one of the companies that had been a previous customer of his. The issues with the fine was discussed. While they did not have any jobs for Peter, he was given a contact, and a referral to Colad, a company that made binders, office equipment, supplies, graphics, and other things. Over the next couple of months there were meetings that resulted in the first job for Pro-Pak: assembling product for various companies. Soon other companies came calling and more contracts were signed, resulting in more jobs. Peter was back, making as much money as before the fine.

Pro-Pak was the only business in the area with a fleet of trucks, a long history of excellent work, pristine evaluations by various companies, and a reputation for a fast turn-around in the outsourcing business. We were back in business, ab e again to build a reputation for excellent work. At this rate the fine would be paid off in two years. By January of 2000, we had paid $15,000 of the fine, with only $35,000 remaining.

By April of 2000, the business growing every day. Peter was invited to submit a bid to fulfill a job through Colad for Walmart to collate 3-ring notebooks, folders, and spiral notebooks, which were to be assembled and then shrink wrapped and put in display boxes. The product was being used as a test market for a back to school fall promotion. The colors of the product were bright and sassy. They were rich hues of cherry red, bumble bee yellow, electric blue, emerald green, and eggplant purple. It would be a huge job taking most of the summer.

In order to secure the contract, shrink wrap machines, carton sealers, and another conveyor belt had to be bought, or leased with an option to buy. We went to KeyBank, a business friendly bank located along the main street in the Village of Orchard Park. Sitting at the desk with the gentleman in charge of business loans, it was suggested we lease the equipment with the option to buy it for $1.00 when the lease ran out in three years. Signing the lease, the equipment would be delivered within ten days and we would be ready to go. As we left the loan office. Peter called Colad and informed them he had secured the machinery. They replied, "Good because your bid was the lowest, and we have just sealed the deal with Walmart."

We had to do more to prepare for this job. We had quickly to renovate the building to handle the machinery. Peter called on the contracting firm Wagner Brothers, who had worked on our home and Advanced Massage Therapy the previous spring and early summer.

Peter, renewed in his spirit, stated, "We need a renovation quick. A big job is coming my way, so I have to build a mezzanine to handle the workload, reinforce the floor over the main office adjacent, to serve as a third work area if there is an overflow."

He also added that we needed outside, along the adjacent loading dock, four more docks to accommodate deliveries coming and going. Attached to this area would be a storage space located inside the building for added storage. This would ease the pickup and delivery system into a fast-paced zone.

The renovation was completed on schedule in June and was ready for the first delivery. The staff would pick up the pallets loaded with the various items still loose, putting them in a designated spot to be broken down into separate areas. There they would be rebuilt into a "back-to-school promotion" to be used in a few stores throughout the country.

The constant rush of deliveries had different deadlines set to coincide with the wide array of dates the kids had to be back to school for the New Year. The joy among the employees, and in Peter, was infectious and good to observe. We were back and reclaiming our lives.

While Peter was running his business, I was running mine. I did not get a chance to go to his business often, and I had no reason too, as I owned the building not the business. Pro-Pak was all Peter's. I had enough to keep my hands full with the two locations for massage in Orchard Park and Williamsville. If I did go to Peter's business, it was to help with cleaning the lunchroom and offices.

The staff would often give Peter "boss jabs" - sneaking in a few shots about the fine. He took it in good nature, dashing about to make sure everything was going smoothly. Usually there was another smaller job going on at the same time as the Wal-Mart job.

Within weeks it was decided by Peter that two shifts, seven days a week, was needed to keep up with the demand. I would come on the weekends and do my part to help keep everything clean.

One day, an employee turned on the radio to a local station while he worked. One-by-one, employees started singing as they went from one job to the next. It was a fun place to work - except for the plastic wrap used to seal the cartons of product being shipped out.

When the product was ready to be wrapped for shipment, the staff used hand-held dispensers. The tape would come off the rollers and gobs of stickiness adhered to everything but the cartons. Sticking to clothes, hands, and shoes was bad, but the worst was the hair.

Peter, knowing this was costing more in time lost along with the wasted tape, ordered an automatic box sealer to be put on the conveyer belt along with stronger tape. It was a relief to everyone that worked with the tape. Now the boxes would slide along the conveyer to the end, an employee would seal the top and the bottom at once, then it was off to the forklift to whisk it away to the loading dock. A second forklift would be brought in to repeat the scenario. Finding this to be faster and cheaper, Peter would go into his office to make notes. This small bit of information would result in still lower bids to be placed for Walmart or any other company in the future.

The Wal-Mart job took six weeks' total, finishing at the end of July. The last day, after shipping off some product, I was on the upper floor deck of Pro-Pak sweeping up loose clippings of paper. As I looked through the large window towards Route 20, a car slowly passed by the front of the building. I found this unusual because the 18 Mile Creek Bridge, less than a mile away, was closed due to repairs over the summer.

A man was sitting in the driver's seat leaning towards the passenger window shaking his fist and yelling. As I leaned towards the window to get a clear view of the person shaking his fist, I thought I recognized him from years ago. He gunned the petal of the car and it quickly lurched forward and peeled away for parts unknown. "That's weird," I thought, before going back to my broom and wishing it could fly.

Late that same day, the last of the semi-trucks had pulled out from one of the loading docks. Not only had Pro-Pak met its goal but it had gotten the job done early. It looked as though we had already secured the job for the following year as well. All the suppliers were happy. Very happy.

As July turned into late August, the summer was reaching an end. People wanted time off to spend with their families, leaving a skeleton crew to continue cleaning up the excess paper product, paint the floors, and break down the boxes to be returned to Colad. There were more jobs coming in the next day and whomever wanted to work could. It was that easy.

We had also planned to take some time off, as we were taking a family vacation to the United Kingdom, including Scotland and Ireland. The scheduled date for departure was August 30, 2000. It was a welcome relief for both of us. We had been working for the past seven years to make up for lost time in both of our lives.

Two days before we were to leave on vacation, Peter went to Pro-Pak to finish up his paperwork. My first appointment was in Williamsville at 9:00 a.m. with two more finishing up at 12:00 p.m. The rest of the day would be spent in Orchard Park, filled with massage appointments until late that evening when one of my regulars would be coming in at 8:00 p.m.

As the last client left, I reached for my phone to check the messages. One was from Peter asking me if I wanted to meet for lunch at Friday's in Blasdell. Returning the call, I asked him if he was already there.

He said, "No I'm at Don's. He is going to check the building and get the mail out of the letterbox in front of Pro-Pak while we are gone."

Good, I thought, as the bridge on Route 20 was still closed so not much traffic would be passing while we were in the UK. We just needed someone to watch the building and get the mail in case the staff forgot. We had a security system on the building during the off hours, so Don would check that too.

Peter said, "By the time I leave Don's house and you leave Williamsville, we should get there about the same time."

I headed out to the parking lot, hopping into my beloved 1974 Volkswagen. Peter had bought it for me on a whim three years before, at the end of summer. It needed a ton of work and had spent the winter of '97 and Spring of '98 in a car repair shop. Many parts had been replaced, including the canvas top, which was now black with white piping as trim. It had red and black plaid seats, and was newly painted cherry red. That previous year, for my birthday and Christmas, Peter surprised me with gangster white wall tires. I thought the car was the bomb. I guess I was a late bloomer making up for lost time.

Heading towards the thruway, it was a beautiful day. The sun was brilliant coming across the entrance of the road to take me to Blasdell. Splashes of the sun's rays bounced through the trees of mixed pine and maple as I drove to my lunch date.

Passing the main line connecting the thruway to the city of Buffalo, a cluster of life size buffalo cast in bronze were clustered on the small hill. Smiling to myself, thinking it was good to be from Buffalo, "The City of Good Neighbors."

Suddenly my cell phone rang, bouncing me back to the present. Picking it up, I heard a voice say, "Is this Jo Anne Gleason?"

"Yes," I responded, not recognizing the voice.

"This is the Hamburg Police Department. Your building is on fire!"

Laughing I responded, "Who is this? I haven't lived in Hamburg for years!"

The voice countered, "Is this Jo Anne Gleason?"

Still not getting it I asked, "How did you get my number?" followed by, "this better not be some joke coming out of Hamburg, this number is not given out to anyone!"

Suddenly I realized the person on the other end was in fact the Hamburg Police, and he was fed up with me. He said, "You own a building on Southwestern Blvd in Lakeview, New York. It's on fire!"

It hit me like a ton of bricks, shocking my system, and the echo of his last words pounded in my head.

He said again, "Your building is on fire!"

I had forgotten I owned it at all.

When Peter bought it, he had put the building in in my name in case something happened to him. Bringing me back to reality, I told the caller I was on the thruway coming back from Williamsville and would be at the scene right after calling Peter. Hanging up from the phone call, I looked at the time. It was 12:24 p.m.

Hastily calling Peter, who had just pulled into Friday's parking lot, I heard "Hello" in a cheerful voice.

I yelled, "Peter, your building is on fire!"

He responded, "Cut it out, that is not funny! I just left Don's house to give him an extra set of keys to Pro-Pak while he was still home. I'm going back to the shop right after lunch to finish paperwork."

Once again I shouted through the phone, "The Hamburg Police just called and your building is on fire, I'm driving out there now, you better meet me, joke or no joke!"

I continuing along the thruway as fast as the Volks would go, until reaching the Camp Road exit in Hamburg, hoping to get to Lakeview faster. I made a quick left turn onto Southwestern Boulevard. It would be a straight run to get to Pro-Pak.

What I saw was traumatizing. White billows of smoke intermingled with angry black shades of soot filtering around it, reaching high into the beautiful sky above.

Arriving at the scene, I parked the car on the side of the road opposite the building. Along the side of the building were multiple fire trucks, with water spurting from the hoses into the flames coming from the left side of the first floor. More water was being hosed onto the same side of the second floor.

As I got out of the car I saw Don, our insurance agent whom Peter had just left. Walking along the side of the road, looking from Don to the building then back again until I reached him, he started pointing to the right side of the building.

Don said, "Peter is over there talking to the police and the firemen."

Looking down on the same side of the street, I saw Peter distraught with worry. Don and I walked to the group to join in on the conversation. One of the firemen told us the fire investigators and police were already in the building. Someone asked what the time was.

"One o'clock," a policeman said as he walked across the street to the front of the building.

I thought to myself, "if I got the call only about 45 minutes ago how bad could it be?"

Don, Peter, and I looked at each other with disbelief. What would cause this to happen? The shop had been cleaned up from the debris of the Walmart job, the floor painted and all the repairs from the massive job had just taken place. A new delivery was to come in the next day, and to be completed with a 24-hour turn around before being sent back to the supplier.

The stench of the black smoke filled the air, soot now landing on cars, firemen, police, and us. A man of apparent authority walked towards the three of us. Introducing himself as a detective for the police force, he indicating to Peter, "Will you come with me to my car?"

As they sat down in the front seat, Peter proceeded to tell him the chain of events he had performed that morning, leading up to the impromptu lunch date with me and including my phone call back to him informing him of the fire.

The conversation was finished and I was called to the police car. Getting in the front seat, the detective seemed okay. Not the warmest of persons, but he seemed interested.

The detective said, "Please explain to me how you found out about the fire."

Referring back to the phone call with the Hamburg Police dispatcher, I told him I thought someone was joking with me from Hamburg. We looked into each other's eyes as I told him what I recalled. It was an odd moment and nothing more was said other than, "You can go now."

I got out of the car to rejoin Don and Peter. We stood, watched, waited, with the air now heavily permeated with smoke. Soot kept falling from the sky. It was getting hotter and hotter, the day now in full swing with the sun beating down on us.

A fireman approached Peter asking him to move one of the delivery trucks away from the loading dock, so they could quench the hot spots. He then asked, "By the way, what is on the second floor that won't burn out?"

Peter had no idea, while I announced, "I bet it is the polyester plaid lime green leisure suits I wanted to save."

Laughing, shaking his head, the fireman proclaimed, "Now that is worth saving!"

Suddenly, we heard a loud thump coming from inside the building. The ceiling had caved in where the leisure suits had been stored, falling on the shoulder of one of the woman firefighters. The joke was over and thankfully she did not have to be transported to the hospital for care. She was able to continue her dangerous job.

As the afternoon progressed, it was nearing 3:00 p.m., the hottest part of the day. The fire was under control, the firemen hustling in and out of the building and surveying the grounds. It was an education for us to see the precision they used, without a break, to reach the core of the blaze and keep on it until it was defeated.

Peter noticed the sweat coming from one of the policeman's brow standing close to us. Asking if he was alright, he replied he was hot and thirsty. Peter told him he had a refrigerator in the front right hand side of the office. The policeman disappeared into the building, and within a few seconds he came out, his arms filled with bottles of water and passing it out to whomever wanted it. I reached for a bottle to share with Peter. Drinking it in, tasting the ice cold water swish around our dehydrated throats, we had no idea how parched we were.

Looking at his watch, the policeman informed us it was nearing 4:00 p.m. The once raging fire had now turned into a black smoldering, stinky frump with sporadic licks of fire giving its last gasps of wrath. The policeman, who had been with us for the entire afternoon, encouraged us to leave and get something to eat at one of the local restaurants. "I'll be here when you get back, it's going to take a while to make sure this thing is out," he said

Hungry without an appetite, we got into Peter's car and headed to the West End Hotel, a local restaurant in Hamburg. It would be a quiet place this time of the day. Maybe if we got away from the current scene we could absorb what had just happened to us.

Arriving at the restaurant filthy with soot stuck in our hair, eyes, and clothes, we headed to the respective restrooms to clean up. Soon after, we met in the hallway and ventured into one of the smaller rooms. Sitting down at a table, we were exhausted from the past four hours.

Within minutes a waitress came to the table holding two glasses of water. Setting them on the table, she inquired, "What happened to you?"

We explained we had just had a fire at our business, now under control, so we stopped in to get something to drink and a light meal. It was then we learned a local drugstore in Eden, New York, had also caught fire at approximately the same time. Peter and I looked at each other overwhelmed, thinking this had been a very strange day in Western New York. Little did we know how many strange days would be in our future, extending for a very long time.

The heightened emotions of disbelief, sadness, confusion, and shock had tilted to our systems in less than eight hours. We picked at our food, bringing our forks to our mouths, pausing and setting the forks down on the plates again, not knowing what to do next. We drank what seemed to be gallons of unsweetened ice tea that was brought to us by the kind waitress, as we sat on the old fashioned chairs without saying much of anything. Tears came to our eyes as we sat and quietly discussed what to do with this mess. Soon, without asking, the waitress brought us to-go boxes and told us how sorry she was to hear we had the same troubles as the drugstore.

I had called Advanced Massage Therapy earlier in the afternoon to cancel all appointments until later that night. As we left the restaurant, I called again to cancel my long standing appointment for that evening.

It looked like we would be at Pro-Pak until well after office hours. As we drove to Peter's business, the cleanup had been initiated by the firemen and Envior-Care, a service used for flood, fire, and smoke damage. Watching them board up the windows and secure the building, a few police had remained on the premises.

Getting out of the car, we walked to the group. One of the police turned and stated, "This has been a terrible day for us, there was a fire at a drugstore in Eden, and we have been stretched pretty thin, trying to take care of them at the same time. It started about the same time as yours, lucky for you both businesses were only a couple of miles apart."

We agreed, thankful for the dedicated fire volunteers in our community

The investigation by the police and the fire department had been progressing throughout the afternoon. As we continued to stand in front of Pro-Pak, an investigator walked from the building to us, handing Peter the orange reel that held the battery charger supplying the electric to the forklift.

The investigator said to us, "Do not throw this away or replace it, this is how the fire started."

He invited us into the building to see the exact spot where the reel had been lying on the floor. As we approached the area, we saw the concrete scarred black from the sparks coming from a short in the reel.

As we turned and walked to the front of the building, I pointed my finger, saying, "Look the time clock stopped at 12:25 p.m."

The investigator made a note in his book and we continued to the front door reaching the outside of the building and fresh air.

Within a few minutes, the police and fire department left the scene. Don had left a few hours earlier and had told Peter he would call the fire adjuster for our insurance company, Peerless Insurance. As the scene was winding down, Don called Peter to tell him to he would be meeting with an associate of Gary Gable Fire Adjusters the next morning at the shop. There was only one option: the building had to be repaired and cleaned, and opened as soon as possible. New jobs had been bid on and they were being delivered the next day, with a twenty-day turnaround.

Peter and Peerless Insurance Company had to move fast to get things done. Thankfully he had increased the insurance coverage to comply with the new machinery and business interruption insurance.

Dusk was turning into night. At 8:30 p.m. that evening we finally prepared to go home. Hot, tired, and the ongoing soot adhering to our clothes and cars, we were also coughing up a brownish liquid junk. It was time to go. Getting into our respective cars covered with the same ash, we drove the fifteen miles to our home, take a shower and try and calm down from the miserable chain of events that August 28, 2000.

After cleaning up, we sat on the couch each with a glass of wine. We discussed what to do about the upcoming vacation with Peter's niece that was scheduled to start in two days. We wondered if we should take a hit on the reservations for the airlines and hotels and just stay home.

We decided to wait until Peter talked to Gary Gable Fire Adjusters, who represented Peerless Insurance, the next morning. We were convinced he would provide some insight to the situation. Exhausted from the drama of that day, we snuggled with our dogs Minnie, a Lhasa Apso, and Chanel, a Bichon. Sensing something was wrong they clung to us the rest of the night.

CHAPTER 5: THE CHESSMEN RULE THE DAY AFTER

We both slept restless throughout the night, tossing and turning, waiting for daylight. Looking at the clock it read 6:00 a.m. Tossing aside the covers, we were witness to another beautiful day in Buffalo. As I walked into the kitchen, looking out the large window, the sun filtered through the trees surrounding our home. Peter joined me soon after to enjoy the first cup of coffee of the day, followed by a discussion of where each of us would be throughout the morning and afternoon.

Peter was to meet with the fire adjuster from Peerless Insurance at 11:00 a.m. at our building to discuss the situation of the burnt machinery and the startup of the business, while I had a morning filled with massage appointments. As I left the house, I mentioned to Peter I would be checking the appointment book and possibly moving people around a bit to try and meet up with the fire adjuster from Gary Gable Adjusters. I felt it was important since I owned the building.

Peter stayed at the house making phone calls to his suppliers explaining what had happened. Leaving the house early for his 11:00 a.m. appointment, he drove the fifteen miles to his business. As he pulled into the driveway of the now pretty sad looking building, puffs of soot rose from the wheels of his truck. Surveying the front of the building, the windows were covered with plywood, the grounds were worse for wear and the bushes in front had been smashed down, probably by the fire equipment. It would all be an easy fix, he thought. We would be back in business within two weeks.

Walking to the front entrance, the door was covered with plywood with a small peephole left open for the office key unlock it. It easily unlocked, and Peter stepped into the vestibule that thankfully had not been damaged.

The interior of the building contained four rooms on the right hand side. Walking into the first room, there was a large picture window overlooking Southwestern Boulevard. This is where the businesses "Girl Friday" was located. She was a jack of all trades: answering phones, taking deliveries, monitoring the invoices, preparing payroll and assigning jobs. There was no damage to this room, other than leftover smoke.

Leaving this area, Peter ventured into the second room. It did not have a window. This room was occupied by Peter, who ran the day-to-day operations of outsourcing the jobs, bidding on future jobs and doing the schematics of bidding down to a fraction of a cent to get the job secured. There was no damage to this room.

Peter turned, leaving the room to enter the third. This room was used as a conference room and had a large window overlooking the woods. It was used by key employees who needed information for various jobs. It contained the usual office equipment including filing cabinets, office supplies and a large conference table with the ability to seat 10 to 12 people.

As he walked through the door into the room, Peter noticed a large cinderblock sitting in the middle of the table with broken glass scattered on the table and the floor. The broken window had been boarded up by Envior-Care the previous evening. Knowing we did not have any cinderblock on the property, he stood and stared at the scene wondering how and when this window had been broken. Had it been done before, during or after the fire?

Thinking for a minute, Peter pondered the events of the previous day, including a visit by a strange man a few hours before the fire. The visit occurred when Peter had been cleaning up remnants of the Walmart job. Peter had been outside in back of the building trying to charge the 4,000 lb. forklift that was stuck in mud from the rain the night before. The battery to the forklift had run out of juice just as he was doing the final cleanup. Peter plugged in an extension cord to give it a charge.

Hearing footsteps coming from inside the building, a man dressed in jeans and a white tee shirt, with a tiparillo cigarette clenched between his teeth, approached the back door.

"How did you get in here?" Peter asked.

Disregarding the question, the man asked, "Got any pallets here?"

Peter replied he did not, as the pallets the man had seen belong to the supplier. Peter added, "If you give me your phone number, I'll see if they want them. If they don't you can have them."

The man responded, "Nah that's OK" as he flicked his ashes on the cement floor.

Peter barked, "Hey you can't smoke in here. We have product that has to be worked through yet."

The man spun around, and walked through the warehouse to the open loading dock facing Southwestern Boulevard.

Peter's mind came back to the present as he walked the hallway to the lunchroom. It held the refrigerator, microwave, tables, chairs and a radio. There was no damage to this room. Proceeding from the lunchroom, Peter made another right to enter the storage room which held larger supplies for the day to day cleaning. It was filled with the lingering scent of smoke. Other than the smell there was no damage.

Next he walked the short hallway with the restrooms at the end of the area. To the right was a 8' x 6' portable office which was occasionally used was by staff working in the warehouse. The fire had begun to melt through the plastic components of the computer on the desk

Leaving the area, proceeding to the warehouse, Peter noticed the sun peering through the second story window in the back of the building, providing enough light for Peter to survey the damage to the rest of the interior contents of the now broken building. Noting the compressor had been burned through, he made his way up the mezzanine that stretched the length of the building. The two shrink wrap machines, the plastic wrap for them, and the conveyer belt were all destroyed by the heat and the flames of the fire.

Reflecting with wonder, Peter realized that the machinery made of metal could not sustain the damage, yet the wood floor that held it had. The floor appeared unstable but it still held all the damaged machinery.

Peter thought of the firemen from the day before. It was a blessing that none of them, including the woman who had gotten hit on the shoulder, had not been seriously hurt.

Circling the area before making his way back down the stairs to the first floor, Peter walked to the rear of the building. He went through the back door covered by dirt and stone where the forklift was still stuck. He surveyed the damage, including damage to the large hundred-pound forklift battery charger. Thankfully there was no damage to the forklift or the charger.

Then, for the second day in a row Peter heard footsteps. Peter turned to see a man of medium build, average height, dressed in wrinkled clothes, with a camera and an accompanying pack approaching him.

Handing Peter a business card, he stated, "I'm John Shera from Gary Gable Independent Adjusters. Peerless Insurance Company has hired us to look over the damage and make an estimate of the loss."

Peter was impressed that Peerless Insurance wanted to get the building fixed as soon as possible without interrupting the business's day-to-day business.

As the two men turned back to the building and proceeding to go through the back door. Mr. Shera was taking pictures as they slowly moved through the debris. Peter showed him the reel from the battery charger, and the scorch marks on the floor where the fire had started according to the Hamburg Police and Hamburg Fire Investigator.

As they continued through the destruction, Mr. Shera turned to Peter and asked, "Do you know what happened to me while I was getting on the elevator from work this morning as I was going from the fifth to the fourth floor?"

Peter looked at him waiting for him to continue.

Mr. Shera added, "I saw a few pretty girls and sucked in my belly to make me look thinner and almost lost my pants because I forgot to put on my belt this morning."

Peter looked at him and smiled thinking what a ridiculous statement to make as a representative of Peerless Insurance to one of their clients. He thought that Mr. Shera needed some training in continuing education of professional behavior in the field if he was going to represent Gary Gable Insurance Adjusters.

Ignoring the statement, trying to keep it professional, Peter and Mr. Shera continued through the building. Peter pointed out the damage from the hole in the roof visible from the first floor. Mr. Shera, remarked, "That looks like a perfect square, we can cut a square and fit it in!"

Peter then pointed to the ceiling on the second story towards the delivery garage doors, stating the insulation had fallen during the fire.

"You don't need to replace that!" Mr. Shera exclaimed.

Peter protested, saying that it was needed to protect the employees during the winter months. The Lake Erie winds blew right through and the employees needed some protection. Mr. Shera did not care. He had an agenda of his own.

Turning to the mezzanine at the back of the building which had been severely damaged, Mr. Shera continued, saying, "You may be able to shore that floor up."

Again Peter protested, telling Mr. Shera, "There is heavy machinery on the second floor, I do not need my employees in danger without a stable floor!"

Peter then mentioned one of the two heaters was damaged, but this it was met with Mr. Shera replying, "You don't need two heaters, one is enough to heat the whole place."

Making their way back through the warehouse, Mr. Shera continued his analysis. The overhead fans, along with the exhaust fans, which were used to keep the air as comfortable as possible during the severe climate changes, were deemed unnecessary, along with the automatic thermostat that controlled it. The newly installed six paneled doors could be patched and painted. Peter was becoming disgusted.

Peter told Mr. Shera the policy clearly stated we were paying premiums for total replacement and not a patch job. Mr. Shera rambled on aimlessly about nonsense as he continued to pull up his pants.

Meanwhile, I was in Orchard Park working on another one of my great clients. I felt lucky to have these people in my life. Hearing about the devastation the previous day, they easily slid from one scheduled time to another. As soon as I was able to switch my last client. I called Peter to see how he was faring. He told me he was still with the fire adjuster hired by Peerless Insurance.

As he was talking to me on the phone, I realized I had a two hour gap between appointments. I told Peter to keep the adjuster there as I wanted to speak with him personally about the damage to the building, since it was in my name. Also, a decision had to be made about whether to cancel the trip with Peter's niece.

Getting in my car and driving the short trip from Orchard Park to Hamburg, I pulled up to the driveway of the building. I saw Peter walking with the fire adjuster from the left side of the building to the front. Thinking they must be doing a walk around to see if there was damage to the grounds to the exterior of the building, I got out of the car and approached them.

Peter introduced Mr. Shera to me. My first impression of Mr. Shera was that he appeared sloppy, as if he had just rolled out of bed. He was careless in his dress, and was not exactly what I was expected from Peerless Insurance company that is a subsidiary of Liberty Mutual.

Sensing what I was thinking, Mr. Shera declared, "I'm dressed like this because I had to inspect the property." I dismissed my initial thoughts as Peter and Mr. Shera continued to carry on a conversation while we stood next to the sad looking building.

What followed next was an odd, if not illegal. Mr. Shera proceeded to tell Peter that he had "people, relatives" that he could hire to do repairs on the building. Some of them were relatives who would be able to do a patch-up job. He told Peter to look no further for people for the repairs, as he had it handled.

I wondered if Liberty Mutual had any idea what one of their subsidiary companies was doing and the people they hired to represent them. It was outrageous behavior, but it was not going to be the end of it either.

It became eerily quiet as the three of us stood in front of the building. Here was a man suggesting that if we did it his way everything would be taken care of. If we didn't well…. who knows? I watched as a sporadic car passed along the highway as Mr. Shera continued his suggestions of his special people that would handle the cleanup and repairs.

Listening patiently, Peter mentioned to him we had vacation plans and were supposed to leave in two days for a long ago booked holiday.

"Should we cancel?" Peter asked.

Mr. Shera replied, "No go ahead everything will be cleaned and repaired by the time you get back."

With that he got into his car and left probably thinking he had sealed the deal for Gary Gable Adjusters and his people.

Peter looked at me and announced, "I'm going to call Frank Pappas from National Fire Adjusters and see what they think of the situation. John Shera and Gary Gable Adjusters only want to pay for a patch-up job, not the full policy."

He continued, "Since we are not over-insured, and only for the interior contents including the machinery, damage to the building and we have business interruption for up to $50,000."

After hearing about the suggestion to do a patch-up job to a floor that was holding heavy machinery, I agreed. I said, "We do not need to have a floor cave in on people because a fire adjuster who was hired by Peerless Insurance said to patch it. It's not safe."

We got into our respective cars, with Peter going to the house to make phone calls and me to my office to finish scheduled appointments. I had an uneasy feeling about the fire adjuster.

Peter called National Fire Adjusters, making an appointment for the next day once again to go over the damage to the building and the machinery. I canceled my appointments. This time I wanted to be there for the proceedings.

As I waited with Peter for the new adjuster to arrive at Pro-Pak, Peter commented of the beauty of the day. The leaves had already started to change with the slight shading of orange, yellow, and a slight tinge of red just beginning to cover the woods adjacent to the building. While we remarked about what a beautiful time of year it was, a car pulled into the driveway. A man got out of the car and introduced himself as Jeffery Wendling. He was neatly dressed and professional, with a crisp look, and he was precise in his statements.

After doing a quick check of the property, Mr. Wendling offered Peter a contract for his company to send a crew out to list the damages and put a dollar figure on it. Peter jumped at the chance of having a professional look at the building and a crew that would do a thorough job.

As Mr. Wendling got into his car, I noticed a yellow rubber duck on his dashboard. I laughed and chided, "You have a rubber duck in your car!"

He replied, "I love my job, but sometimes I need to squeeze it when it's been a rough day."

Laughing back, I said, "Maybe I should buy Peter one since the last two days have been more than stressful."

Little did we know how brutal and horrible it would get with Peerless Insurance, the evil child of Liberty Mutual.

Once again, Peter and I got into our respective cars. He was going home and I was going to finish up the last of my appointments. This would be an early day and we were both exhausted. We packed for the trip to the UK, getting the luggage into the car parked in the garage. It would be less to do in the morning. That night we semi-relaxed, knowing that everything would be taken care of while we were gone for the two weeks. Mr. Shera said it would be done while we were gone, that he was ready to roll, and we believed him.

CHAPTER 6: SEPTEMBER 30, 2000

The next morning, August 30, 2000, was the day of departure. Getting into the car, we drove to Advanced Massage Therapy to make sure everyone was on board fulfilling appointments, banking, and the general running of the offices while we were gone. Just before leaving for our flight, Peter stepped into the storage room and called Michael Drumm, bringing him up to speed of the events of the past three days.

Peter told him he had signed a contract with National Fire Adjusters, adding Gary Gable Fire Adjusters had not even given him a dollar value, was not following the rules of the contract, and, in Peter's opinion, Gary Gable was not an independent fire adjuster as he was working for Peerless Insurance. He also told Michael that Mr. Shera had not made a good impression on either one of us.

National Fire Adjusters, however, was a well-known company in Buffalo. They were an independent firm with a long history for personal attention and honesty. No one we had contact with had ever heard of Gary Gable Fire Adjusters.

Peter finished his conversation with Michael, who assured Peter that things would work out. He agreed with Mr. Shera that we should continue our plan to go on vacation.

Leaving the office, we drove to the airport with an uneasiness that things were not quite right. We continued anyway, taking a flight from Buffalo to Cincinnati, and meeting Peter's niece and leaving for the UK. She was a delight to be with and Peter had missed seeing her after helping to raise her after a personal tragedy until she graduated from high school. Now that she lived in Florida, visits were sporadic at best. The trip had been suggested by the Surrogate's Court in Buffalo as a way for her to so enjoy the outside world.

We left Ohio for an overnight flight. We landing in the UK and spent a few days first in Scotland and then in Ireland. It was interesting to see the beautiful countries and the various cultures. Soon it was time to go back home. We had spent 10 days visiting the UK, including Scotland and Ireland. It was not enough time and I vowed that this trip would result in a redo. We left from Dublin and arrived at La Guardia airport in New York City, then on to Buffalo. We got home late in the evening.

Glad to be home, the sense of uneasiness that had accompanied us throughout the trip intensified. It felt like a double edged sword. If we had not gone on the trip we would have lost the money for the reservations since the person that made the reservations had not gotten insurance. We also would not have seen Peter's niece. We heard Mr. Shera's voice saying, "Don't worry, everything will back in place by the time you get back."

CHAPTER 7: THE CHESS GAME BEGINS

Most of us have heard of or played chess. Each player has sixteen pieces. Usually, one side is black and the other beige or white. The pieces for each side consists of one king, one queen, two rooks, two bishops, two knights, and eight pawns. The pawn is placed in front of the other pieces as the front defense or offense, and is often the weakest because it takes the brunt and has to protect the other pieces. Chess is like a war: you are not only protecting your space on the board, but stopping the advances and conquering the opposition.

A chess game was about to begin. It was longest game of our lives. It appeared every dirty and illegal trick was used by a Peerless Insurance and their fire adjusters and attorneys, and we were the pawns. It was all over a sweet young girl whose mother died during her birth. It involved greed, jealousy, and hate. The game was spontaneous and evil, and had to be stopped. We were forced along for the ride and had to make sure it stopped when we said so, and not by an attorney, a judge or the courts of the Western New York District.

Arriving home late in the afternoon on Saturday, September 9, 2000, we immediately went to bed, falling into a sound sleep. It appeared the jet lag had caught up with us. We would unpack the next day and see what was going on with Pro-Pak and Advanced Massage Therapy.

Early Sunday morning, Peter went to Hamburg to see what progress had been done with the building, while I went to the office in Orchard Park to check my appointments for the next week. As I was writing down my schedule for Monday, the phone rang on the desk. Answering it, Peter on the other end of the line relayed the news to me the building looked the same as when we had seen it almost two weeks before. He was going to come to the Orchard Park office and make some phone calls.

Arriving at the Orchard Park office, Peter told me with frustration, "Everything is the same, except the battery charger and the reel to the forklift are missing. We have been lied to by Gary Gable Adjusters!"

It would be the first of many lies by Peerless Insurance and their representatives either told or written about us. Slander and Libel by the people that acted for them.

Peter slumped into the chair at the reception desk before picking up the phone to call to Michael Drumm, our insurance agent Don, and Gary Gable Adjusters offices, hoping at least one of them was at work Sunday. Unfortunately, it was not to be and we would have to wait until Monday. We left shortly after in our separate cars to go home.

On his way back to the house, Peter stopped to pick up the mail for Pro-Pak from the post office box in Orchard Park. As he reached into the hollow space, a letter fell to the floor. Picking it up, Peter saw it was a letter written by Mr. Fitzgerald, the attorney for the Department of Labor to Ms. Schroder, our former labor attorney.

In this letter, Mr. Fitzgerald asked whether Ms. Ginger Schroder still represented us. After he read the letter, Peter turned over the envelope and noticed it was postmarked August 28, 2000. It appeared that while we were standing in front of Peter's business watching firemen extinguish a blaze, Mr. Fitzgerald was getting the news out at the same time. Apparently the phone lines were burning up that day with the news of the fire and Michael Fitzgerald needed to get the news to Ms. Schroder as soon as possible.

Things had changed rapidly while we were gone on vacation. On August 31, 2000, without our knowledge or our permission, Peerless Insurance had Gary Gable Insurance Adjuster's main man, Mr. Shera, and apparently another man from Stauffer Investigative, inspect the property. Peerless Insurance had pulled a quickie behind our backs. It looked like the call had been made as soon as Gary Gable Adjusters located in Buffalo, had known we were out of the country. They took the opportunity to illegally enter the business property

Gary Gable Insurance Adjusters had also taken or stolen evidence while we gone. This was the same evidence Hamburg Police had told us to hang onto. To make matters worse, they did not secure the premises after they illegally entered. The privacy cable that stretched from the left side of the property across the building to the right had been left lying on the ground. The scene had also been altered by Gary Gable Insurance Adjusters. It was done with precision and intent to change and remove the evidence to Peerless Insurance advantage. It was done despite the investigation by the Hamburg Police and Fire Department during the fire, which had proved the cause of the fire was the short from the battery charger to the forklift.

On Monday, we received our monthly premium from Peerless Insurance. The policy included the two businesses, our cars, business trucks, and the house, for the full coverage policy. Peerless Insurance covered everything we owned. We paid the premium confident that everything would be straightened out as soon as possible. It said so in their advertisements and letterhead: "Once you choose us you will know you made the right decision. And if you unfortunately have a claim, be assured it will be handled quickly, courteously and by an expert." This apparently referred to Gary Gable Insurance Adjustors.

The next few weeks were filled with meetings between Peter and his suppliers in Buffalo. Both the suppliers and Peter were waiting for Peerless Insurance to fulfill their end of the bargain and either pay for the damages, the emergency money or the funds to sustain ourselves as stated in the contract.

On September 29, 2000, Peerless Insurance sent us a letter stating they were not going to pay for our damages due to misrepresentation by us voiding the policy. It was signed by Cheryl Hess. That same day Peter went to Michael Drumms office, bringing the letter from Peerless with him. As they discussed the fire damage, loss of business, and the letter, Peter felt it was becoming ominous.

Michael declared "You could be running out of the building with a gas can in your hand, it means nothing! I'll send them a letter right away!" his voice engaged with authority.

Peter felt more at ease now, Michael was his friend and he knew what he was doing, plus he worked for a firm highly respected that was a great firm and specialized in corporation law.

On October 9, 2000, without a building to go to, or machinery to work with, Peter signed a short term lease for a business rental within a few miles of our house. It was a month-to-month occupancy, so we would be ready to move back into the building in Hamburg at any time. The premises were in bad shape but it would do for the time being. We were convinced Peerless Insurance was getting ready to pay for the damage done to the building and the equipment. We had to continue: there was work to be completed. The costs for the move totaled over $4,000 plus another $2,085 for the first and last month's rent.

Gary Gable, the president of Gary C. Gable Professional Adjusters, had refused to give up the battery charger for the forklift, stating it was now so called evidence for Peerless Insurance, and he was keeping it. We had to spend another $400 was spent for a new charger, smaller than the original and, without the bells and whistles.

On October 19, 2000, the monthly invoice came from Peerless Insurance for our insurance coverage. We paid it.

Peter called Michael and advised him that we fulfilled our end of the bargain, and asked what Peerless Insurance and Gary Gable were up too. He was angry, venting to Michael. Michael told Peter he would call Gary Gable and have us go to his office to make a statement. Within minutes, Michael called back and told Peter we would all be going in to Gary Gable's office to make a statement on October 28, 2000. Lost wages were piling up, bidding on new jobs had stopped, and they could not be fulfilled without the machinery. We needed to get everything on the table, the sooner the better.

On October 28, 2000, the seasons were changing into fall. With the crispness of the leaves crunching under our feet, we got into the car to meet at Michael office, and then we would go to meet Gary Gable. Picking a parking space as close to the Ellicott Square Building as we could get, we entered the building to ride the elevator to Messerendino, Celniker & Estoff, the law firm where Michael was employed. He greeted us with a cheeriness and assurance that this matter would be taken care of very soon, we just had to go through the motions.

While Peter and Michael conversed about the procedures of the insurance company, I looked around the room amazed at the clean and pristine office. Usually sitting in an attorney's office there would be mounds of paperwork everywhere, with folders and files loaded with cases set before the attorney. Here there was nothing, not even a pen on the desk. I again dismissed it as a very neat attorney.

Michael did have one claim to fame. He had gotten "Kathy's Law" passed in in New York. It was a law that protected patients from abuse in nursing homes within the state. I decided to ask him about it since there was some time left before our meeting, which was occurring a few floors below Michael office. He gushed with pride at the story of getting the law passed, which will help stop abuse to the elderly by their caretakers and nursing homes. I chided him with the statement that I was 56 and Peter was 61, saying, "Kudos to you for having this passed, we will probably need it by the time we get done with Peerless Insurance's abuse." Peter and I laughed while Michael went into his desk, pulling out a pen. This would turn out to be a very special comment made to him.

Within a few minutes, we walked the hallway to the elevators, riding a few floors down to Peerless Insurance adjuster's office. As we walked into the receiving room of Gary Gable Adjusters. Present was Gary Gable, his wife, his sister-in-law, and John Shera.

We went into a separate room, where there was a small card table which held an old tape recorder. As we all sat down, Mr. Gable proceeded to explain what was going to happen. He asked Peter to raise his right hand, explaining he was going to put him under oath. We both turned our heads quizzically to Michael, wondering if Mr. Gable had the legal right to do this. To our knowledge, this was only done within a legal setting in a courtroom. Michael nodded his head affirmatively indicating we should proceed as stated by Mr. Gable.

Mr. Gable then attended to the matter with Peter holding his right hand up, he swore him in with Peter's other hand on the table. "We don't have a bible." explained Mr. Gable.

He proceeded to once again ask Peter the same questions that had already been answered to Hamburg Police and Mr. John Shera. I observed Mrs. Gable who was gazing at the beat up recorder with boredom, apparently due to the proceedings. This activity went on for about an hour or so, and it ended uneventfully. I was then asked to be sworn in. The same questions were asked of me: "Where are you?", "What time is it?", "How did you find out about the fire?"

On and on with the same questions and answers. Mr. Gable was trying to find out something that wasn't there, it did not exist, or, as I later found out, he was milking Peerless Insurance Company for all he could get.

My time was shorter than Peter's - probably 30 minutes. The tape recorder was turned off and Mr. Gable explained his wife would be transcribing the audio and that the finished paperwork would be sent out to Peerless Insurance and Michael Drumm. I looked at Peter and Michael with surprise. Really? The wife of the fire adjuster that worked for Peerless Insurance was going to transcribe the handmade oath! This was getting irrational a time killer for us and, adding billing hours for Mr. Gable to submit to Peerless Insurance.

Ending the session, Peter asked Mr. Gable for the battery charger for the forklift that was in his possession. Mr. Gable ushered us out of his office without answering or acknowledging that he had even heard the request. Michael, oblivious to the exchange was fooling around with his tie, said nothing. Once in the hallway, out of the grip of Mr. Gable and his preposterous oath, Peter, Michael, and I had a short conversation about the previous acts we had been witness to as we walked to the elevator. Arriving at his office, Michael commented that we had done a "good job."

I then mentioned what I had observed in Gary Gables office as a woman.

"Gary Gable has a problem, he is dressed sloppy, dirty, unpressed clothing, and his shoes were filthy. I'm not sure, but I'm pretty convinced it is gambling, drinking, or he has a girlfriend the latter which I highly doubt. He needs money and he needs it now, he has a habit, or his company is not in good financial shape, something is out of place, not sure what it is but, as a woman, we know these things. We sense it and pick up on it."

Michael leaned forward from his desk and Peter came at me from the right side. Looking at me with superior attitudes they giggled and laughed like little girls as they humored me about my comment. Leaving a short time later, we went home, Peter confident that Michael would have this matter solved within a short time as he had promised.

On October 31, 2000, Michael wrote to Sevine Rowe, Senior Claims Representative for Peerless Insurance. In the letter, he stated that in his opinion Peerless Insurance was in violation of Insurance Law Sec. 2601.

He continued saying: "65 days have passed and your adjusting company, run by Gary Gable, is still not complete nor has he even started the examination and evaluation of the battery charger to the forklift he removed from the premises. No request was even made to take a statement from Mr. Kirisits until almost fifty days following the notice of the loss. If this letter is not completed and my clients claim accepted within the next ten [10] days from this letter, I will proceed to file a complaint with the New York Insurance Department with your violation of Sec. 2601."

That same day, Michael sent a second letter to Mr. Gable and Mr. Shera. Apparently Mr. Gable had asked Michael for our personal records which were not under the contract. The corporations of Evans, Pro-Pak and Advanced Massage Therapy had the contract. Michael told them, "You are overstepping your boundaries. Hamburg Police and the Hamburg Fire Department concluded it was accidental. The financial records you are requesting are completely irrelevant." As far as we knew, there was not a response from either Gary Gable the fire adjuster or Michael Drumm. Perhaps the records were destroyed.

On November 6, 2000, the report from National Fire Adjusters was issued by Jeffery Wendling. Damage to the building totaled $225,055. With deprecation at 12%, the total loss came to $198,048.90. The damage to the contents totaled $101,907.22. The policy from Peerless Insurance stated we had business interruption protection of $50,000 to get us through for up to one year. Clearly, we were not over insured. We thought Peerless Insurance would pay us for the machinery now and start the rehab on the building.

To our, knowledge Gary Gable Adjusters to this day never did fill out an estimate for our business fire. It has never been found in any records, including Peerless Insurance in our possession.

On November 7, 2000, Michael wrote two letters. The first was to Lawrence Rubin, the first out of the four attorneys representing Peerless Insurance. Apparently the attorney, Mr. Rubin, along with Gary Gable, had asked for the personal records of Peter and myself.

In the letter, Michael explains the obvious: the contract for the insurance is between Pro-Pak and Evans Services, not Peter Kirisits and Jo Anne Gleason.

He continues, "If you can prove to me with compelling evidence that either party caused the fire, I will reconsider my position. We are reserving the right to pursue an action of breach of contract and breach of good faith and fair dealing. I will hold your client Peerless Insurance personally responsible for any and all damages suffered by my clients of their bad faith violations and fair dealing in New York State. I am going to issue a complaint to the New York State Insurance Department. I want a certified copy of the insurance policy between Peerless and my clients."

The second letter was a complaint filed by Michael for the violation of insurance codes against Peerless Insurance to the New York Insurance Fund, located at the state's capital. This was a big deal, because if any company has their main offices in another state and crosses state lines to do their business, they must follow the rules of that state. They are considered a foreign corporation. In this case, Peerless Insurance's main office is located in Keene, New Hampshire and does business in New York State. They must follow New York State's rules.

On November 14, 2000, Michael filed another complaint with the New York State Department of Insurance for Peerless Insurance's code violations. They were punishable by a very hefty fine. Peerless Insurance was laughing at New York State's code of rules as they continued to harass us, as they had a number of other litigants within the state of New York and throughout New England.

On November 19, 2000, Peerless Insurance sent us the monthly invoice for coverage of our insurance. We paid it.

It was now becoming apparent to us Peerless Insurance was going to delay payment as long as possible. We were informed by KeyBank we could not get more machinery to run the business, until Peerless Insurance paid the remainder dollar value of the lease to them. We had to make a move soon. Real soon.

The winter of 2000 into 2001 was particularly brutal. Blowing wind and ongoing snow almost every day. The rental space for Pro-Pak in Orchard Park was not the best for business. The trucks could not pull up to the doors for deliveries coming in or shipping out for the lack of a good driveway. The relentless snow was backed up to the doors every day. The added expense of having a snowplow come and remove the snow every few days did not help, because the snow blowing right back in again.

Peerless Insurance continued to ignore their responsibilities of emergency money assistance, including the $25,000 requested by National Fire Adjusters' to get us enough to start up until the rest was taken care of. It was a tough time without the machinery, and the bidding on jobs could only include the use of manual labor. Everything had changed: the jobs, the biddings, and the profits.

As the weeks passed we anticipated payment any day. We bit the bullet, hoping that Peerless Insurance would see that we were people who paid their insurance. After all, we were never accused of anything. Why wouldn't Peerless Insurance pay?

We continued to pay the premiums in good faith, Peerless Insurance continued to accept payment and send us a new bill every month for our coverage. Meanwhile, we were on edge. Everything except the necessities had to be given up. I had to work longer hours at Advanced Massage Therapy in an attempt to hold the glue together for the house, business, utilities, and groceries for just a little while longer.

"Here comes the check" is a verbal statement made to warn your opponent that you are making a move and would possibly win the chess game.

One horrible snowy afternoon just before Christmas, Dick Manfreda, who held the mortgage for the burned building, came to Peter's rental in Orchard Park. Standing in the forlorn room of the dismal space, Dick and Peter faced each other - one small business owner to another. They conversed about the issues with Peerless Insurance, including those giving Peter problems over paying for the damages to the building. Peter could not pay the mortgage on the building he had just renovated, because he could not take bigger jobs due to the lack of the machinery. Mr. Manfreda was also having problems with Peerless Insurance. Dick explained his position, along with his wife's, who owned the building. Mr. Manfreda had to foreclose on the building and take it back. It was not his choice but a business decision. If it was not reopened soon, the county of Erie would rezone it from commercial to residential.

It was a very stressful and sad time for both of us. The burden and money lost was increasing every day. The holidays came, but we barely got through the supposedly happy events, pretending we weren't worried even though most of our friends knew what was going on since the fine.

On January 10, 2001, Moss & Sullivan, the Insurance Company that had signed us up with Peerless Insurance, sent Peter a fax for Michael. There was a notation on pages 17 and 18 that stated that in the contract we signed with Peerless Insurance they had the right to see only the corporation papers, the books, and records for Evans Service, Pro-Pak, and Advanced Massage Therapy, not for Peter or myself. It also stated that that the insurance was with the three companies, that whatever money we received from the companies was considered personal income, and that we had no personal insurance with this company. Our income was none of their business. Peerless Insurance had violated the insurance codes of New York State and our contract.

Peter put in a call to Michael with the notice of the contract. Michael asked to see it, since he had still not received the contract he had requested from Peerless Insurance or Lawrence Rubin five months prior. The billing practices for the never ending new evidence must have made billing hours a breeze for the attorneys. Along with the regular stalling tactics of Peerless Insurance, they also conveniently had hired another attorney, named was David Sleight from the office of Brown & Lustig, who asked for and got delays and extensions. It was getting profitable for everyone but the victims. We wondered about the other small businesses, and other consumers that paid the premiums to this company.

CHAPTER 8: WOW, CHECKMATE

On January 15, 2001 a letter from Brown & Lustig arrived. It was a Notice for Examination under Oath. We were to be at their office in Williamsville, New York, on February 20, 2001. This was great news. Finally, this mess would get settled. We were to bring all of the following:

1. Our taxes from 1997 through 2000, both federal and state.
2. Records of all liens and judgments prior to 2000, both federal and state.
3. All mortgages and deeds for 6246 Southwestern Blvd. in Hamburg, New York.
4. All leases and deeds in effect on August 28, 2000.
5. All work orders from January 1, 2000, to August 28, 2000.
6. The incorporation papers from Delaware, property taxes, foreclosures.
7. Also the records for Advanced Massage Therapy.

The letter was signed by Maurice Sykes. Was this the third attorney for Peerless Insurance? We were not sure.

We had just gotten the foreclosure papers for Pro-Pak. It was the beginning of the end for the building.

Peter was surprised that the records were called for from Advanced Massage Therapy. Putting in a call to Michael, his advice was: "Let them get a court order for it, they are stalling."

On January 18, 2001, a document came to the house from Michael. It was the statement from the meeting at Gary Gable Adjusters the previous October, which had been transcribed by Mr. Gable's wife off the tape recorder. It was an odd document filled with non-essential questions presented by Mr. Gable as time fillers for Peerless Insurance to pay him for. Peter called Michael and requested the tape to be produced. Apparently the tape they had made such a big deal of had been lost by Mr. Gable. He should have been fired by Peerless Insurance, however they appeared to find him useful for their insurance coverage stalling tactics.

As Peter vented to Michael, Michael assured Peter the statements could not be used in court, that it was not a legal document, and that Mr. Gable was not an attorney. I had my doubts about Michael at this point, wondering about his motives. So far, this was a charade being played out for money and it was going to get wilder and more aggressive.

On January 19, 2001, five months after the fire, the monthly invoice came from Peerless Insurance. We paid it.

On January 31, 2001, knowing it was impossible to build a business in the building in Orchard Park, Peter signed a lease with a rental property in Lackawanna, New York, hoping with the increase of space, a cleaner environment, and the loading dock he would be able to bid on jobs with more volume. The workforce had been downsized to eight people.

On February 6, 2001, Michael sent the tax returns to Maurice Sykes for both businesses for the years 1997, 1998, and 1999.

We still had hope that Peerless Insurance would see the light and notice we were trying as hard as possible to keep our heads above water. So far they had paid nothing, but we would be going to a deposition soon and all the facts would get out in the open. It seemed that everyone had been paid except us: we had lost thousands of dollars and without a single accusation against us. Peter kept in touch with Michael, who assured us it would be settled within three months right after the deposition that had been scheduled to be held on February 20, 2001.

I wondered if Liberty Mutual, the parent company of Peerless Insurance, knew of the things that were going on. In our opinion, they were more than aware. It appeared to be standard procedure for all the companies they were involved with. We had provided all the information they needed and if there was one thing "Pete the packrat" had, it was paper he was a fanatic about hanging on to.

CHAPTER 9: WHAT IS A DEPOSITION?

A deposition is a gathering of facts related to a case and occurs before a trial. It's like a face off in the beginning of the chess game. In our case, the situation we were deposed about was the fire. During a deposition, you answer questions an attorney asks of you, and you tell the truth. So long as you tell the truth, you will not make a mistake at trial.

A little secret is most attorneys are not very good at trials and will do anything to avoid them. They do their pretrial motions through letters and phone calls, and they build up their hours, you know, just in case they do poorly before a judge who, often, has his or her own issues.

On February 20, 2001, at 9:00 a.m., we met Michael at his office in Buffalo. Boasting again of our open and shut case that would be settled promptly, within three months, he said, "Peerless had to put up a bond [savings account] in case they went out of business."

As it turned out, this was not the first time they had been sued for non-payment of an insurance claim.

Within a few minutes, we left his office and headed over to Brown & Lustig just around the corner from the office of Advanced Massage Therapy in Williamsville.

What had started out as just another freezing day in Buffalo with a dark, gloomy atmosphere, would turn into a day that would come down on us with a force of accusations, lies, falsehoods, inaccurate information, and bullying by Peerless Insurance attorney David Sleight, who had replaced attorney Maurice Sykes.

At 10:02 p.m. we entered the conference room and Mr. Sykes was nowhere in sight. David Sleight was now the third attorney for Peerless Insurance in a little over a year. He explained to us the reason for the delay over the past few months was to give him time to go over the case.

"It takes time, you know, and it has to be done right." he told us. The more time the better for Peerless Insurance who continued to ignore three insurance codes of New York State Law.

In the room were Mr. Sleight, Michael Drumm, Peter, and myself. Peter would be up first. He was asked where he was born, about schooling, marriages, children, homes, and his career - using billing hours for Peerless Insurance to pay the new attorney.

On Page 38 of the typed out deposition, consisting of questions and the answers, Mr. Sleight finally cut to the chase, asking Peter questions related to the business. He continued waddling around to page 59 when he asked Peter if he had fire insurance. On page 79, he asked Peter about the labor fine, specifically about attorney Mr. Michael Fitzgerald of the Department of Labor, and about attorney, Ginger Schroder, our labor law attorney. Ironically, we had just heard some interesting news about Ms. Schroder, as she was making a career move.

Killing more time, Mr. Sleight told us we had gotten a "consent judgment" not a labor fine as Gary Gable had said in his office the previous October. Peter brought up Ms. Coleman chasing one of his employees up her driveway to her front door, yelling at her to give her information about her job.

It took to page 134 for Mr. Sleight to ask Peter about the August 28, 2000, fire. He had spent all the previous questions asking about things he already knew the answers, and most of it irreverent to the case. It was easy money, and Michael sat apparently bored twiddling his pencil on his yellow legal paper. He interjected a few times to clarify questions being asked.

The deposition was getting boring to me with the constant repetition of the same facts over and over along with the same questions. Nothing on our part had or would change. What would change was the deals being made in the dirty, smelly back rooms of the attorney's offices.

Finally, the end of Peter's deposition came to a close. The entire deposition was 179 pages long.

The National Fire Adjusters report was brought up during the deposition. Apparently seven months later, Gary Gable still had not filled out a fire report. Michael said he needed a copy of the report. Peter told him he had already been sent one in November of 2000 by Jeff Wendling of National Fire Adjuster's and from us as well. Mr. Sleight stopped in his tracks and asked for the same fire report also. Apparently we were the only one with the files of the fire report in the deposition room that day.

At 2:00 p.m. we broke for lunch. Peter, Michael, and I went to a small local restaurant around the corner from Brown & Lustig. It was getting ominous outside, with dark clouds coming in off Lake Erie. We needed to get this over with. Peter asked Michael to see if he could discuss with Mr. Sleight the emergency monies National Fire Adjusters had requested to rebuild the business. Michael agreed to discuss this with the attorneys from Peerless Insurance after the deposition, but he never did.

I was up next. The time was 3:05 p.m. and part two of the deposition was starting. Mr. Sleight drug me through the same questions that had been presented to Peter. Where were you born, how many marriages, how many children, their ages, how many massages a week do you work, are you engaged, what is the difference between what you owe on the labor fine and what you make a week, where was I when the fire was being called in, who called me, etc. I gave the short blunt answers as suggested by Michael. "Don't give them a reason," he had told me. When I asked him "a reason for what?" he ignored me.

During the deposition, Mr. Sleight noted that a tax lien for Evans Services had been sent to Advanced Massage Therapy. Handing me the letter, it appeared that the lien had been sent to a business down the street. This was the first I had seen of it and once again denied owing taxes - which he already knew since Michael had sent him the taxes for both businesses a few months before. I then noted to him we had only been in business for a year under that name, due to the labor fine. Also, the letter he had handed me was not for us but for another business down the street as was noted on the envelope. He put the letter in his file ending the question.

It was becoming clear to both Peter and me that someone had decided we made a couple of million dollars during a six-month time period.

Michael continued to sit doodling on his yellow notepad. He would at times say the minimal or go off the record to interject something that would not be transcribed by the stenographer. I kept wondering why he did not say anything about the taxes since he had them in his possession and, in fact, had already told Peter he had sent them to Brown & Lustig. I had to go along with his judgment since he was our attorney and he knew what he was doing.

Towards the end of my deposition, Mr. Sleight shockingly pounded his fist on the table making accusations to me about owing taxes between $179,000 and $750,000. "Where had he gotten this information?" I thought. It was crazy. Not only was it wrong, but he stupidly had gone into Peter's guardianship information for his niece and attached my name to it.

Perhaps it was because the Buffalo News had reported in an article a few years before that Peter had in fact been awarded a significant award of money. His niece was under age at the time, the courts wanted to keep her protected, therefore the media had reported it as if Peter had won the money.

The deposition was making me sick to my stomach. How many other people in this town believed this rubbish? We had to continue to protect her along with the Surrogate's Court decision even to Peerless Insurance Company.

Finally, we got to the lease of the machinery from KeyBank. It was on page 79 of the typed out deposition, and only one sentence was devoted to the machinery we needed to get back into business.

Suddenly Mr. Sleight asked me about my restored 1974 Volkswagen and the robbery that had happened to the house on Cloverbank Road in Hamburg, years before. When I mentioned how I met the insurance agent, his voice slowly rose to a whining pitch and he asked me about a lien again. His voice continued to rise until practically a scream. "You have a lien with the labor department!" he said, with his face turning a slight color of red. Looking at me with disdain, staring at me, his arms shuffled through the paperwork at the same time. I decided to give him back the same business by looking at him with the same attitude he had given me.

"It is a labor fine, we decided to just pay it." I said.

Plaintiff to Defendant

"Why did you just pay it?" his face ruddy with the anticipation of finding something exceptional he could use.

Once again I explained to him, "It would cost $60,000 up front according to Ginger Schroder to fight the labor fine. We had owed $50,000, had paid off $15,000, bringing it to $35,000 in less than a year. It was better pay it off, shut up, keep quiet, and go the safe way." Continuing I said, "You agree right? Besides another company sued Michael Fitzgerald and won a million dollars from his war chest."

Now my voice was rising. "You need to just pay me for the fire damages done. The labor fine is not an issue here, not the Volkswagen, nor the robbery in my house in Hamburg. We are here for one thing: a fire insurance case."

He shut up.

We left the deposition late in the afternoon. By now the February winds of Buffalo had turned miserable. Blowing snow, high winds, the sky was dark, dull and gloomy. We were exhausted from the day. As we bundled up to face the rush hour traffic from Williamsville to Orchard Park, we parted ways with Michael as he faced both us he stated, "You both did a good job."

Peter, shivering, answered, "We were telling the truth Mike; we have nothing to hide from anyone."

Responding, Michael stated, "If I thought you were guilty, I would not represent you, this case will be wrapped up within three months and you will be back in business."

A little later I will write what Michael really thought about his clients, written in his handwriting, in his personal diary. He had a bad habit of not totally purging his files. He should have kept them as neat as his office and desk.

On March 14, 2001, attorney Maurice Sykes sent letter to Michael about the tax liens and policy. Michael called Peter - apparently he did not have the previous tax records in his file. We gave Michael another copy of the taxes and checks paid to the IRS. Peerless Insurance was now using two attorneys for our case. Attorneys David Sleight and Maurice Sykes had replaced the first attorney Lawrence Rubin.

On March 19, 2001, the monthly invoice for our coverage came from Peerless Insurance; we paid it.

On March 30, 2001, Michael sent a letter to Brown & Lustig citing various legal cases along with the violation of yet another Insurance Code, New York Code ICS Sec. 3404. The letter included a bid for a $90,000 job Peter had gotten three days before, on March 27, 2001. Peerless Insurance's attorneys ignored the letter. Peerless Insurance continued to laugh in our faces over the violation of the New York State Insurance codes.

There was a lot of gossip during this time period between Peerless Insurance representatives. Gary Gable made the ridiculous remark that Peter was a very wealthy man and Peerless Insurance did not have to pay at all. This came back to Peter through Michael Drumm via the Peerless Insurance attorneys.

It was disgusting and vile to hear they had now incorporated an underage child lawsuit into the fire insurance case. Peter had to keep protecting her and so did I, it came with the territory, but I wanted to slap all of the attorneys for even relaying this cheesy gossip to us. My parents and sister, Leslie, who was born with a brain tumor that left her helpless, had gone through hell and so did I. I grew up knowing I had to protect her too. I had passed this to my children. I would tell them, "Do not use, abuse, make fun of, laugh at, use the word retard, or short bus, it is offensive and you will answer to me but for the grace of God go you or your children." Knowing I had to hear gossip about such trash from Peerless Insurance and the people that worked for them was beyond comprehension.

On April 19, 2001, Peerless Insurance sent the monthly premium. It was almost nine months after the incident. We paid it ... you know, in good faith.

On May 17, 2001, four months from the date of the deposition, Michael sent another copy of National Fire Adjuster fire report to attorney David Sleight. Gary C. Gable Professional Adjusters still had not made a report of the estimate of damages to the now lost in foreclosure building. Apparently Mr. Gable wasn't finished with the investigation, and continued to refuse to give Peter back the forklift so he could continue his business.

On May 19, 2001, the monthly premium came from Peerless Insurance. We could not pay it. By now we had gone through savings, emergency monies, and had cut back more on day to day living. Peter called Michael explained the situation to him. Michael assured Peter it would be settled within a few months. Probably three at the most.

On June 1, 2001, Michael wrote a letter to Attorney Maurice Sykes. Apparently Mr. Sykes had not responded to phone messages left by Michael. Peerless Insurance was now in violation of three New York State Insurance Code Secs. 2601, 3213 and 3404. These codes were used in New York State to protect the consumer. Peerless had been laughing in the face of New York long enough.

In the letter to Mr. Sykes, Michael stated he was going to charge Peerless Insurance with a attorney's fees and disbursements associated with the lack of "good faith" by Peerless Insurance. He continues in this letter saying, "Let me know whether to go forward with a summary of judgment or proceed to go to trial."

A Summary of Judgment is a tool used by the attorneys to counterclaim the other party before filing a lawsuit. It is usually done by the plaintiff, in this case Peter and me, against the defendant, or Peerless Insurance.

On June 1, 2001, we received a letter from the Department of Labor. The letter requested the 2000 income tax returns for Advanced Massage Therapy, Evans Services, Peter, and myself. We sent copies to Michael Fitzgerald. It appeared everyone understood the situation we were in. So many people had copies of our income taxes for both Federal and New York State, we felt lucky Peter had kept copies of everything back to the early 90's.

On June 15, 2001, Michael sent a letter to attorney David Sleight of Peerless Insurance. In this letter Michael stated, "You have not responded to my letter of June 1, 2001. National Fire Adjusters submitted their report to you, they have not heard from you either. Peter is my friend; I will not let you treat me as badly as you have let Peerless Insurance treat him. You have submitted settlement proposals twice, then ignore the settlement proposal you asked for." Clearly, we had a complaint issue for the New York State Insurance Department.

Peerless Insurance, Attorney Maurice Sykes and Attorney David Sleight continued to spend their billing hours laughing at us. The letter was not answered. The stalling tactics continued and apparently Peerless Insurance was a pro at it. This had been the general business they played in New York but, in other states through New England as well. The game to have people pay them for their services of protection and then not fulfill their end of the bargain was commonplace. I wondered if Liberty Mutual the parent company acted the same way as well.

In June of that same year, Dick Manfreda had to start foreclosure proceedings to regain the building that Peter had put so much money into. The land was in danger of reverting back to residential if he did not have a business running out of it. He had called Peter apologizing and told Peter he was going to lose as well if the insurance that Peerless Insurance owned was not paid. As it was, he was going to take a beating from Peerless Insurance just to keep the building as commercial property.

Peter hung up the phone and looked at me with defeat. "All we worked for is gone, all the money we put in is gone." His voice was resigned, sad, and defeated. He had not run across anything like this before in his life. True evil was seeping out of some very immoral people in this town.

Shooting back sharply at him, bringing him back to reality, I said, "So we paid the insurance company for fire and damage coverage, and they are paying the damages to Dick Manfreda?

"The fat lady hasn't sung yet, we still have time to get it back together, forget about the malicious people in this town, show them and Peerless Insurance we will fight for justice. Peerless is too big for their britches, and I want to see where and how the narcissistic attitude is coming from in Buffalo. I also want to see how many other people this has happened too, it has to stop and stop now or the whole system of democracy is going to go down the tubes."

He suddenly looked better knowing we had each other's back.

On July 20, 2001, a letter was sent to attorney David Sleight from attorney Carl Tronolone, Dick Manfred's attorney. Money was needed to make the building safe after the fire. The request was necessary, proper, and under the authorized terms of the policy. Peerless Insurance was unnecessarily delaying the resolution of the case and holding out on paying Dick Manfreda as well as us. It looked as if they had no intention of paying anyone. They needed to be booted out of New York. I made a mental note to myself to find out the history of nonpayment of this company.

The summer of 2001 was full of work and not very much play. Peter was continuing to do start up without the needed equipment. It was increasingly difficult to continue with the expenses of both the house and the business. The attorney's letters had stopped over this time period. Michael continued to state, "It will settle soon." Peter was fortunate he had a good reputation with the other small business owners in the community. They would wait as long as possible, and then join forces again.

PART II

Sometimes you need a friend who will look out for you and stay in the sidelines. This happened before, with first time during some difficulties during the late eighties. It was time to call that friend once again. We needed help finding out information about Peerless Insurance and the newly formed cast of characters in Buffalo surrounding the problem.

Snoopy, a friend who I also called Snoop, and later Buffalo Snoop, would meet with me when we needed clarification on the proceedings against

Peerless Insurance and the attorneys on both sides representing both the Plaintiff and the Defendant. Snoop had told us to watch our backs right after the first meeting with Gary Gable. Apparently, Mr. Gable had his own set of problems and had been looking for money around Buffalo. His business was in trouble and other insurance companies and agents had stopped using him because of his underhanded ways of doing claims. Snoop also said, "You were right about him; he is a mess!"

In mid-July, I had a meeting with my old friend, meeting in the village square in Hamburg. Snoop told me a number of lawsuits had been filed against Peerless Insurance for violations and not just in New York. They had been violating various insurance codes in a number of states - mainly in New England.

Snoopy told me, "They, [whoever 'they' were but, somehow I figured it out with the next statement] want you out of Buffalo now," continuing with, "do you remember that guy screaming out of his car on Southwestern Boulevard last summer during the Walmart job?" My memory floated back to the previous summer day.

"Yes I remember, why?"

"He is one of them. Be careful, they want you gone for good if you get my drift." Snoop carried on, "He hates you."

I laughed. "That guy hates everyone in his life."

Sometimes Snoop used so much drama.

I got in my car heading back to Orchard Park with a new calm entering my mind, things were oddly coming together. I finished the rest of my workload for the day peacefully.

Snoop and I had met secretly for many years, to discuss things that interested us. We did not hang in the same social circles but it was fun to hear the gossip from our respective professional areas of our lives. Usually the meetings were short but sweet usually over coffee and a light snack. I would tell anyone working around me that I had to go to the store, or run an errand. Later, Peter would be included in these various conversations. He was stunned to hear what he would be witness to in learning about the legal system in Buffalo.

For the rest of the summer, conversations continued between Michael and Peter. "The case will be settled soon, within a couple of months Peerless Insurance would be paying in good faith soon." Michael Drumm would tell Peter. August 28, 2001, the first anniversary of the fire came and went. It had been 365 days of pressure induced by Peerless Insurance and their attorneys. We were not aware a life changing event would soon happen in our country.

Plaintiff to Defendant

CHAPTER 10: THAT DAY IN SEPTEMBER 2001

September 11, 2001, was a glorious morning in Western New York. I had gone to Ellicottville, New York, to take an 8:00 a.m. Pilates lesson. As I entered the 219, a highway constructed some years before to shorten the time to get to the south towns of Buffalo, I looked at the clock in the car. It was 9:10 a.m. plenty of time to get back to my office for a 10:00 a.m. appointment.

Suddenly, I saw a plane approaching over the right side front of my car. It was so low I could see the faces of the passengers peering out the windows of the plane. It was too low, the mountains used for skiing were just a short distance away. They would crash if they did not pull up. Chills overcame my body as the phone rang. It was Peter. Someone had flown a plane into the World Trade Center in Manhattan.

"Get back as soon as you can." he told me.

Suddenly, the plane climbed into the air as I looked out the driver's side of the window. It had just missed the foliage of pine trees hovering over the top of the mountain. Hopefully it was landing at the Bradford Pennsylvania airport. Continuing on the highway, it seemed empty with only a few cars approaching the other way. It was quiet. Keeping the radio off to try and absorb what was going on, the periodic clicking of the tires over the pavement had an odd sense to it. Normally, it would be hardly noticeable, today it sounded dense and thick. The sun once again filtered through the green scrub pines surrounded by the colorful leaves starting to change on the trees.

Arriving at the office in time to make the first appointment, I wanted to cancel the rest of the day. This particular client had a number of neck injuries, which required massage to the surrounding areas to heal. I turned on the radio in the office only to hear another plane had crashed into the Trade Center. When my client arrived she was in a lot of neck pain. We headed back to the massage room, keeping the news on the radio. Soon we heard another plane had crashed in Pennsylvania. The country was under attack.

Finishing the session, canceling the rest of the appointments, we clustered around the television Peter had brought in, the color screen only showing black and white - the true colors of the horrible scene. It was worse to look out the window and see a brilliant sun filtering through the trees, shadows bouncing along the parking lot. Our problems were minor compared to the horrific events happening across the country. I wondered about another client who was a flight attendant. I prayed she was safe. Peter and I felt guilty as the vast amounts of killing was being reported to the world. We could not take our eyes off the television screen nor could we watch. Why is this world so hateful and spiteful? It was so much easier to be peaceful and kind. The quest for power by a certain few was just downright incredible.

That day, watching the thousands of families looking for their loved ones that worked at the Trade Center, was too much to bear. It seemed that everyone knew of someone who had died that day. Even in Buffalo, five hundred miles away, we had lost people who had moved to work there. As the hours passed, we discussed the possibility of the Niagara Power Plant, which supplied the northeast with electricity, would be coming under siege. If that happened, the east coast of the country would be thrown into total darkness.

The police had closed the bridges going into and leaving New York City. Fearful, we canceled our plans to go to a wedding of one of my best friend's daughter in Milford, Connecticut, where I had grown up until high school. We were too nervous and cautions, with thoughts of the unknown, thoughts that they had us right where they wanted us – whoever "they" were. A country living in fear but, not for long. Soon the rise to anger flowed like a tremendous wave through the country. A sense of patriotism filled the air, we would fight back for all those lost on our own soil. We would stand behind the military with whatever it took. The flags flew, there were courteous drivers, and there was a politeness that had been missing for a few years. The events of September 11 would burn in our memories forever. We had gotten so used to the violence of the world we were becoming desensitized to the tragic events.

CHAPTER 11: THE ROOK MAKES A MOVE

On September 12, 2001, (newly named day-after 9/11), our attorney Michael Drumm filed a Summons and Complaint against Peerless Insurance in New York Supreme Court. He filed two lawsuits: one for Evans Services with the case number 8326/2001, and one for Pro-Pak with the case number 8329/2001. The cases demanded $988,000 as in damages to be paid compounded at 9% annually until it was settled. He called Peter and told him proudly, "This is going to be settled. You got a good judge. It's Judge Joseph Glownia, he will get this thing moving fast. It will settle soon within three months."

We had lost the building and the monies put into renovating our future had been shattered. We could not understand why Peerless Insurance had treated us so horribly. Little did we know how bad it would get before they were done with us.

On September 19, 2001, another monthly invoice came from Peerless Insurance. We did not pay it. We were being attacked by a company located in our own country, doing business on New York soil. They had used every method in the insurance business on the "do not do" list.

CHAPTER 12: THE SECOND ROOK MAKES A MOVE

Odd things started happening to us right after filing the lawsuit in 2001. We started getting hang-up phone calls day and night to the house phone, our number that was unlisted and only a very few people knew it. We lived on a dead end street, surrounded by woods on our property. During the fall of 2001, people would pull up in their cars, parking at the edge of the woods, sitting and watch the front of the house. Often it happened on Saturday mornings. We would wake up to a beautiful day, pass by the front of the large doors at the front of the house, and a car with one and sometimes two people would be parked in front next to the woods.

Our driveway was especially long and winding, curving along the opposite side of the house. Peter would go out to ask what they were doing and the car would speed away. Coming back into the house the phone would ring. Picking it up there would be a loud click and it would be disconnected. More than one night there was banging on the windows of the house. Peter would go out and whoever it was would vanish through the woods, passing through the yard next door to get to wherever they were going.

One night, around 10:00 p.m., Peter was in the morning room off the kitchen. I passed the front door to the house and a man was peering through the length of the front window along the side of the door. I ran through the house to tell Peter a man was looking through the front window of the house. Peter ran to the bedroom drawer to get his gun. By now the man had made his way to the side door of the garage next to the kitchen window.

Yelling to Peter, "He is at the side door now!" he came rushing through the house, waving his gun in the air yelling at him to get off the property. The odd man ran off to the shallow part of the woods on the other side of the house.

Call the police? We had no proof of anything except the phone calls that, in the next few months, sometimes reach forty a day. I commented to Peter this had happened to me once before when I was living in Hamburg. I had called the phone company and they told me they would put on a detector of sorts. When the parties who were calling got caught - and they would, the representative told me - I would have to press charges. There would not be a choice. Instead, I revealed to the situation to some people in Hamburg, and suddenly the phone calls stopped.

Back then, I was living alone; this time I was not. I thought we would take care of this situation also. It was just getting creepy to be alone in the house. We decided to get a caller ID and the calls stopped. For a while, that is.

The winter of 2001 started coming in with a force of wind, dark days, and snow. I was working later in the evening with one of the local sports people in Orchard Park. A snowstorm was in progress with the winds raging. I had bolted the front door to the office from the inside to keep things in check.

In the middle of the massage, the hairs around the base of the back of my head stood on end. Had I heard someone in the front office? I excused myself opening the door from the massage room. Standing on the other side was a man, perhaps in his middle to late thirties, dressed in black from head to toe.

"Are you open for any appointments?" he asked.

"How did you get in here? The door is bolted shut."

He countered with, "No it was open when I got here, is someone back here?" as he made his way to the massage room.

"Yes, there is, and I don't think you want to get in his way!" I replied.

He turned to look at me with an attitude like he had something on his mind. I met him with a fake confident look on my face, checking him out for anything outstanding on his person. My index finger pointed to the front door, escorting him to the entrance.

"If you need an appointment, please call the office for one tomorrow we can usually fit you in right away." I told him.

Once again bolting the front door, he walked to the left side of the shop to get into his equally black car. When my client left that same night, I had him wait until I locked up the office so we could leave together.

Relaying the story to Peter when I got home, he started staying with me at the office during after-hours. Between the cars in front of the house, the hang up phone calls, and this latest event I was certain we were being watched. We never saw or heard from the man dressed in black again.

After the next few weeks without any new episodes, I was convinced it was a fluke, and my confidence once again built up. Orchard Park is a small town, and a safe one. Maybe it had been my imagination. I told Peter I would be fine, giving him a break. I told him, "No worries I'll be fine. It was someone probably perfectly normal, I'll be fine and I have my cell phone." He had enough going on in his life with the problems with Peerless Insurance.

One night later that month I had an appointment with a special client, a doctor who had given most of his waking hours to the research of Lymphoma. The time and day would vary according to his schedule but he usually came into the office around 8:00 p.m. on a Tuesday. Feeling I was doing my part to keep him healthy, we would laugh and in general tell each other things that good friends talk about.

I would wait for him to fight the blustery winds and snow whipping around the streets as he came in from Buffalo. Calling me, he told me he would be arriving late, the traffic was clogged and the visibility had been reduced to near zero. It was Ok. We were good friends. The previous week, we had been to his home for Thanksgiving dinner with his family, enjoying every moment of the day. His children were a delight and both Peter and I had enjoyed watching them growing up.

He arrived shortly after 8:00 p.m. The winds had suddenly died down and the snow that had been relentless for most of the afternoon had stopped. As he was leaving, I looked at the clock in the front office. It was 9:30 p.m. We had spent the past hour plus a few minutes in our usual manner, laughing and rehashing the events of both our lives. Usually we would say our good nights, he would leave and I would clean up the office before going home.

As I opened the door to let him out, I noticed movement across the now empty parking lot. It was at least fifty feet away. It looked like three figures, dressed in dark clothing, lined up, crouched low, behind the leafless bushes, the snow before and behind them, along with the security light of the building to the right or them had filtered the shadows of them behind the hedge. I turned to my client who was now in the parking lot next to his car.

"Do you see figures behind the bushes?" I asked.

"Where?" my client responded.

"In front of me as I look towards the bushes, I see something."

"I still don't see it."

"Well I do and you need to wait for me, I'll clean up tomorrow." I said as I quickly locked up the office jumping into my car.

I no longer wanted to be in the Orchard Park or Williamsville office alone. I felt trapped in my own business, trapped in my home. None of this had happened before, at least not since the robbery in Hamburg and the hang up phone calls back then. It was time to tighten up our lives to watch, listen, and wait.

For the second year since the fire, the holidays came and went. We did not show being worried to family and friends. They did not ask and we did not offer. We had to keep it tight, just the two of us. There was a new normal of life, a hesitation, guarding, making sure we did not give out any information.

We were getting harassing letters from Peerless Insurance for not paying our monthly premiums. They had ignored us in our time of need, we would ignore them after paying for almost a year on a burned out building and stop their "protection money." We were now just another trashed small business in western New York.

On January 25, 2002, Peerless Insurance referred us to a collection agency for payment on the invoices they had been sending. In words to enhance their pristine reputation, the letter stated: You have an outstanding bill of $700.00 and you had better pay it or we are going to take you to small claims court.

We laughed at the emotional abuse of this corporation, and put the ever growing file of Peerless Insurance paperwork to be used in the trial that would take place in Supreme Court. Keeping the original we sent Michael a copy. "A few more months," he declared, "and everything will be settled."

CHAPTER 13: CONTROL YOUR CENTER

Good things were happening to us during this time as well. For example, a friend and fellow business owner, Kate and I were accepted to work as massage therapists for the Olympics that were to be held in Salt Lake City, Utah, in 2002. It was difficult trying to figure out how I was going to be able to go while fighting with Peerless Insurance and Peter trying to carry on to his business. The problems were endless.

Russ, another great friend of Peter and mine from Advanced Massage Therapy, came in for his appointment one afternoon carrying a glass jar. "This is how you are going to the Olympics!" he boomed throwing $25.00 into the jar to commence the start of a fund. During the next few weeks, one by one, my clients contributed to the jar. So generous, so kind, they believed in us, knowing we were going through extremely hard and difficult time with the lawsuit against Peerless Insurance. Soon I had enough money for the plane flight round-trip. The rest would be figured out when we got there. The Olympics in Salt Lake were scheduled from February 8th - 24th. We were scheduled to be there in the middle of the event to the closing ceremonies.

Leaving Buffalo, we arrived in Salt Lake City in the early afternoon. We were to stay with a friend of Kate's. As we made ourselves at home, the quarters were a little tight but we managed to find a space on the floor, falling asleep after the long day of flying and getting our bearings in Utah. In the darkness of the night, my cell phone rang. Answering "Hello" it clicked into dark space. They had started again - over and over all night long and throughout the next day.

September's attack six months before, along with other public safety problems, had almost canceled the Olympics. Here we were, amid the tightest security in the world, and I was getting hang up phone calls.

During the next day, with yet more hang up phone calls, it was suggested I report it to the military police and let them catch the idiots that was getting such joy out of stupid tactics. The military had enough to worry about in Salt Lake City, and whomever spent their next two weeks calling me clearly had to be from Buffalo. They wanted to let me know they knew where I was, and it had to be someone who had either gotten my cell phone number or it was someone close to Peter and myself.

"Screw them." I thought. I was here for a purpose and it did not include the cowardly caller. I would deal with it when I got back to New York.

The security was intense during our stay in Utah. A bus would be located in a parking lot far from where the village was. It would fill with volunteers and participants. Approaching the gates of the Olympic Village, the security would be heavier, lining the road with vans, trucks and car with artillery forces sitting inside. The gates would open and the military would step inside the bus, walking the aisles looking at our Identifications with rifles posed, dogs sniffing looking for anything out of the ordinary.

Rumors continued throughout the Olympics that they were going to be attacked, and, if this was the case, the military was ready and they would not be taking many prisoners. One night, we finished our stint early and as we walked through the village, we noticed an odd sense of wariness. Thinking we were being filmed, and perhaps audios were in the bushes and trees, we felt safe. The village also had stores open that were not privy to the public.

We had been allowed in where the media and other professionals had not been allowed. We went through the stores looking for the famous berets that were so popular. We did not find them that day so instead we got large posters to celebrate the event. As we continued to walk the peaceful grounds, I turned to Kate and remarked, "Have you noticed my phone does not ring when I'm on the grounds of the Olympics or on the bus?" Nodding, we walked with our own thoughts on what was probably coming out of Buffalo. Secretly, I wondered if someone had followed me and knew when I was volunteering at the Olympics.

Over the next two weeks, with the periodic hang up phone calls having become the new norm, we finished our stint in Salt Lake City. We had visited Park City, a beautiful village within driving distance, and bought berets, t-shirts, and pins for family and friends. Our energy was spent, and we were ready to leave the area where so much had happened in such a short time. That evening we packed our stuff, getting in the car at 2:30 a.m., and drove to the airport for an 8:00 a.m. flight to New York. What we thought would be quiet and calm trip, allowing us to continue to unwind, turned into one of the most chaotic nights imaginable. Arriving at the airport, we opened the doors that gained access to the ticket area. We were then stopped at the door, unable to close it behind us. There were long lines in front of us. It appeared that everyone all had the same idea. Whoops, not quite as planned.

As we made our way through the small airport, it was controlled chaos, and we were soon at the ticket counter where we were told we were on standby, ticket or no ticket. It had taken us four hours to make it this far and we had time to kill. However, there was not an empty spot to sit or, for that matter, stand in the airport. We managed to find a small spot near our gate, which would be taking us back home to Buffalo. Within a few minutes we were called to get on the plane. Leaving early, we later heard stories of people taking days to get home. We felt blessed it had been so easy for us.

Arriving home, Peter had surprised me with caller ID on our cell phones. After this the calls stopped for a while, but other things replaced it. Good thing that friends and clients only wished the best for us. While others, including Peerless Insurance and their attorneys, were giving us nothing but grief, others in the community gave us, strength, support, and encouragement. We stayed the course working as hard as we could to keep everything on track.

CHAPTER 14: THE CHESS GAME HAS BEGUN

Winter turned into Spring of '02, and every few weeks Peter would call Michael for new information on the now almost two-year-old lawsuit against Peerless Insurance. He would assure Peter that Judge Glownia had this as a business involved civil case, that it would preceded before any other private lawsuit, and it would settle soon. "Buffalo did not need to have companies go out of business." he would continue. Civil cases involving businesses in Supreme Court usually would be settled within five years he said, which was a drastic change from the three months he had touted before. He would continue chattering to Peter, saying Judge Glownia is a fair judge, a good judge, and a liberal judge. We didn't know where the liberal part fit in but we were assured he would get this mess to trial.

I would often speak with Peter about Michael. He was insistent that Michael was a good attorney, that he had been one of Michael's first clients, and they were friends. I was not so sure. His desk was too clean, as if he had nothing to do.

The papers had been filed in Supreme Court September 12, 2001. I found this odd. Who files court papers the day after a major tragedy hits the nation? Michael continued to boast that he had the case in the palm of his hand and we would be in Supreme Court having a trial in Buffalo soon, very soon indeed.

What we did not know was that he had not gone back to the courthouse on our behalf until May 15, 2002, for "the first time on," meaning for the first meeting in Judge Glownia's chambers. It also appeared to be a meeting with the law clerk of the judge. The law clerk for the judge handles the judge's day-to-day business. The judge has to be the umpire of the chess game. Both sides start out even. Supposedly.

The next court date was set for June 7, 2002, for the preliminary conference. It looked like it was held with Kurt Sajda, Judge Glownia's law clerk. Michael did not step into the chambers of Judge Glownia again until March 6, 2003. That was 921 days since the day of the fire.

During 2002, three conferences had been scheduled. One on May 15, 2002, the next on June 7, 2002, and the third, scheduled for December 6, 2002, which was adjourned.

Since Kurt Sajda worked for Judge Glownia, we knew the law clerk was likely at the conferences. Also present was likely the attorneys for Peerless Insurance and Michael. We were never informed of these conferences - we would find out on our own. When Peter called his friend Michael, Michael failed to mention them, assuring him it would settle soon be an "open and shut case." He would not step into the court of Judge Glownia again until March 21, 2003 - almost nine months later. The paperwork presented by Michael showed that motions were being filed. This did not make sense.

Michael was busy at the time, making a career move of his own. We were not aware of any of this going on in Judge Glownia's courtroom or the changes Michael was making for himself. He was moving his law practice from Miserendino, Estoff & Celniker to Brown & Chiari, while we were sliding into bankruptcy, losing everything we had worked for.

On January 20, 2003, we received a letter from Michael. The letter said we were to sign copies of the documents and return them to Brown & Chiari. Peter called the office of Brown & Chiari and asked for Michael. Reaching Michael, he told Peter he had moved his practice to the firm in early fall of 2002. He had discussed with Mr. Brown and Mr. Chiari his current cases he was bringing with him, and it was agreed between the three attorneys to keep our case and finish it one way or another.

The documents would then be sent to Brown & Lustig, the attorneys for Peerless Insurance. Good! We were finally making progress. We found out later the papers were not sent until April 2003, almost ninety days later. As the deal was being made with Michael and Brown & Chiari, the dates with Judge Glownia's law clerk Kurt Sajda had been adjourned from December 6, 2002, until March 6, 2003.

In February of 2003, Peter started to feel woozy and lightheaded. He went to his primary physician who then referred him out to a specialist based out of Millard Fillmore Hospital, located in Buffalo. While we sat in the patient room following a test, the soft spoken doctor came in and told Peter he needed a stent on the right side of his neckline. I was worried. I told the doctor the stress we had been under for the last few years, the labor fine, the fire, the ligation with Peerless Insurance, the general ruination of our lives without a reason other than hate.

"Well, stress will cause many things in the body, and certainly you have not been enjoying life the way you should be." the doctor said. Continuing, he described the procedure to Peter. He was to come back later in the week and get it done. Returning a couple of days later, Peter had the procedure and came through with flying colors. He would be staying overnight for safety reasons.

I left the hospital late that afternoon, arriving home, taking phone calls from our friends and seeing those who came to the house throughout the late afternoon. Early in the evening the phone rang. Thinking it was a friend or family I picked it up without checking the caller ID. "Click." Another hang-up. I laughed at the phone caller, what a coward he or she was, the phone always showing unavailable instead of a phone number

The next day I retrieved Peter from the hospital. He was looking much better than he had been. The attending physician entered the room only to tell Peter he needed another stent in a few weeks on the other side. He would be as good as new: get rid of the problem and you will get rid of the stress. He would return the first week in March for surgery of the insertion of the stent on the other side and once again be healthy.

On March 10, 2003, Michael called Peter and told him he needed us to come to the offices in Lancaster New York, to sign a contract. I was in Williamsville for my usual appointments when Peter called me. He assured me it would not take long since the rest of my appointments were in Orchard Park later in the afternoon and evening. No sooner did I arrive in Orchard Park then I was back in Peter's car for the short trek to Lancaster, two towns away. The days of winter seemed to be dissipating into a dull nondescript time. The afternoon was dim, with the snow charred with dark chunks of ice and snow, the temperature would not register higher than 10 degrees. It looked as though we were going to be held in the deep freeze for another few weeks.

Pulling into the parking lot of Brown & Chiari for the first time, it was a new building, and a larger than average law office. Getting out of the car, the snow crunched under our feet as walked across the lot and into the well-appointed reception area. The receptionist welcomed us to sit and make ourselves comfortable, she would notify Michael we had arrived.

Suddenly Michael burst through the door from his office. "My good friend Peter!" he exclaimed. Then I was welcomed also, not exactly with the same enthusiasm but then I wasn't his good friend, I was his client. He guided us into his domain. Michael and Peter made small talk with Michael telling Peter the office move was one he had been thinking of and that it would be a better professional move for him. The office was closer to his home in Eden, with the ability to do more law cases. He had felt constricted in his other firm. While they conversed, once again I noticed the lack of paperwork on his desk or anywhere else in the room.

Peter asked him what was going on with our case in Supreme Court. Michael spent a few minutes assuring us he had been in court not many days before.

"Just a few days ago, I was in Judge Glownia's chambers with Kurt Sajda, the law clerk for Judge." he told us.

Once again I marveled at his clean desk. Michael reached beside the side of his pristine desk, into what appeared to be a file, bringing out the contract. Sliding it confidently across the desk, he stated "I'm qualified to continue as your attorney in this, it's an open and shut case." Handing a pen to Peter and me at the same time, as we signed the contract he had put before us, he smiled as he took them back and slid them into the top drawer of his desk along with the pens. He appeared to now be jovial as he escorted us to the entrance door of the law firm. I'll stay in touch, it won't be long now, I'll continue the lawsuit, he said.

As we got into the car, I felt compelled to say something, anything to Peter.

"Do you think he slapped our butts on the desk as a bargaining tool to Brown & Chiari?" I asked. Peter answered "No."

"Why did we have to come and sign a contract here and not at his previous firm?"

"I don't know. Michael is a friend of mine, he would never screw me over. He has been my attorney for years, I referred a case to him and he went to court and won $180,000."

I had my doubts about Michael. I would start asking around town about him. Perhaps Snoopy knew something. I wished I knew another attorney that I could go to for information or guidance. Stupidly, I dismissed the thought, because I did not know any attorneys that did corporate law. I should have called the attorneys I did know. I found a number of things very odd that had been going on since the labor fine. The lack of concern for the small businessmen, the fine with New York State and Mary Coleman, a number of events with the attorneys that had been using tactics that seemed discourteous. We felt under siege, and I wondered who in Buffalo was running the show. We continued back to the Orchard Park office, where I would finish the rest of the day's appointments.

On March 21, 2003, Michael made his first appearance of the year in Judge Glownia's court. He had lied to us when we signed the contract. He had not been in the court of Judge Glownia since June 6, 2002, and had let us go farther into debt.

On April 1, 2003, Michael sent the paperwork we had signed on January 20, 2003, to Lustig & Brown. Almost ninety days after we signed it.

CHAPTER 15: EN PASSANT CAPTURE YOUR PAWN

It was an interesting time for us, working as hard as possible, we had to make it work, this was our future. The nest egg which had been secure was now in trouble and it was dwindling fast. We had to get this mess with Peerless Insurance straightened out fast. We were told it would be done soon, to just hang on, that the light will shine through the clouds, it always does. We were the plaintiff's in the Supreme Court case, but Peerless Insurance and whomever they dragged along had deeper pockets. We just weren't quite sure yet where the opposition was coming from and why.

I had made contact with Snoopy, meeting in a restaurant in East Aurora, and had to listen to the comments that American National Rubber had been approached to join a union, and if they had signed the contract, instead of fighting, Pro-Pak would have had to follow them. "They want you dead, dead and gone." The "they" I imagined was Peerless Insurance.

I set my spoon in the soup bowl as I retorted, "They will never beat us, and there is a special place in hell for people like this, when they die." Adding, "You get what you give, including Peerless Insurance. Karma is a bitch. There is weird stuff going on, and both Peter and I will get to the bottom of it."

Snoopy countered with, "There have been things going on in the courthouse you do not know about yet, I will tell you when I find out."

Slowly, I picked up my spoon staring into the liquid, enjoying the soup of the day, knowing that things would be discovered that I did not have access too. Evil things going on right here in the city I was living in. Shortly after we left the restaurant, I drove back to the office in Orchard Park, resuming the work that would encompass the rest of my daily schedule. I slept well that night for the first time in months. I had learned to be patient, that all good things come to you eventually.

One blustery day a few weeks later, I was sitting in my office looking the window as the day was turning to dusk the shadows dancing on the snow filled parking lot. A woman around thirty, with reddish hair, medium build, and ruddy complexion got out of her car heading to our business. Opening the door, she entered the inner office where I was sitting.

"Are you Jo Anne Gleason?" she asked, looking at me.

"Yes," I answered, inviting her to sit down in a chair in front of the desk.

"My name is Shawna Hunt."

She started to give me her unasked for history. She had gotten laid off from her job, her husband had not worked in a while, and she had wanted to be a massage therapist. Would I sponsor her so she would be able to go to school to learn the trade? If I did sponsor her the state of New York would cut her costs so she would be able to afford to go. I hesitated for a minute then asked her what difference would it make if I signed a piece of paper whether she went to school or not.

"If you sign this paper it will insure I can get a low cost loan, you have to sign to let the state know that you will hire me, otherwise I can't afford to go."

She seemed nice enough, but my antenna had gone up when she told me a few things. Once again, I ignored it. We had a light conversation as she edged the paperwork across the desk before me. Taking the hint, I picked up a pen and signed the paperwork. Before I gave it back to her, I inserted it into the printer, to keep a copy for myself just in case.

Turning to her and handing the paper over, I remembered how I had struggled to get myself through nursing school a few years before, working two jobs to keep me afloat. Just in the nick of time my mother had come to the rescue helping me financially. I still had the school loan but that was an easy fix. I wished her Shawna well, telling her we would see her sometime in 2003.

CHAPTER 16: KEEP YOUR KING CLOSE AND YOUR QUEEN CLOSER

Later during the winter of 2003, Peter was getting calls from his suppliers. They needed him back. Pro-Pak did a great job, along with the low bidding and fast turn-around. The company was based on volume, getting the bottlenecks out, making the job run smoother, and be more productive. There were jobs to be bid on, money to be made, employment to be created, yet Peerless Insurance and their goons refused to pay for the damages, and still without a reason.

We were in a holding pattern going round and round like a hamster on a wheel that we could not stop. We needed a break. We decided to go to Dallas, Texas, to see my daughter, her husband, and my granddaughter. They had just moved and needed company, and we were more than willing to get out of the Buffalo winter environment.

Peter had recently hired a business acquaintance who had lost his job with one of the dealers that had worked with Peter. This would be a good opportunity for everyone. He had knowledge of the business, and he could give Peter a break. Encouraging Peter to go with me to Dallas, he would take care of everything. Against his intuition Peter, accompanied me to Dallas.

There had been an increase of jobs and one came in while we were away with the timeline of a turnaround of three days. The three-day timeline was not met so the supplier came and picked up the job. We lost $70,000 in one week. Needless to say, the business acquaintance was let go. We could not afford to lose any more money.

On the plane ride back from Dallas to Buffalo that Sunday, we discussed whether Peter should keep the doors open or come and help out at Advanced Massage Therapy. I needed someone to take control. The busier I got, the less I knew what was going on. It was a bad situation. I had to continue as a massage therapist to make money, but that time lost did not give me time to go over things with the day-to-day business itself. I encouraged him to close his business and come and develop mine. We would all benefit and grow, cutting costs, and he could stay on top of things while I continued to work as a therapist.

Monday morning, Peter went to his beleaguered business, and started breaking down the cardboard, removing the remaining forklift, and dissembling various other tools of trade equipment. Talking to him on the phone in the morning, I told him Peerless Insurance should lose their license to practice in New York State. The tools of trade should have been paid for and they had not paid KeyBank for the machinery.

I finished my massages for the day, and headed to help Peter clean out his business. He looked dejected, at a loss for words. I encouraged him to take the business opportunity I had offered him and work for our future. I needed help and I needed it now. I had some thoughts drifting around in my head pertaining to Advanced Massage Therapy, and I needed someone experienced, someone I could trust.

It was unusual for a woman to own the company and have a man run it at the time. We would just change it up a little from before the labor fine when I had owned the business and Peter had run it. Later that night, I presented my proposal to Peter. "You know how to run a business more than I do, come and run it for me. It will free me up to introduce Pilates and massage together as a combination, a one stop affair right here. Buffalo might be the first city to offer it."

During the next week, Peter sadly said goodbye to all his fellow business owners. Clearly, Peerless Insurance had put him out of business. That same week Peter called Michael to find out if he had given the paperwork and invoices to Peerless Insurance attorneys. Did he make it available to the courts? Did Lustig & Brown have the results?

Michael continued to assure Peter that we would be going to trial soon, probably within three months, and all this would be brought out then. On May 15, 2002, he appeared or the first time in Judge Glownia's court. The hearing took place with Kurt Sajda, the Judge's law clerk. Judge Glownia was nowhere to be found - we just had no knowledge of it yet.

In April of 2003, we got wonderful news, my daughter in Texas was going to be a mom again. There would be more grandchildren and this time there would be two at once! We were bolstered by the happiness of this new family. The twins were to be born during the early part of December, just before the holidays. Then I was given more great news: sometime in August they would be coming over the summer for a visit. This was going to be a fabulous year in spite of Peerless Insurance and the attorney bullies from Buffalo.

After Peter took over Advanced Massage Therapy, he found serious holes in the day-to-day business. It seemed I was very close to losing the business in spite of working six days a week. The money didn't jive coming into the business. He tightened up the slack parts, running it as he wanted too, and I could do what I wanted, which was work as a massage therapist and introduce Pilates to the Southtowns.

We would get almost weekly updates of the events going on in Texas. Before long we were informed it would be a boy and a girl. Perfect! This would be so exciting for them and us. Even Peerless Insurance could not stop our happiness.

That same early spring, I had ordered Pilates equipment to be used by Advanced Massage Therapy. I had a great client base living in Orchard Park, with the citizens of the Southtowns and the local sports personalities. The tenant next door had moved out and with the owner's approval, so we cranked open the dividing wall of the two businesses putting in a door to gain access to the large room to be used for floor classes. At the same time, we would be using the equipment for rehab and general fitness. We were on our way again in spite of Peerless Insurance and their attorneys

Peter, always looking for a way to innovate a business, talked about a franchise. I would scoff at him, "It is more than brutal trying to find a massage therapist, let alone a Pilates instructor, in a community who was still calling it pilot's. We need to wait until the community catches up." He would grudgingly agree until the thought would strike again.

One day, Burke, a friend and fellow business owner in Orchard Park, came in. Agreeing with Peter, he chimed, "You could have a wonderful innovative business right here in Orchard Park!" as I walked the hallway going to one of the massage rooms to tidy up before a client came in.

I turned around looking at both of them. "Listen up boys!" I said, looking at Burke first. "For one, Burke you are on your way out of here, moving to Florida!"

Then turning to Peter I said, "You, my man, have just had surgery not once but twice due to stress. Or do you not remember the doctor saying so? So that leaves one person. Me. I'm a massage therapist and I teach Pilates, that's it."

Continuing on, I said, "Peerless Insurance and their goons have ruined our lives, we are living day to day, just the way they planned it to happen. You want to increase business, that's fine do it, both of you!"

I was laughing when I said it, but we should have done it then, we would have been the first, in its infancy, right here in good old Buffalo. Oh wait. We did not have enough money; Peter had just lost his business.

In August, three years after the fire, my daughter and her family came to visit us. I can't remember if she mentioned it or I did, but I assured her I would be coming in December to help her with the new babies. By the time I would arrive, my oldest beautiful granddaughter would need a break from all the excitement. She was still in high school, and was just getting used to the western feel of Texas. After mulling around the dates, it was decided both Peter and I would come out for the Christmas holiday. Peter would stay for a few days; I would stay for a few weeks until things smoothed over for the family. Finally, we were going to have some fun other than work.

What we did not know was that Michael had not made an appearance in the courthouse with our case since March 21, 2003, five months previous, when a motion was granted, probably by the law clerk Kurt Sajda since he signed it.

We also did not know that Peerless Insurance attorney David Sleight had written Judge Glownia on December 6, 2002, informing him that Kurt Sajda had granted Peerless Insurance their request to extend the discovery period. In addition, Mr. Sleight managed to have the date of the pretrial conference tended from December 6, 2002 to March 6, 2003. It looked as if Kurt Sajda was running the courtroom. This was to become a huge debacle in the years to come in the Supreme Court of New York.

On June 6, 2003, Michael sent a letter to Mr. Sleight. The letter included a Notice of Deposition Upon Oral Examination to the defendant, Peerless Insurance, their investigator Gary Gable, whomever had taken pictures of the fire, the firefighters or police officers, and whoever had contact with the equipment. He said in the letter, "We do not have an expert witness, we will call them at trial." and "I have 78 purchase orders for Pro-Pak from April 2000 through August 2000. I think I gave them to you."

"Dear Lord!" I thought. The phrase, "I think I gave them to you," appeared to be ridiculous, almost submissive by our own attorney. Thankfully Peter had given Michael copies, not the originals. Did anyone have control of this case? It was getting more bizarre by the day. Unfortunately, we had given Michael money to complete the case, leaving us with very little funds.

As summer became fall, and then winter, we did not know Michael had not made an appearance on our behalf in the courthouse since March 6, 2003. We found the paperwork later which showed he had finally showed up in Judge Glownia's court on October 3, 2003. This was well over three years after the fire, and Mr. Sleight had been given more time by Judge Glownia to stall the case.

So, while the attorneys and Judge Glownia's law clerk, the new referee of the chess game, were playing a standoff on the chessboard waiting to see if the other attorney would make a move to end the game, our lives were falling apart, Peter was getting sicker and the stress was building up to an all-time maximum high.

I started to listen intently to Snoop, who had assured me the twists and turns were deliberate to lengthen the time period of the court case. He explaining to me the news was going around about Peter getting sick. It was becoming apparent some people wanted us out of the picture and Buffalo ... for good.

That same day, June 6, 2003, which Peter and I found incredible, we got a letter written by Peerless Insurance's attorneys to Michael. It was a letter of objections, seven to be exact. Some were vague and ambiguous; about the policy, the contract with National Fire Adjusters, the labor fine, the one that stood out more than the others: J.K. Harris & Company.

This is the first mention of J.K. Harris & Co that we had seen. Peter had met with two gentlemen right after the deposition of 2002. First with a Jeff Walter, then with a Stephan M. Jacob. He had scheduled the meetings to see if the men who represented J.K. Harris & Co. could find out what was not showing to us in our taxes but was being shown to Peerless Insurance's attorneys. Nothing had been done, he was assured by J.K. Harris & Co. There were no issues.

Why Brown & Lustig brought this up was ridiculous, and even worse, they had already gotten the information from J.K. Harris & Co. and had it in their files for quite some time.

What was interesting was that both the letters - from Mr. Sleight and from Michael - were written on the same day, June 6, 2003, and to each other. Either Mr. Sleight had gotten the letter from Michael early in the day, then shot a back response immediately, or something else was happening. At the time we were not privy to any information. While they were writing letters to show how important they were and taking vacations over the summer, we were working harder and harder.

In any case, they did not go back to the courthouse with our case until October 3, 2003. The first Compliance Conference was held that day, and it the last hearing for the year. This was a meeting to show the court the progress the parties were making in the case. If there are delays the court wanted to know why. What we did not know was if the attorneys had made illegal moves or if they just had no idea what they were doing. Or perhaps there was another reason, as Snoop had suggested.

CHAPTER 17: THE JUDGE FROM THE LABOR FINE

By stalling over the years, with false information and holding back paperwork in a case that had no merit, Peerless Insurance had brought the U.S. Department of Labor back in our lives. If we had been paid for the damages to the business from 2000, or given our emergency funds due us per the contract, we would have been back in business and the labor fine without a doubt would have been paid by the end of that year of 2000. Business was that good, and we owed only $35,000 to the labor department.

On December 11, 2003, Michael filed a Notice and Motion to Preclude against Peerless Insurance, on behalf of Pro-Pak and Evans Services. He had supporting paperwork showing Peerless Insurance and their attorneys had in fact been stalling for over 1,204 days. Exhibits were shown to the court to support this and all prior pleading and proceedings. Relief was demanded for a violation of CPLR Code Sec. 3126. Peerless Insurance had failed to respond during the 1204 days after the business fire at Pro-Pak. Another CPLR Code, Sec. 2214(b), was mentioned which stated answering affidavits must be served prior to the return date of the motion.

This particular pleading would prove to be a huge part of our lawsuit down the rocky road we would continue to travel until we found out the truth.

On December 18, 2003, Michael wrote to Judge Thomas Curtin of the United States Federal District Court in regards to Elaine Chao, Head of the Buffalo division of the Federal Labor Department. It was based on a letter he had received from Donyell Thompson, an attorney for the Labor Department, stating we were misleading the court in the labor fine case.

The attorney, Ms. Thompson, apparently had been sending notices to the wrong address in Orchard Park. In his letter, Michael stated he had told Ms. Thompson this and she did not believe him, therefore he was writing to Judge Curtin. Continuing the letter, he stated Peerless Insurance has been violating a number of insurance laws and regulations within New York State for over three years. Ms. Thompson had accused him of misleading the court when in fact it was Peerless Insurance. He goes on to state at the end of the letter, "Hopefully this unfounded accusation of Donyell Thompson is not an evidence of her character in general." Signed Michael Drumm.

This was the first time we had seen any bad-mannered remarks made by Michael. There would be further unprofessional remarks he had written in his diary about me when we get further in this chain of events.

While the attorneys were running Judge Glownia's court, we had other things to do. We had to get ready for the holidays by selling gift certificates for Advanced Massage Therapy. It promised to be busy with last minute gift buying, and would help during the next year running the business.

Meanwhile, my daughter and her husband had welcomed the new babies into the world on December 8. I needed to get to Texas before Christmas, staying as long as possible to try and help out. I scheduled the flight for Monday, December 22, early enough to make it there without any delays. Peter would follow me out on Christmas Eve, right after he closed the shop for the day. We needed a break from the intense problems Peerless Insurance had caused. It seemed they, or someone in Buffalo, was intent on ruining our lives.

December 20, 2003, was a Saturday. That morning we got up early to sell gift certificates for the holiday. I had previously scheduled massage appointments in the Orchard Park office. The night before the weather had been freezing, leaving chunky ice on the road. As Peter was leaving, he told me he was going to take the car and leave the truck for me. Laughing I told him, "We will be lucky to get out of the driveway with all the ice, let alone down Jewett Holmwood Road. Be careful, I saw a deer in the backyard this morning."

Leaving, he gave the dogs their "Good Girls," and walking into the garage he said the usual, "I'll be right back in a little while."

I turned, walking towards the bedroom to take a shower and get dressed to follow him. The phone to the house rang. Thinking it was a family member, possibly my daughter, I picked up the phone without checking the number. "He lo" a long pause, then click, they had hung up. Looking at the caller ID, it registered unavailable. It had started again, and when I was by myself.

The phone rang again. I looked first, intent on screaming or using a nearby whistle into the phone. But it was Peter. When I answered the phone, he said "Do you believe the brakes went on the car? I was on Jewett Holmwood Road, got halfway down, pressed the brakes because of the ice, and they didn't work!"

"The brakes!" I exclaimed. "That car has just been in for maintenance this week, didn't they check the brake fluid?"

He replied "Yes, they checked everything they always do, I'll call them and see if they can pick the car up and fix it while I'm here at the office."

In the excitement, I forgot to mention the hang-up phone call to him.

I finished getting ready, putting on boots, coat and hat, and I headed into the garage getting into the truck. Pulling out of the garage, I aimed the electric door opener to shut the door. I turned the truck towards the front of the long driveway. Gunning it, I plowed through the crunchy snow without any difficulty. Turning onto Jewett Holmwood Road, I started down the hill to get to the office about six miles away. Suddenly I felt a slip, then a jerk, thinking it was probably the ice, I pushed the button on the panel to bring the truck into low drive pumping the brakes as I went. The brakes were non-existent. Pumping once again furiously, they were gone. I pushed another button to try and keep the truck under control.

The snow had not been plowed and was thick with white chunky snow which kept the truck from going out of control. Finally reaching the bottom of the steep hill, the truck slowed down enough for me to turn onto Freeman Road. Thankfully it was early, there was not any traffic along this residential area. If I could make it to the traffic light in the center of town, I could get to the office. As I approached the light, on the east side a car was pulling up on Route 20. I blew through the light, now turning yellow, barely making it before the motorist would be pulling into traffic. Just a little longer before I could get to the office and safety. The large unplowed parking lot thankfully was empty, giving me time to downshift again and come to a slow stop fifty or more feet from the office.

I walked to the office opening the door. Peter, who had witnessed the event, looked at me with amazement. I then announced, "Guess what. My brakes are gone too!" We looked at each other knowing something evil was going on and we could not do anything about it. Peter made another call to the mechanic, who would be there shortly to pick up the truck. We were stuck without cars for the moment.

Luckily, a friend came into the office to pay a Saturday morning visit. He would drive Peter back to the house to get the '73 Mercedes, which he used as a summer car. At least it had heat and it was a tougher car than the '74 Volkswagen.

Now on the third vehicle in one day, we carried on the business of pre-holiday sales. It was good to see our loyal clients come in, getting gift certificates for each other. As the afternoon progressed, Peter was anxious to get the bank deposits into the bank in East Aurora, in order to register to the account by the following Monday. I was anxious to get home. I had the creepy feeling we were being watched or monitored somehow.

Getting into the Mercedes, we headed over to East Aurora, passing the traffic light intersection of Freeman Road, where I had blown through the intersection earlier in the day. Route 20 was clear as we moved over the hills into the Village of East Aurora, pulling into the bank parking lot of the bank. Peter walked to the deposit slot on the side of the building, putting the bag with the day's receipts in closing the slot he walked back to the car. Getting into the driver's seat, he turned the ignition to start the car. Putting it into drive, the car moved slowly through the bank parking lot pilling to the main street of East Aurora. Stopping at the edge of the road he pressed the brakes. Once again, nothing.

Exasperated, Peter called AAA who would come and tow the car back to the mechanic in Orchard Park to be fixed. Now three cars down, we hitched a ride home with the same friend who had driven Peter to pick up the Mercedes. "What are they tryin' to do, kill ya?" He chuckled. Here was the "they" again.

After arriving at the house, we both needed a stiff drink. Taking off our coats and boots, we greeted the two dogs who had been keeping each other company for the day. I suggested some soup and wine, saying "I'll light a fire in fireplace and we can relax."

As we sat before the sparks in the fireplace, my eyes drifted across the room to the house phone. "I got another hang up phone call after you left this morning." Looking at me and laughing, Peter suggested we were probably being watched, then added the phone call was to see if we were still home. Maybe someone was waiting at the bottom of Jewett Holmwood Road to see if we crashed into something. I cautiously returned the laugh as I gazed at the phone.

I then asked Peter if he wanted to walk around the outside of the house, especially where the deep side of the woods was located. He agreed to keep me amused. We put on our heavy winter clothes and boots and I grabbed a camera. Peter opened the garage door, walking through the open area to the front of the house. I dawdled behind him looking for anything out of the ordinary along the walls and floors of the garage.

As we crossed the front of the house, the deep woods faced us to the right. Passing the bedroom window, I saw deer tracks. The bushes directly in front of the window had the snow brushed away. Looking along the yard, I saw more tracks and human footprints. As we followed along to the side of the woods, we picked up just footprints going along the side of the yard. As we walked the path of the large human prints, they appeared to be encased in ice. We continued to follow the footprints until they once again entered the woods behind the back of the house, only to be picked up again a few feet later along the side of the house where the garage was located. There appeared to be a clump of footprints located at the side of the small entry of back door below the kitchen window, which is hidden from the street.

The garage is attached to the house. When we entered or left the garage during all the seasons of the year, we would use the hallway door to the house that took us to the garage. The only person that would use the back door was the cleaning lady. But these footprints were large, men's footprints, not tiny Katie's prints. Who had made the large footprints come from the woods, where no one could see them approach the house or the garage door from the street or the neighbor?

Someone had gotten into the garage while we were in the house sleeping, had been at work, or both.

Once again we thought of calling the police but, what would we say? We are in a lawsuit against Peerless Insurance and someone is out to hurt us? Someone cut the brakes to three cars in one day? Someone is following us and banging on our house and windows at all hours of the night? Someone is calling us, and when we answer they hang up? We think we are being watched wherever we go? It would sound preposterous. We had to ride it out by ourselves; if we were in a horrendous situation we would then call the police. They were for emergencies, not harassment and abuse from unknown people.

What had been a heaven was turning into a hell and I was glad we were not going to be here for Christmas. We would be in Dallas, a much happier place. I had just two more days to go and I could get out of the snow and the depressing atmosphere of Buffalo.

Arriving at the Buffalo International Airport, I was glad Peter would be following me to Dallas on December 24, scheduled to arrive late in the evening. He needed a break too. This garbage presented by Peerless Insurance was getting on my last nerve.

Landing at the Dallas Airport in the mid-afternoon, my son-in-law was waiting for me. Giving quick hugs, we quickly walked to the car. The sun was shining, the air was clean, and there was beautiful green grass. We carried on a conversation about the new babies, and the joy both Deb and he were experiencing. I felt caught up in this great news, Buffalo felt dark, gloomy and depressing by comparison. I felt free, free of the creepy things going on at my business, my home, and the challenging court system, including the attorney's behavior of stalling the case.

It seemed within minutes we were pulling into the driveway of house and my beautiful daughter standing near the front doorway looking fabulous. She was holding one of the babies and said, "Here is your new grandson!"

Peering into his perfect face, she gently handed him over to me, as she leaned over the cradle to pick up their darling little girl. They were absolutely beautiful, as close to identical as you could get with the same features, eyes, hair, and just a slightly different bone structure. Soon after, my oldest granddaughter came in from running errands. She had gotten so grown up! After getting hugs, one of the babies, who by now were back in their cradle, started crying. She swooped him up with an assurance of knowing exactly what to do. I thanked God she was there to help, she was a natural with her brother and sister.

The next two days were hectic and would be followed by little sleep for all of us. The babies would either take turns getting up or one would be settled in then the other would be up for a go at it. It was now Christmas Eve, another warm day in Dallas. Peter would be arriving by direct flight later in the evening, barring any hang up with the weather on the East coast. As the afternoon evolved into dusk, my cell phone rang. It was Peter and he sounded excited.

"I left the office early, leaving one of the therapists in charge. The weather was looking ominous so I left for the airport, as soon as I got there I asked if any empty seats were left, as it turned out they had one on the next flight leaving in a few minutes. I ran to get to the gate and just made it." Continuing, he said, "It's a good thing I did not have to check any luggage! Come and get me at the airport in Dallas."

As I was relaying the news to my daughter, she called her husband. Surprised as the rest of us that he had made it so early, my son-in-law left his office to pick him up. Within minutes they were at the house and Peter had the babies in each of his arms. He seemed talkative as he looked at the babies followed by being very quiet and rocking them.

As the day flowed into early evening, my son-in-law and I decided to go to Fort Worth to one of the well-known markets. Buying steaks, shrimp, and the accompaniments that went along with it, we came back to find Peter had gone into the guest bedroom to take a nap. Waking him up in time for dinner, he sat at the table picking his food. He said he felt tired from the trip, stating he had a headache of sorts. He turned in early, sleeping through the night.

The next day was Christmas Day. It was filled with the excitement of two new little lives who seemed to have more energy than anyone in the house. We exchanged small gifts among us, went outside when we wanted with a general sensation of freedom. We hung around the house relaxing with the babies, who spent the time sleeping or waking up for more food and a quick change of diapers. We met the neighbors who, thankfully, had helped this new family get adjusted. That night,

Peter again turned in early to catch up on some sleep. He said had a headache, and he felt tired.

The day after Christmas was another beautiful day in Texas. The air held a smell of freshness and a cleanliness without the blustery cold of Buffalo. The twins were up early, bathed, and had their liquid breakfast. Sleeping for the moment, my daughter suggested Peter and I go for a ride and explore the surroundings. After assuring me she would be fine without us, we decided to go to the nearby town of Arlington and check out the scenery.

Getting into the car, it wasn't far before we hit Arlington. Driving through the main roadway, we decided to hit the nearby mall and take a little walk. As we circled the parking lot, we suddenly found a spot close to the entrance. We walked through the entrance doors, the mall was packed with the locals exchanging Christmas gifts. We edged our way through the stores into the hallway, the air clogged with a dense heaviness. Seeing an escalator, we hopped on expecting the environment might be less thick on the second floor. As we walked along the hallway, Peter grabbed my arm and told me he felt dizzy from the congestion and too many people. I agreed, feeling overwhelmed by the bottleneck of shoppers.

As we started our way back to the house in the car, Peter suddenly pulled into a tavern located along the right side of the main road announcing with glee, "Let's have a drink with the Texans!" We got out of the car and moseyed in, thinking it would be fun to see what a Texas bar was like. Entering the building, we saw two empty bar stools, waiting for us to sit, relax, and have a conversation about the holidays. We were both happy to be in Texas this Christmas, sipping from two drafts we had ordered.

Suddenly Peter was quiet and speaking softly. His headache had gone away early that morning, telling me he felt great after his big sleep. We could enjoy the next few days before he had to go back to New York and deal with Peerless Insurance, their attorneys, Advanced Massage Therapy, Michael, and the ongoing court case in Judge Glownia's court. By then the holidays would be over and he could sit down with Michael, who had just submitted paperwork to have the lawsuit progress through the court.

Finishing our beers, we headed for the door, "Y'all have a good holiday and come back and see us soon!" Turning, we wished him well also. They were friendly here and in good spirits, people smiled all the time. I made the decision right then and there I would be back as much as I could. I had plenty of reasons to visit, all of them good.

Peter sat behind the driver's seat, starting back to the house. He commented his headache was back with an intensity and he needed to lie down.

"Do you want me to drive?" I asked, concerned.

"No, I'm ok and I know where we are. You get lost when you go around the block!" He retorted.

Laughing, I kept my eye on the landmarks, making casual conversation to keep his mind off the returning headache.

As the minutes passed, I suddenly saw Peter waving his right arm around making circles in the air. Out of the corner of my left eye, I looked first at his arm then up to the profile of his face. He looked tired.

"What's the matter? Are you feeling ok?"

Peter replied, "I'm looking for a drugstore to get something for my headache."

Those were the last words he said to me for what seemed a lifetime.

Babbling was now coming out of his mouth, waving his right arm wildly in the air, he was trying to tell me something. Looking at him with astonishment I spoke loudly. "Peter you are having a stroke, pull the car to the side of the road now!"

He stared intently ahead as if he did not hear me, he continuing along the highway.

"Peter stop the car you are having a stroke; someone is going to get hurt!"

He kept driving, pulling up close to the back end of the fenders of a car ahead of us. I still do not know why he did this but, then again neither does he. We passed my daughter's street.

"Peter pull into the street, you can stop now, get some aspirin and take a nap."

He probably knew I would be calling 911 to take him to the hospital. Knowing his persona, he probably did not want to have the family witness this disaster. He kept going another twenty-two miles, heading back into Arlington traffic which, by now, was congested with people getting out of work. Someone was going to get hurt and soon. My mind was racing, people were everywhere and they were as helpless as I was.

Suddenly I remembered the last words out of Peter's mouth before he started babbling. He needed to stop at a drugstore to get aspirin for his headache. Within a few minutes, a plaza with a grocery store came up on my right side.

"Look pull in here they have the aspirin you want." I told him.

Pulling in he jumped out of the car, running into the store. I grabbed the ignition keys running in after him. Seeing him run down an aisle, I ran up to a cashier and told her to call 911, he was having a stroke. She relayed the message to the manager who called 911 and, within thirty seconds, the EMT's were at the scene, leading Peter to the ambulance after finding him at the back of the store.

Gingerly, they put him into the ambulance. I called my daughter telling her what had just happened.

"Where are you?" she said.

"I don't know." I answered, crying.

One of the EMT's took the phone and told her the location and where we were going. Hanging up the mobile he told me, "We have to get him to the hospital before he has another one, he is in grave danger." This was turning once more from a wondrous holiday event to a nightmare.

By this time, the police had shown up and taken over the situation. It was decided one of the officers would take me to the hospital, leaving the car in the grocery parking lot. As he led me to the car, the huge letters Arlington Police Department glared at me from the side of the car. Sitting me down in the car calmly, the officer stated, "I will take you to the hospital, it's only a few miles away, then we will get someone to pick up the car at the store. Don't worry, it will be ok when we get to the hospital." I felt safe with him, as I looked into the side mirror, the car would be fine for the day, and everything else would be alright.

As we drove to the hospital the policeman divulged, "If you knew how many people have strokes and heart attacks while they were driving it would amaze you. You were lucky, sometimes it is fatal, it is a mess."

I wish I could have told him the nightmare we were living in Buffalo. Like the footprints, the banging on the house, car brake lines cut and hang-up phone calls. I turned to him, thanking him for being prompt, efficient, and telling me how it was behind the scenes. Arriving at the hospital, he walked in with me directing me to the emergency department to wait for the news of Peter's condition. The staff had whisked him into one of the treatment rooms. Within seconds my daughter and her husband had arrived at the hospital leaving the babies with my granddaughter, who luckily was home at the time. We looked at each other with shock and a sadness that this had happened to Peter. Always happy, always in a good mood Peter. We would wait outside the examining room until the doctor had finished, and tell us the results. Damn Peerless Insurance. hoped they and their personal rotted in hell.

Feeling stifled by the air and the flurry of the activity in the emergency room, I realized I needed some air, and fast. The whole thing once again was crumbling around me. I leaned on the cold concrete outside wall of the entrance of the hospital and sobbed tears everywhere. With my daughter at my side I wailed, "Why are they doing this to us?"

"Who?" she asked.

I looked at her, knowing I could not tell her of the banging on the house, the hang-up phone calls, the people boldly in their cars staring at our house and property, the footprints, or the brakes of the car being cut a few days before. I could not tell her who they were, I didn't know for sure, and I could not accuse anyone without proof. We stood for a while then went back into the hospital emergency room.

A few minutes later the doors from the treatment rooms flew open, banging against the wall. A very angry doctor approached me, saying, "This man has had four other strokes this week and you didn't notice anything?"

"I was here in Texas and he was in New York!" I protested.

"And no one noticed anything in New York?" the doctor said.

I told him they did they did not mention anything to me.

He countered, "Well it's a good thing he was so close to this hospital, he needs a test and we are going to have to gamble, if we gamble wrong, it will kill him."

I looked with bewilderment at my daughter, her husband and the doctor. A gamble? Really? He could have another stroke and die, or gamble and hope he doesn't and makes it through.

We went back into the room where Peter was helpless to decide. As the doctor explained the situation to Peter, Peter would try to commutate and could not. During this four-way conversation between the doctor and the rest of my family, I leaned into him making a bold move. I whispered in his ear and told him that a certain few people in Buffalo would love to hear what had happened to us and he better "buck up" to the task before him. He must endure this to get to the next step in the court trial we had asked Michael to schedule.

Thankfully, the decision was taken away from us. The doctor made the decision, and he made the right one. Peter was administered the test and he was going to make it through. In addition, the physician wanted Peter to stay in the Arlington area for the next three months, because he need rehab and to get healthy. Peter was paralyzed on the right side and unable to speak. We were told he would be held at the hospital until further notice. They rolled the gurney around he was then transported the critical care unit.

I could not let him be there alone. Not in a new environment or with people he did not know. Staying with him that night, the nurses gave me blankets to spend the night in his private room across the hall from the nurse's station. I rolled up the blankets, laid on the floor as close to the hospital bed as I could get. Peter's hand dropped from the bed and found mine. Getting up to see if he was alright, he had tears in his eyes, a sad look. We spent the rest of the night like this - his hand periodically dropping to meet mine, then I would put it back in the bed only to have it come to the side and find mine again.

Yours truly was now bound and determined to make Peerless Insurance be held accountable for this and whoever else was going along for the laughs. It was becoming an evil game and we were the pawns of the game. The next day, I went back to my daughters to change and get cleaned up. I called Michael with the news of Peter's stroke. It was met with, "Oh no, so sorry to hear that."

Continuing, I repeated what the doctor had told me. The stroke was stress induced with apparently the length of the court case to blame. Peerless Insurance ruining his business by not paying us had either been the cause, or part of the cause, since his tests had come back negative related to anything else. Michael responded with a half-hearted "that's good."

There was an uneasy tone to the conversation, something not quite right. Shortly after the exchange, hanging up the mobile phone, I hugged the babies, took a shower, and went back to the hospital. Whomever was after us seemed to be succeeding in whatever relationship I had with other people. The time at my daughter's home now had been destroyed.

I headed back to the hospital to see how Peter had fared through the morning. He was out of intensive care, in a private room, and had gotten some of his color back. Within the hour, lunch arrived consisting of soup, salad, and a mixture of chicken and pasta. Being right-handed, Peter tried to eat with his left hand. He was frustrated with the outcome of using his left hand with lunch falling off his fork and of course not letting me feed him. Finally, he picked the pasta up with his hands and ate, his appetite hadn't been lost. This guy had a great constitution.

Soon after lunch, the Physical and Occupational Therapist came in to give Peter encouragement and instructions to improve his dexterity. The therapist asked him to write the numbers one through ten on a piece of paper. He could write two through nine but not the one or the ten. She explained to us this was the part of the brain affected and he would have to be patient. He still could not talk but was making an attempt to be understood by all of us. The staff remarked at how fast he had progressed in a little more than twenty-four hours, especially since it had been a major stroke. By the end of the day, Peter was tired, and as he started to go to sleep, so I eased out the door to see my family. I was feeling a little better than I had the day before.

Around 10:00 p.m. that night the phone rang. Recognizing the number, I answered saying, "Hi Snoop, what's going on?"

"What the hell is going on there?" Snoopy retorted. "It's buzzing all over town that Peter has had a stroke and he's in bad shape!"

Ahhhhh ... the rumors and phone calls had started; how disappointed people will be when we get back to Buffalo.

I relayed the information from the hospital staff, that progress being made, and what was hoping to be the outcome. I continued with the information of the odd phone call to Michael. "God, can't keep the old boy down, Peerless Insurance should be charged with attempted manslaughter! I'll dig around here to see who has a guilty conscience, although I doubt it, too lazy, and narcissistic." Snoop said. Click and the phone call ended.

I looked down at the phone and smiled. If anyone could, Snoop would handle it.

The next day was mind-blowing. As I entered the room I heard "Hello Sweetie-Pie." Peter had gotten his voice back and able to carry on a conversation as if nothing had happened. He spoke of his treatment from the emergency room right to the present moment. The staff was excited as I was, he was back with full force! Soon the doctor came in and we discussed the stress we had been under with Peerless Insurance.

"You have been under more than enough stress to bring this on, I'm surprised you are still standing." the doctor told us. It was then that Peter relinquished any idea of us staying in Texas for any length of time. There was too much going on in Buffalo, more than we even knew had been going on.

Peter got out of the hospital on New Year's Eve, an amazing feat with an amazing staff to help him through it. He felt so sad and unhappy. He felt the trip had been broken into pieces. Dejected, he said, "I feel like I have been hit by a truck, I ruined everything, but I want to go home." Reluctantly I agreed. That would be the end of any bonding with the twins, my granddaughter, or my family.

Peerless Insurance had us in a vice for over three years and they were not about to give up now. Sadly, I looked at him. "You did not ruin the trip, you could not help it. We have had people on our tails for three years and we have to get through this year. It will go down as one of our bad years. 2004 will be better."

Once again, there were five appearances scheduled in Supreme Court in 2003. Out of the five, there were two adjournments and one a no show. Kurt Sajda, the Judge's law clerk, had to be there, so it was either Peerless Insurance's attorney or Michael who did not show. We were not informed of the continuing situation. We found out later.

On January 2, 2004, we boarded the plane to go back to Buffalo. What had started out as a happy time had been trashed, brought on by outside sources. We left Dallas and were to change planes midway to connect to the Buffalo flight. Moving through the terminal Peter suddenly looked pale. He told me he felt dizzy and weak. We gingerly made it to the gates of the terminal to go back to the dark, cold, snowy, northeast. Back to fight some more. We arrived late that evening, exhausted from the trip, soon falling into bed and more court ligation to follow.

Within a few days Peter was back to his old self, however, we were more cautious, always looking out the window, locking the side entrance to the garage, looking for footprints. We pulled the curtains of the back of the house overlooking the woods shut. There would be no more enjoying the woods. It was funny, there were no more phone calls, but to this day we lock before we pick up, and never if we do not recognize the number.

CHAPTER 18: THE BISHOP

One of the pieces in chess is called the Bishop. He has to stay on the color assigned, and work well with other Bishops because they cover each other's weaknesses.

On January 23, 2004, after adjournments and delays throughout January of 2003, Judge Glownia signed his first order. It was an order on a Motion to Preclude submitted by our attorney, Michael Drumm, the previous December 11, 2003. This motion would let Michael continue to trial since Peerless Insurance staff had lied about unfounded information about Peter and me. To preclude means to stop, hinder, prohibit, oppose, or reject. This would bring on the trial. We just were not informed of it yet. We had gone 1,277 days without an income and Peerless Insurance was still laughing.

On February 25, 2004, two months after suffering his stroke, Peter and I wrote separate letters to Magistrate Judge Hugh Scott, who was standing in for Judge Curtin, regarding the labor fine. We wrote of the ongoing antics of the Supreme Court case. In the letter, we explained the situation with Peerless Insurance. We mentioned the order that had been issued by Judge Glownia against Peerless Insurance the previous January, and we were waiting to continue the court case soon. We were the plaintiffs, good guys, and we were innocent. I wrote of the consequences of Peerless Insurance not paying "in good faith", and that we had to take a second mortgage out on the house. The second mortgage was to be for 30 years at 12% versus the original 15 years that has been in place at a considerably lower percent. The case had taken a financial toll on my credit which had always been supreme, as had Peter's.

Three weeks later, on March 18, 2004, Attorney David Sleight, the attorney for Peerless Insurance, sent Michael authorizations for us to sign for IRS taxes 1998, 1999, 2000, and 2001. This was the second time we would be providing the information for Peerless Insurance. It would not be the last, and it was another stalling tactic being made by Peerless Insurance attorneys in the scheme of the chess game.

Peter had felt pretty good until the end of April, 2004. Working at the office, he had turned around Advanced Massage Therapy, making a profit for the first time. We were working six days a week, continuing on the hamster wheel unable to get off. Peter would call Michael and listen to the ongoing chant. "We will be going to court very soon" had replaced "we will be finished with this very soon, within three months."

One day, towards the end of April, while walking to the mailbox, Peter could not get his breath, feeling woozy, and out of sorts with himself. Knowing it was not another stroke, it had to be his lungs or his heart.

That evening, I mentioned what was going on with my old standby client, who was a doctor. "I have a friend in Buffalo, he is a heart guy." he said as he wrote his number down on a piece of paper, handing it to me. "Get in to see him as soon as possible, in fact I'll make the call for you tomorrow." It was good to have someone in Buffalo not listen to the deafening constant rumors and try and help us out at least with our health.

Peter got in to see the specialist within two days. By that time, he was having angina pain in his jaw, shoulder, and arm. After the tests were run a diagnosis was made. "You need open heart surgery, and you need it very soon, as soon as possible, we are looking at a quadruple bypass to the heart."

The doctor continued and looked at me. "The stress of the lawsuit has taken its toll on his life."

In almost four years and Peerless Insurance had not budged refusing even emergency money to start up the business.

On May 7, 2004, one day after his birthday, and never having an illness in his life, we drove to Millard Fillmore Hospital to have the surgery done. This time, I was really worried about the situation and the toll Peerless Insurance had taken on our lives. Would the loss of the financial status and the subconscious play a role? This time we would take the chess game right to the end with Peerless Insurance. How many others had suffered sickness or, worse, died over similar crap by this corporation?

Five hours later the doctor came out of the surgical theater.

"We had to take some moments with this, he made it in here just in time. He has made it through quite a bit in the last few months. He needs to stay in the hospital over the weekend, one of the staff will come and bring you to the room when he is ready." I thanked the doctor for his kindness, for getting Peter into surgery as soon as he did, and for saving his life.

After another hour of waiting on the recovery floor, I felt overwhelmed. I was sitting alone, waiting for the nurse to come and get me, and I kept wondering who wanted us dead and why. Slowly the hour passed and then the attending nurse came into the waiting room, leading me into Peter's room across from the nurse's station. As I went into the room, I saw he was surrounded with tubes and machines, a very sick man, who over the last soon to be four years had gone through hell. He gave a weak smile as he looked at me, saying "Hello Sweetie Pie." We gave each other a hug as he drifted off to sleep, apparently content. Leaving shortly after, the nurses assured me he would probably sleep for the rest of the day. I left the hospital, driving home to get some rest myself.

That night the phone rang. Making sure it was not another hang-up, I looked at the caller ID. It was my daughter. "How is Pete?"

Grateful to have a family member ask, I rattled on how great he was doing. "No worries here!"

I was scared stiff. The rest of the evening calls came in from well-wishers, "He will be out by Monday and it's all good." I would chant, scared to go to bed, scared someone knew I was alone, scared of someone breaking in. And I could not tell anyone, we did not know where it was coming from. After the news of Peter's latest sickness, we never received another hang up phone call again. It appeared to be coming from someone in Buffalo.

On Monday afternoon, Peter came home weak and exhausted. All he wanted was to sit in the living room in a recliner and regain his strength. Looking weak and sickly from the ordeal, he was happy to be home. Well-wishers welcomed him with phone calls and short visits. The doorbell rang as the florist delivered flowers from a friend, within minutes another basket of flowers, then a large fruit basket was delivered. His friends left shortly after as Peter was drifting off to sleep. About a half hour later the doorbell rang. I opened the door with a big grin on my face happy so many people cared about us. It was a man standing on the front porch.

He asked, "Are you Jo Anne Gleason?"

"Yes." I replied as he handed me a subpoena.

Obviously, he knew we had just gotten home and he had taken advantage of it.

Shocked, I returned to the living room handing Peter the envelope. He turned a brighter shade of white as he reached out for the paperwork. "I can feel my organs moving as I turn and it hurts." He read the paperwork stating, "I need to put a call in to Mike Drumm."

Picking up his cell phone, he called Brown & Chiari's number. The secretary answered, "Mr. Drumm is in court, he will be out for the rest of the day, he will be in tomorrow morning."

The next day Peter called Michael again. The secretary put the call through. Peter told him we had gotten a subpoena, and had to be in Judge Magistrate Hugh Scott's courtroom over the labor fine. Michael told Peter he was not authorized to practice in Federal Court and we would have to go on our own.

On May 12, 2004, just three days after getting out of the hospital, we were to appear before the Judge early in the afternoon, representing ourselves. As we drove to the courthouse, Peter was visibly tired, this new stress was taking a toll on his mind and body. Entering the courthouse, we went through security, taking the elevator to the proper floor. We noticed a guard, a retired state trooper, in front of the chambers to protect the judge. I laughed to myself, apparently the judge needed protection from us. Who was standing up to reach out and help us? Suddenly I was mad as hell, sick of Peerless Insurance, sick of the lying attorneys, sick of the narcissism, sick of Supreme Court, sick of everything. I wanted to right all the wrongs that had come under the claws of the monster insurance companies.

We were checked in and were directed to the huge wooden door leading to his courtroom. Entering the room, we were alone except for the court stenographer. Sitting down on the left hand side facing the stenographer, we waited for the next move to be made. Suddenly hearing the chant "All Rise" coming from somewhere on the side of the room we stood up for Judge Hugh Scott to take his place on the bench. He appeared eloquent, a tall man with a quiet elegance. This judge seemed different, maybe he would see the light.

As soon as he sat down, Judge Scott picked up the telephone and placed a call. It was to Donyell Thompson, the attorney for the Department of Labor. Her voice came over the loudspeaker of the phone seething with anger, stating she had been at the courthouse in April and had sent a letter for us to be there also. I looked at Peter who appeared pale and weak from the surgery, but had a quizzical look on his face. We had never received a letter from her or anyone else from the Department of Labor.

We had not shown up, Ms. Thompson continued.

As she haggled on, within a few moments it turned out she had sent the letter to the wrong address. On top of that it was discovered that Judge Scott had changed the date from April 8, 2004, to May 12, 2004.

Maybe Michael had been right in his letter to Judge Curtin. Ms. Thompson was rude without merit. She apparently did not read her mail. Ignoring her own mistakes, the abuse continued.

"Throw these people in jail Judge, they are in contempt of court they were no shows in April!" Ms. Thompson yelled.

The verbal abuse continued on with Ms. Thompson verbally raping us as we quietly sat and took it, as we had done for the past now five years. Finally, I had enough, standing up and started going berserk yelling, "What in the hell is the matter with you people? We had a business fire! Peerless Insurance to this day has not told us why! They will not pay! Why out of all the days in the year do we get called to court three days after Peter has gotten out of the hospital? Is it a plan? What are you all doing?" I wanted to bring up everything that had been done to us.

Ms. Thompson cut me off as she started again. The minutes passed, the ranting continued, finally Magistrate Judge Hugh Scott, with the smoothness I had never seen before, held the receiver high in the air with his right hand, the voice on the other end still ranting, dropped it perfectly into the cradle of the base of the phone. The now familiar "click" on a loudspeaker and Ms. Thompson was gone.

The Judge looked at us and said, "Send me whatever you have." Then he stood up and left the courtroom.

It appeared he had read the letters we had sent to him. We got up also walked through the doors got our phones from the guard and left the building. By the time we got in the car, I was happy and mad at the same time. A judge finally saw what was happening to us. Three days after getting out of the hospital for heart surgery, sitting in a federal courtroom trying to defend ourselves without an attorney, the chess pieces did not fit, and we were running out of time. Someone wanted us out of Buffalo, bad.

Peerless Insurance was making it as hard as possible to continue, and over the next few weeks and months the accusations continued about the taxes, money, and once again the "they don't want you here" line came up. The "they" were getting on my last nerve.

It did not help when Michael Drumm told Peter that Gary Gable had made the comment to Peerless Insurance attorneys that "Peter Kirisits is a very rich man so we don't have to pay him." It may have been a reference to the story about Peter that was in the Buffalo News a few years ago - the story that was told to protect a child. It was repulsive to say the least. Peter was incensed and so was I. Where Gary Gable had gotten this information we were not sure, perhaps he looked it up on the internet.

CHAPTER 19: TWO KINGS

There are two kings in chess. They can move in different ways than the other pieces, they can move over, or plow through the other pieces. They can go two squares at a time, then move at a 90-degree angle, changing the chess game. It's like a free for all as long as they don't get checkmated.

There was paperwork that existed, we did not know it at the time, but Peerless Insurance did and so did some attorneys.

May 24, 2004, was the first time a new law firm, Hurwitz & Fine, entered into the picture. A letter had been received by Michael regarding the building in Lackawanna that Peter had rented to start up again after the fire. Included in the letter was an order from Justice Marrano, stating we were behind in our rent for the startup business. Not much could be done about it, since Peerless Insurance was holding their ground and not paying us. This was the first contact with Hurwitz & Fine and attorney Katherine Fijal. Later they would be representing Peerless Insurance under the helm of the same Katherine Fijal. The fourth attorney to be use by Peerless Insurance. New Faces, new delays.

The same day, on May 24, 2004, Michael sent Peter and me another tax authorization to be signed by us. Peerless Insurance need another copy of our taxes. This would be the fourth request that was fulfilled by us.

Also on May 24, 2004, Michael made up a handwritten draft for a Motion to Preclude. This would be the second, since Judge Glownia signed the first in January 2004. It never showed up in the Supreme Court files or entered into the court system or in Michael's diary. It is written in his hand writing on a scratch pad.

On June 3, 2004, a letter was sent to Brown & Chiari, specifically Michael, from Lustig & Brown's attorney David Sleight. In the letter, Mr.

Sleight wrote: "The reason we have not provided you with Howard Dematties' report is because it does not exist. Just because Howard Dematties made an exam of the electrical evidence, does not mean he made a written report. If he had made it, we would have produced it to you with the court's prior discovery order. You [Michael Drumm] were going to provide us with a settlement demand in pre-trial conferences you have not done so."

Attached to this letter were color pictures of the fire scene. Some of the pictures had rays of filtered sun coming through the top of the building, in others it was very dark. They had been altered. The cord to the forklift had been placed in the same outlet as before, however, it was not secured the same way Peter had done four years before. More pictures displayed the reel to the forklift being placed in a number of places throughout the building. They also took the reel to the forklift that day with them when they left, in spite of the Police telling Peter to keep it for evidence.

The pictures indicated there were two men in the building, one dressed in jeans and the other writing on a tablet, with the one in jeans watching the other man write. They were standing in front of blackened, charred beams. A third person, taking the photos, had situated himself about thirty feet away. None of these pictures matched the first batch, we had been privy too. It was almost as if they were taking two batches of photos. And it had been done while we were in the UK. Why were these pictures attached to the letter and not the others? They had altered the scene.

On June 4, 2004, another letter was sent to Michael. Peerless Insurance had issued an objection to something in my IRS taxes for Evans Services. It appeared to be another stalling tactic by Peerless Insurance.

That year, there were thirty-one letters sent between Michael and Mr. Sleight - time fillers and stalling tactics. They had the records since 2001 and continued to press us against the wall until we got sick, died, or had a mysterious accident. Ours wouldn't be the first deaths from a lawsuit.

In 2004, there were five scheduled court dates, one was adjourned without a new date, and the other just adjourned. The attorneys would not go back to the courthouse until June 6, 2005. We were not made aware of this information; we were not notified by a letter or a phone call.

We were barely hanging on at this point. Peter's health had gotten better in spite of Peerless Insurance. The house had been put up for sale without success. I was exhausted.

Peter called Michael over that summer to get information about our case. We were not informed of anything happening in court, probably because nothing was materializing. During the call, our increasingly difficult financial situation was discussed. Michael suggested we file bankruptcy. He suggested Dennis Gaughan, a bankruptcy attorney in Hamburg. Mr. Gaughan had been appointed Town of Hamburg Prosecutor, along with practicing general law at his office.

Continuing, Michael said, "Make sure you mention my name as referring you, sometime I go to court, I will remind him of the referral, he might help me in the courtroom."

Peter came back and told me what had transpired. My antenna went up immediately again. I kept my thoughts to myself for the moment. It went along with his neat desk. I felt Michael was up to something and none of it good. I could not put my finger on it; something had to be lurking in the background hiding behind the attorney's skirts, periodically peeking out.

Looking back, Michael had referred us to Dennis Gaughan for one purpose: to benefit himself. To get himself noticed. You believe your attorney, that's what you pay him for. I listened to the referral and waited a few minutes. Peter was going to go to the bank and put the receipts for the day in the bank in East Aurora before it closed.

I wandered into my massage room to place a call to Snoopy. We made light conversation, as if I was speaking to another massage therapist. Then Peter left the office for East Aurora.

"Who is this guy?" I asked Snoopy.

"No one special, you will see when you go in. These attorneys have you spinning on a dime constantly, who wouldn't be bankrupt? It's been almost four years. Gaughan is known for saying 'These are my friends' in the courtroom to the people who had had brushes with the law. It could be a speeding ticket, a fight, stealing, small stuff, small town."

I said, "I know. I feel something is lurking in the background, something is going on but, I don't know what, someone is out to get us."

Snoop replied, "A lot has changed in the past fifteen years. Everything is smoke and mirrors around here."

CHAPTER 20: 202 WEEKS

In chess, use all your pieces or you will lose. This includes the rook, which moves to any number of unoccupied squares, including the one where the enemy piece sits.

We had now gone through our savings and our retirement money. We were behind the 12% mortgage payment and the house was falling apart at the seams. Our property taxes were overdue; we could not go on. Peerless Insurance had forced us into bankruptcy. Peerless Insurance had been told we had money that did not exist. The stalling tactics had worked. The fumbling and lying attorneys had worked. No matter how many times we submitted our tax authorizations, Peerless Insurance would wait a few months and ask for them again.

Advanced Massage Therapy was trying to hold on to pay the house debts. In spite of constantly thinking of ways to improve the situation, it was becoming clear that even working six or seven days a week doing physical labor could not go on indefinitely. I was fifty-six years old, in okay shape, but it was catching up with me. If I wasn't careful, Peerless Insurance and their attorneys would make me sick too. I imagined it was just what a few people wanted. Well they would be wrong, this case would be over when we said it, not Peerless Insurance.

Peter called and made an appointment July 12, 2004. It was a cold rainy day in Buffalo. The summer had been dull and nondescript. In six weeks, the fourth anniversary of the fire would be coming up and we had to make a move. Putting on my sweater, we headed over to Hamburg to file bankruptcy. It was a fairly small office, indicating he either operated it himself or had a small staff. His advertisement for the law firm stated he would work hard for you. It read good, he was supportive and experienced, having been an attorney for a number of years.

Pulling into the small parking lot, we walked into the small office, greeted by one of the staff who offered a seat in the outer office. Suddenly, Mr. Gaughan loomed in the doorway, his reputation had preceded him. He was a loud boisterous man, overweight, with thinning hair. "Come into my office." he said, gesturing with his arm.

Entering, he appeared to be a proud Democrat, with photos and certificates scattered about the room. Apparently, he spent a lot of time running for office in one election or another, obviously not winning, at least according to Snoop, but I hadn't paid attention to the elections in Hamburg in years. As he walked behind his desk, he gestured for us to sit in the two chairs facing him. He started rocking back and forth in his chair, discussing the bankruptcy and what would happen to us regarding the house, the business, and our future down the road. I noticed piles of legal paperwork neatly stacked behind him. It was also neatly placed in various open spaces along the walls of his office. A far cry from Michael.

Peter, looking defeated, spoke first. "The labor department is on us for non-payment of the labor fine. Credit companies are calling for business related expenses. KeyBank is on us for non-payment of the equipment that burned in the fire of the business. Our credit is ruined. How did this happen to us?"

Mr. Gaughan answered, "You know how insurance companies are - they do not pay!" Drinking a soda, jamming potato chips into his mouth.

He turned to his computer, ready to enter into the computer the questions that would follow.

"What do you owe?" Mr. Gaughan asked Peter as he was chomping away.

"Thirty-five thousand to the labor department." Peter answered.

"What else?"

"Nothing that I know of."

"What credit cards do you have?"

"Chase, Bank of America, and Capital One, all for a couple of hundred dollars."

The attorney entered the information into the computer as Peter spoke. Within minutes it was over. Peter was officially bankrupt. It went that fast. I was next. I sat forward to listen to the questions that he would be asking me. I wanted to kick Peerless Insurance and their staff in the butt.

"What do you owe?" the attorney now asked me.

"Mortgage, taxes." I replied.

"What else?"

"KeyBank for machinery on Pro-Pak that Peerless hasn't paid for."

"What else?"

"Pilate's equipment for my business."

"Do you have credit cards?"

"Yes I owe a couple of hundred dollars also."

It was done. I was now bankrupt for the first time in my life.

Mr. Gaughan announced he was going to put the bankruptcy in the hands of Harold Bulan, a local attorney. We had never heard of him, but apparently he was well known in the community of bankruptcy attorneys. He then stated proudly, "I'm going to write Harold Bulan to ask him to be trustee in the case. I call him Your Majesty!" Once again the antenna went up, thinking "what the hell was this about?"

We continued to discuss what was going to happen to us, Dennis told us to stop making payments on the house. Peter asked him how long it would take to lose the house, "About a year, just pay the utilities, you don't have a chance of saving anything." Peter slouched in his chair and looked at the attorney.

"I think I was set up for the labor fine." Peter said.

"Of course you were!" he replied, as he laughed with a weird kind of mirth.

It put a dagger in Peter's heart. This was the place where he was born, had lived his whole life, contributed to the community, and they had turned on him, without any reason other than greed, jealousy, and hate over money that did not exist. Mr. Gaughan turned to me, stating, "They hate you and want you out of here." Shocked by his absurdity, I was staring, still not knowing for sure who the "they" were.

I challenged him. "Dennis, if you are in a room with the 'they', you better not leave the room first, because 'they' will turn on you, make fun of you, the minute you turn your back to open the door and leave."

Peter chimed in, "If 'they' think for one minute this rubbish will break us, it won't."

Mr. Gaughan now seemed to be the surprised one. "These are my friends!"

Oh my God, there it was coming out of his mouth with full force.

"They were after her, not you. You got in the way!" he said.

I questioned him, "Who are you talking about?"

His face turned red, his hands fidgety, hovering over his desk. Ignoring me, he stood up realizing he had said too much. "Well it's time to end this meeting, I'll keep in touch with you about the details that will happen."

We paid him a hefty sum in bankruptcy fees to go through the abuse. It was money well spent. Now we knew we had not been exaggerating things. It was time for us to move on, disregard this ugly gossip, not only were we not privy to it, we did not care. We were finding out a lot about ourselves we had not known over the past few years. As we walked out of his office, getting into the car, Peter turned to me and said, "Do you believe what he just said to us?" He was astonished to hear of such hate. It did not exist in his world. But it had in mine.

As we drove back to Orchard Park, heading home, Peter mentioned he was going to call Michael to see what Harold Bulan was about. As the call was put swiftly through, Michael affirmed Harold Bulan was going to be the trustee in our case. Apparently he knew before we did. He told Peter that one of the partners in his firm was related to one of Harold Bulan's partners in his firm. He stated he would call him and write a letter explaining the situation we were in and we would continue to prevail in the case against Peerless Insurance. He added it might prove beneficial in our case.

Peter told me the conversation. I went to the white pages of the phone book and there it was, Goldstein, Bulan & Chiari. This firm's partner was the brother of Chiari of Brown & Chiari. When I questioned the ethics of this case, I was told that the Chiari for the other firm only did real estate, as if that mattered. I then asked Peter how Michael knew we had Harold Bulan as our trustee, before we did. Peter responded, "I don't know, Harold Bulan had nothing to do with our case and Chiari's brother is partner of his firm." I wondered how much of a setup we had been in since 1999 and how much more we would go through. It would prove to be a wild and crazy time in good old Buffalo as the years progressed and we refused to cave in to the corruption.

CHAPTER 21: 341 HEARING

The 341 Hearing is a meeting of the creditors, the trustee, and you, that happens within thirty days of you filing for bankruptcy. You are required to have documents, home expenses, tax returns, bank statements, paystubs, and any other proof of monthly expenses. If you do not have the information the meeting will be canceled. No exceptions.

It was August 10, 2004, and we were due at a meeting in downtown Buffalo with the trustee Harold Bulan, who had total control over our lives. It felt cold that day, as if summer was cruising a little too fast into fall. We wondered what Harold Bulan's plans for us were. We were met by a young attorney; Dennis Gaughan could not be at the meeting due to a conflict.

The plan with the attorney was to get into our respective cars, drive separately, and meet in Buffalo for the meeting. As we entered through security, we passed into a large room filled with people who had filed bankruptcy within the last few weeks. Sitting down, I saw what appeared to be a tall man in his fifties, with a receding hairline. He was elevated higher behind a desk. He had a no nonsense persona and asked automatic questions to the claimant before him.

As the proceedings progressed, one by one claimants would stand before Harold Bulan, the trustee for all of us. Some of the claimants had illness or college loans, we were the only ones with a lawsuit. Some had needlessly spent their money on jewelry, clothes, and trips. "Hand me all your jewelry." he would demand, then necklaces, bracelets, and rings would come off to be handed to him, as he casually put it in a place you could not see from the front of the podium. One woman protested, "This is my Mother's ring!" He didn't care. "Hand it over." he proclaimed dropping into his stash at the side of the desk. I wondered where the newly acquired trinkets and family possessions were going from there.

Peter's name was called.

"You have a lawsuit." Harold Bulan stated.

"Yes." Peter replied.

"How much is the equipment for Advanced Massage worth?"

Peter hopped on it while I was wondering what Harold Bulan was doing. Peter did not own Advanced Massage Therapy - I did. Plus this is the first time Advanced Massage was brought up. Peter did not own it I did. And I was filing personal bankruptcy not corporate.

"Seven hundred dollars." Not quite correct but, he said it. Keeping in mind that Harold Bulan seemed to go for the trinkets and low funds put before him

Harold Bulan told Peter to send him a check for seven hundred dollars and he was done. There were no other questions asked, about anything including our monthly expenses, utilities or work history.

I was called next. Standing before him, I felt I had two television antennas sticking out of the top of my head.

"You have a lawsuit." he said.

"Yes, I'm not here because I overspent. I'm here because Peerless Insurance will not pay for a fire in 'good faith' for over four years." I replied.

What came out of this man's mouth was outrageous. He said, "I'm going to take the top 20% gross of your lawsuit for me."

I looked at him wondering where he was getting his information. Obviously, he had talked to another attorney in Buffalo, and he was looking for a cut of the lawsuit – a big cut. There was a cash flow into this room that was unbelievable, and the sitting pawns were lined up in front. It was as if we were being led to slaughter and only one person held the money box. I was dismissed, feeling my antenna waving and jumping over my head as I walked out of the proceedings.

This man never asked anyone in the room about anything. No questions about expenses, lifestyle, sickness, college loans, nothing. It was abhorrent to listen to and watch. Harold Bulan, trustee for all of us, did not care about any issues other than what he could get including jewelry and money. This so called meeting would become very important in the future with our lawsuit against Peerless Insurance, and the growing cast of characters from both the State and Federal courts.

On August 20, 2004, we received a copy of a letter Harold Bulan had sent to demand Mr. Gaughan the books and records of Pro-Pak and Advanced Massage to be turned over to him, the same books that we had talked about in the deposition of February 2001. They had been stored on the second floor of Pro-Pak, the same floor that had fallen on the woman firefighter. On the letterhead, it was confirmed again Goldstein, Bulan and Chiari LLP. Why was the only tie between the attorneys and the two brothers?

I got on Peter's case then. What was the problem in this town, not one person had asked us what we lost in this nightmare with Peerless Insurance? Not one question of what Peerless Insurance had done to us? Not one shred of proof did Peerless Insurance have. Yet they had entered property illegally, while we were in the UK, moved evidence, and Gary Gable still had the stolen forklift battery charger. Neither Peerless Insurance nor Michael had ever called a witness, the only statements were ours - once at Gary Gable Adjusters, and again at Brown & Lustig. The business was lost, people were out of work, lives had been halted, trashed, and other people in Buffalo felt this was hilarious. A cancer was flooding the system; it was going to be fatal. Sick of the "they" and the vicious rumors. We had to make a move or at least think of an alternative. It had to be precise and to the point. We couldn't tell anyone either, not in 2004. We would start the process sooner than I thought.

CHAPTER 22: PROMOTION

Pawns have a wonderful ability if they reach the other side of the chess board. They can become any other chess piece, getting a promotion to a higher rank, and sweep the game.

The fall of 2004 proved to be very lucky for us. It was during this time that friends of ours came into the office at Advanced Massage Therapy. During the last exodus from Buffalo, the year before, Burke and Sue had moved to Florida. They loved it from the day they arrived.

Burke is an interesting guy, shaving his head before anyone else, had owned a motorcycle business, taught classes to drive them, owned a printing business among anything else that might peak his interest. A free spirit, he had hooked up with Sue who had been an registered nurse, who saw what was ahead of her and left that profession to become a bartender in Orchard Park. She was as funny as Burke, more practical, also moving to her own pace. They had met in Orchard Park and were forever joined at the hip.

I used to love it when they came into the shop. He was perhaps the best massage non-therapist I had ever met. It was instinct with him, the power of touch, giving me pointers on different stretches. Never going to school for training, he was without a doubt the best I had ever met, then or now.

September was turning to October when they popped in to see us. They were thrilled with the choice they had made. Content and happy, Sue sang, "You should move there too." with animation and a tan. We made plans to go out that night for dinner. Deciding we would meet in North Boston, away from anyone that would recognize us, we could sit and just be friends. Knowing we could tell them anything and it would stay among the four of us.

Sitting at the table, we told them what had happened with Peerless Insurance, the fire adjuster for Peerless Insurance, the bankruptcy and Harold Bulan, the antics going on in the courthouse, the footprints, hang-up phone calls, banging on the house, the shadows in the bushes, the guy who looked like a hit man showing up at Advanced Massage Therapy through a locked door, and the rumors. The never ending rumors about us in Buffalo.

A calm fell upon the four of us, Burke looked at Peter and me.

"You need to get out of Buffalo, the sooner the better. Come to Florida you will love it." Sue said.

"How do we do that?" I asked.

Burke responded, "I know people that will help you, they drive semi-trailers to Florida and you can share a space on the truck, it is cheaper, and no one in this town will know. The guy will call you with a little notice and off you go!"

I asked, "You can tag and share?"

"Done all the time and most of the time from Western New York."

We finished dinner and headed back to Orchard Park. Finally, we had a plan and a significant one. What a great idea, time was running out in Buffalo, clearly we were not wanted in this community. Burke assured us he was going to get this done, and done right. "Just be ready when I call, most of the people leave right after winter when they decide enough is enough. Have your stuff packed, all the small stuff from the house in boxes, the furniture you don't need sell, the rest we take."

The latest march out of Buffalo had started in 2000, it had increased to 12 people a day, every day, seven days a week. Some had come back unable to deal with the change, but not many. It was time to turn the page and fight the case long distance. We were losing the house within a year and our credit had been smashed, we could not even rent a place in the area. We were done here, forced out.

Thankful we had a house, a very small house but promising, until Michael settled this mess with Peerless Insurance. We would not tell a soul, not even him.

Snoopy would be the only one to hear the news. A meeting was planned for the following Monday in my office in Williamsville after my clients left for the day. We spent the weekend planning the packing for the move that would come on short notice. On Monday, after completing the day's appointments, I walked back into the parking lot behind the building. The building with dimly lit with lights that filtered on to the lot. Snoop popped up from one of the cars still parked for one of the other offices.

"You will be safe there, this is not a good place for you. No one will know and I will not say anything. Hell, no one knows we even see each other! It is getting rough for you, some of these idiots want you gone and they don't care how, so they will be ecstatic. I'll call you when people get too close to you in Florida. It seems fair." Off Snoop went into the dark of the early evening.

Leaving that night, I thought Snoopy was just plain weird sometimes, too much drama. But then again Snoopy had an inside view of things and had for years and probably would for years to come. You don't get many friends like that.

Thanksgiving and Christmas that year was strange, to say the least. We could not let anyone in the house, it had become a packing center. The drapes were kept closed at all times to protect our privacy from too many eyes. If anyone wanted to come over we kept them at bay, saying the house was being renovated, with nails and drywall everywhere, chirping, "We aren't putting up a tree this year so if it's ok we will come to your house." The boxes were slowly climbing up the walls of the dining room and two of the back bedrooms.

That New Year's Eve we packed up and closed off the rooms we were not using on a daily basis. Over the holiday, boxes were then brought in the living room. We would be more than ready when the phone call came that the semi was here to take the contents of the house.

PART III

CHAPTER 23: BYE BYE BUFFALO

The year 2005 brought snow and sleet. It would come in puffs followed by sleet, mixed often with rain if the weather warmed up enough. Looking out the window from the kitchen to the side of the house, five-foot-long icicles leading from the roof to the porch. Boxes were now lined up throughout the house, pictures off the wall covered with newspaper from the day. More rooms closed off what had been our house and it was turning into cave. When we had conversations the words would echo off the walls. What had been our forever home was turning into a forever hell. Concerned about Peter, I made light of the situation, "Nothing like a brand new adventure." I would harp. "Trust me when you leave, you will never look back. You are going to join the real world not some shameless mess ruined by the court system and attorneys in this town."

As winter turned into early spring, Burke called from Florida. "Be ready, the first load is going in a couple of days, I'll be there to take over. You are starting to leave now, and I'm taking over for you, half the semi is yours." Apparently Burke felt the craziness of the previous four years were too much for Peter, and frankly so did I. I just wanted out from what had been my home for forty years. There was an undercurrent of animosity and loathing, and it was just plain weird.

The day of the big event proceeded as if nothing was happening out of the ordinary. Peter called Michael to ask about the court case. The secretary said he was unavailable and would not be in the office anytime soon. Finding this unusual, Peter hung up the phone, telling the staff, including me, he had an appointment in Buffalo. He would be back in the late afternoon.

He drove to the offices of Brown & Chiari, only to find out he did not recognize any of the cars parked in the lot. Michael was known to drive a Subaru, which was also missing from the lot. He was probably in court, perhaps filing paperwork or he was meeting with the law clerk to the judge.

Driving the ten miles back to the house, the semi-truck had arrived. Burke and the semi driver helped Peter load the truck for the first part of the move. The three of them started stripping the house with a friend of ours, while I continued working at the office, answering the phones and making appointments with Shawna, who had by then graduated from massage school. I had done as promised, I hired her within days of her getting out of school, fulfilling my promise to the State of New York.

Casually, I continued through the afternoon as if nothing was happening until Burke and Peter arrived at the office, nice and clean as if they had just met shortly before in the mid-day. "Let's go out to dinner just the three of us." Peter suggested. I knew the first truck loaded and on its way to the Sunshine State.

We headed to the Globe Restaurant, known for their fried fish and beef on kimmelwick. The best in the Southtowns. Peter and Burke explained to me what had gone on that day, how much was loaded onto the semi, and that it was gone. We would need another semi-truck, and we would rent a smaller truck to get the last of it out and drive it ourselves. Burke explained for us to finish whatever was left, the stuff from the shed, and whatever else. "Make sure you have it all, whatever you don't get you will have to leave at the house. I'll be up again and we can ship the rest and get it out of here." We would ship the cars to Florida using a place in Hamburg, a few miles from Orchard Park, and be good to go by the time the auctioneer comes and gets rid of the house.

It was a relief and a sadness at the same time that Burke and Sue were the only ones to show up in our hour of need. We had a couple of drinks, celebrating our new life to come. "You will love it in Florida. Half of upper state has moved there."

My family had moved quite a bit during my high school years, my sister Leslie was getting to be too much to handle for my mother and father after suffering a brain tumor at birth she had been left deaf and blind. A beautiful sister with blue eyes and blond hair she had a tenacity of a warrior.

We had ended up in New York because at the time it was the only state that offered care to the disabled who were too sick to be in a home environment. Bouncing around, I had ended up at Hamburg High School barely squeaking by to graduate. To me, moving was always a new adventure to look forward too. Peter on the other hand was leaving the place he was born, spent his childhood, made his living. He had lots of memories and experiences.

Crestfallen, with sad eyes, Peter said, "If I need to go to the hardware store, I know where it is, going there I won't know where anything is, I don't like change."

Burke and I looked at him. "You have no idea what you are missing, so get over it." I said, trying to make him feel better. What I did not say was that in my opinion the attorneys for Peerless Insurance and the various courthouses in Buffalo were probably trying to kill him with the stress.

That evening Peter and I arrived back at the house. Entering through the garage, through the back hall into the kitchen, I felt lost and unsure. It looked as if the soul had been taken out of the empty rooms. The interior of the living area was in mourning, going from room to room when we spoke there was an echo bouncing off the walls. There was a darkness from the drapes that had continued to be closed shut so whoever was watching could not look in. Closing off more of the house that spring had made the bright light of the season turn into a darkness and gloom.

Suddenly, I asked Peter, "So when you were moving the stuff out of the house did any cars go by?"

"Just the neighbors," he said, "and we parked the truck so close to the garage so they probably would not have even looked."

The driveway was pretty long and curved toward the house, I felt secure.

On April 21, 2005, Michael wrote to Harold Bulan, the trustee for our bankruptcy. In this letter, Michael wrote there was a $240,000 fine levied against Peter and me. Michael had to know this was a lie he fabricated since clearly in the fine had been $50, 000, of which we had paid off $15,000 in less than a year. Michael had this paperwork in his file next to his especially clean desk. Harold Bulan did not answer his letter, and we did not know Michael Drumm wrote it until later when we found it in some files. But then Harold Bulan had never replied to his or our letters or phone calls either. It was a very bad habit for an attorney, if not illegal under the rules of ethics. But you see, there were a lot of ethics questions in our case.

Were we privy to this information? No, we were not. They held the little secret between them. Goldstein, Bulan & Chiari, and Brown & Chiari. We would find it out later, in the paperwork we would discover. Both men had taken our lives and held them in a vice with lies and untruths, along with Peerless Insurance and their thugs. The reason we would find out later. Right now, we were both plaintiff and defendant. Plaintiff in the case against the insurance company, and defendants in the bankruptcy case. Without our knowledge things were going on behind our back, without us knowing. You see, "they" wanted us gone and out of the picture.

CHAPTER 24: A SALE

Over the past year, Shawna had expressed an interest in buying out Advanced Massage Therapy and had brought along a friend of hers, Lisa Plaster, who had worked in Ellicottville, New York. Having never heard of her, Shawna told me she was an upstanding woman who knew how to run a business. "It will take both of you, and you have no idea how hard it is." I told her.

Signing the contract was a ho-hum event and my antenna once again was wiggling and jerking around. Dismissing it, I reasoned I signed a contract to help Shawna go to school, surely she would be accountable if she signed the contract to buy Advanced Massage Therapy. I actually wanted to shred the paperwork, take all the equipment, and do the same thing in Florida. I wanted to combine massage and Pilates to enhance a person's therapy.

Peter negotiated a contract with Shawna and Lisa. It was signed August 4, 2005, just before we were to get thrown out of the house. The sale was for $60,000, with a payment schedule of $630.00 a month for sixty months. It would work out to be just three massages a month for each therapist to pay for the loan.

On August 22, 2005, we received an order signed by Judge Glownia ordering our tax records again, for the fifth or sixth time we were losing count. The original order was signed July 15, 2005. The weird thing about this order was we were not privy to it and the order would not show up anywhere until 2012, seven years later.

The contract was signed by Shawna Hunt and Lisa Plaster. The first payment was deferred until the end of the contract; they did not have the money. Skipping the next few months, they made the first payment for $630.00 in December, on and off skipping payments until August 12, 2006, when we got a payment from Lisa of $315.00, and in September

Plaintiff to Defendant

12, 2006, when we got a $315.00 payment from Shawna. Apparently, this had been the plan from the beginning for both therapists, or clearly they did not know how to run an established business. Or they just for fun ran it into the ground.

Over time, we made phone calls to them both, without an answer on the other end. It was not a surprise to me, Snoop had done some digging around and found some interesting information. They had no intention of paying, perhaps they got their clues from Peerless Insurance. Once again, I wished I had pulled up stakes and let them start without any help and do it on their own, I would have been better off. But then I wished I had listened to my antenna and never signed a stupid piece of paper allowing Shawna go to school on New York taxpayers dime. I was also curious to know if she had done this to other people.

On August 25, 2005, we received notice the house was going to be auctioned off August 29, 2005. We had to get out and get out fast. The auctioneer would keep anything that was left. We had packed everything up for two weeks. We grabbed two lawn chairs from the store around the corner and slept on the mattress on the floor until the weekend before the auction. Then we packed up the remainder of our belongings, leaving the lawn chairs to the highest bidder. We were exhausted from the stress of that day, getting into the rental truck, hauling the work truck behind us, and our Bichion, Chanel. Sadly, her sister Minnie had passed away six months before.

Heading down the hill for the final ride along Jewett Holmwood Road late in the afternoon, we were dirty, sweaty, and more than ready to leave the hell that someone had created for us with intention. Driving along Southwestern Boulevard and passing Rogers Road in Hamburg, I flipped the bird out the right side of the truck. Laughing, I turned to Peter, saying "That was done with meaning! Let's get to the border, we can stay overnight in Erie."

Minutes passed as we continued along for the next few miles. We had forgotten what was going to loom alongside the roadway straight ahead. Soon we passed the building we had put into so many dreams that had been shattered with intention. We looked at each other, knowing there was an evil in this area of Buffalo.

It took two days to get to Florida. It was hot and humid, but we were thrilled when we crossed the border. Our summer clothes from New York would prove to be winter clothes here. Florida was going to be great, no more judgments, no more evil. Everyone marched to their own drummer and somehow it worked out, getting along pretty well. The troublemakers were slammed down and asked politely to leave. This was a state with southern values, the northerners had better learn how to behave or there would be some cackling and mockery done. The population from Western New York was vast, and we were informed it wasn't the snow that drove them out of the upper New York State area.

This nonsense with Peerless Insurance was getting old and we were convinced they would not be happy until we were homeless. They had taken our last dime and continued to harass us. We would be safe here, or so we thought. We filled the house with what we could, with boxes lined up the walls from floor to ceiling. The furniture we put in a storage unit, on the property, and bought an air conditioner and prayed. Michael assured us we would be going to court soon. Peter had gotten a copy of the letter that Michael had written to Harold Bulan. Calling him from the cell phone with our New York phone number, he set him straight on the amount of the labor fine, stating it was not $240,000 but $35,000 left to pay out of $50,000. During the same conversation, he told Michael I had to finish Pilate's classes in Miami from the previous year and we would be here for the winter.

My antenna had been up for quite some time. There were too many discrepancies in this case, set forth by Peerless Insurance or the participating attorneys. I did not believe a thing any of the attorneys said, or any of the firms they worked for produced, but we were stuck. We had paid him and they were slacking until we had lost everything. I told Peter to play dumb until we got to the bottom of it, someone or Peerless Insurance was hiding something and it probably had to do with money or power if not the downright ruination of us, or worse. We were stuck, there was something Brown & Chiari forgot to tell us, something big and probably illegal and not just with the code of ethics either.

We settled into the cramped quarters. With the storage around us we probably had about 240 feet to lounge about in. It would suffice for now, the attorneys and the courts had it handled. A few days later, on

August 25, 2005, we turned on the TV to the news. Hurricane Katrina was hitting the gulf coast of Florida gaining strength, with surging waters and accompanied with strong winds heading straight to Louisiana. The winds were blowing wildly in Tampa, although it was mild compared to what was going to happen along the borders of Georgia, Mississippi, and Louisiana. The devastation was immense, lost lives, homes ruined, people unable to work. In New Orleans, the population had been hustled into the Superdome, where there had been too many people in too small a space. Food, water, and restrooms had all broken down.

We were thankful we were not still driving from the north through Georgia as the damage was immense to these states. It was a good thing they had insurance to help recover from the damage.

On October 24, 2005, Hurricane Wilma ploughed her way through South Florida, decimating many homes and businesses left in her wake. $20.6 billion in damages, barely a drip in the bucket compared to Katrina. I called my Aunt Madelene, who was the same age as myself. She had come over from the UK and had been staying at her place in Naples, Florida. They were without power and could not get a flight back to the UK as of yet. "You must come here, it will be safe, the hurricanes seem to pass through the Tampa Bay area because of the loop around St. Petersburg."

Within a few hours, Madelene and Chris, her husband, left Naples for drier land. Despite having a few bumps trying to get gas for the car, they made it without too much trouble. They would spend time with us until it was safe to go back to the southern part of the state.

We had a great time over the following days. I learned much about the history of my grandfather, who had been in World War I in Europe defending his homeland. He had paid the price for it, suffering for the rest of his life with physical and emotional trauma.

CHAPTER 25: WELCOME HOME TO FLORIDA

Our first winter in Florida was heaven. Continuing with my Pilates classes, driving my '74 Volkswagen around town, as if a breath of fresh air had started to pour into our lives.

We had lost everything in Buffalo but our pride, and the intense feeling this whole lawsuit was missing something. It seemed ridiculous that fire would take six years to settle for us, while the drugstore that had caught fire the same day had reopened within a few weeks. We would push until we found out what was going on, knowing already some of the antics of Peerless Insurance were illegal and the attorneys on both sides knew it. Something continued to smell moldy and old, we just did not know how badly the mold had encrusted the case.

A Compliance Conference had been held in Judge Glownia's court January 4, 2006. We would wait for Michael to tell us what the next move would be.

"It takes time, this is an open and shut case, they will have to make amends and pay all court costs, my fees, plus 9% interest since the day of the fire." was the continued answer by Michael over that Spring and Summer of 2005.

On February 6, 2006, we received a letter from Michael enclosing a letter once again from Peerless Insurance requesting authorizations from J.K. Harris & Co. Once again, Peter called Michael and told him he did not have any formal dealings with J.K. Harris & Co.

The last entry of Michael's attorney diary was April 4, 2006. It is a letter from Lustig & Brown enclosing a letter from J.K. Harris & Co. In this letter, Peerless Insurance attorneys had received a letter from them stating they did not have a file on Evans Services, Pro-Pak, Peter, or me. The whole thing had been a sham. This would pop up in an attorney's unpurged file in 2013. They had to hide the evidence and would be pulling more attorneys into the deep dark hole

We were three for three. We did not owe taxes, we did not owe $240,000 in labor fines, and we did not have a formal deal with J.K. Harris & Co. We were ready for trial and we were going to ride that train to the end.

As the months marched through 2006, we adjusted to our new life. Thankfully, the availability of things to enjoy in Florida without spending too much money is immense. Almost every area in Tampa Bay had something: from wineries, antiques, craft shows, and events throughout the season. The '74 Volks could be driven throughout the year, with a little help from a portable fan with an attached spray bottle for the hot humid days of summer.

As October rolled around, the weather was cooling off. Ditching the spray bottle, I popped the canvas top down and jumped into the car to go to work two miles away. Taking the back roads to avoid the traffic on the main roads, I pulled up to a stop sign, turning right along the two lane road, a woman was passing me in the opposite direction.

Screaming out the window of her car, "Your car is on fire, get out!"

Not fully understanding of what she was pointing to, I followed her gesture, looking into the rear view mirror of the car. Flames shooting five feet into the air were coming from the engine located in the back of the car. Grabbing my paperwork, I jumped out of the car knowing I could not save it. I called Peter to come and help me. Other drivers were calling the Police.

Strangers stopped and offered words of comfort. "We watched this car all year, great little car." Soon, the fire department arrived and tried to save what they could, without too much success. The police were on the scene within the same time period.

"How far had you driven Ma'am?" a police officer asked me.

"About a mile." I answered.

"Did you see anything unusual in the road, clumps of trash or paper?"

"No." I said, and continuing to answer questions.

Peter came squealing through the stop sign, parking on the side of the street. He marched towards our entourage he looking at me with puzzlement and dismay. What had been one of my most prized possessions was literally blowing up in front of me.

As the fire was extinguished, the flatbed truck arrived to carry the burnt out mess away. Peter and I got in his car and went back to the house. Upset with the shortness of the drive back, I kept wondering how a car could get that hot to start on fire less than two miles from the house. As we entered the cramped living quarters, I started calling the clients for the day to cancel their appointments and reschedule. That done, I was at a loss to what I had just gone through.

Suddenly, my cell phone rang. Checking it first, the number was from a 716 area code. It was Snoop. Relaying the events of the morning, Snoop as bizarre as always, retorted, "I bet if you checked the plane flights going to Tampa within the last few days you would find some interesting names on the list." I started to get mad as hell. I yelled, "When are these idiots going to leave us alone and why? What are they getting out of this? We lost everything our business, the massage therapists aren't paying me, our house, Peters health, when is enough, enough for these people? By the way how did you know about this I just got back to the house?"

Snoop, never at a loss for words, replied, "People here are getting nervous, you will not let it go, I for one do not want you to. You have a law in Florida called 'Stand Your Ground.' Get your permit and start carrying a weapon. If anyone needs protection you two do." The phone went dead; Snoop had left the scene. I vowed immediately to take that advice.

In 2006, there were six appearances to be held in Judge Glownia's court. Three were cancelled. We again were not told about this even though Peter had tried to keep an open honest communication with the attorneys and Peerless Insurance.

CHAPTER 26: THE SIXTH ADMENDMENT

The year 2006 rolled over to 2007. Peter had once again asked Michael to request a trial. Peter was informed by Michael that since we were the plaintiffs, the law ruled we had to wait until Peerless Insurance had enough time as the defendant to prove their innocence. They were protected under the sixth amendment, but we were not. When Peter protested Peerless Insurance had seven years to prove they had not acted in "Bad Faith" there was total silence on the other end of the phone.

Peter then continued, "How could I be a plaintiff in this case, because Peerless did not pay us then we became Defendants in the bankruptcy case?" It was followed by the explanation that we were in the Peerless lawsuit as corporations and the bankruptcy was personal because Peerless Insurance did not pay the corporations. This comment by Michael would play a key role in the future.

Peter once again said, "Peerless has never found anything detrimental on us. They refuse to pay us, lies consistently filled the paperwork, with continued tax authorizations, and you are telling me they have not had enough time?" Once again there was total silence on the other end of the phone.

On September 6, 2007, Peerless Insurance offered us a global settlement of $20,000. It was turned down by both Peter and me because not only had we lost everything that had been insured by Peerless Insurance, we knew there would be a non-disclosure. Michael also advised we turn down this offer, writing a letter to Harold Bulan he mentioned he could not make a recommendation to us to accept it. We also wrote Harold Bulan. He did not answer either letter.

On December 12, 2007, another offer came in for $45,000, another low blow from Peerless Insurance.

Harold Bulan didn't get involved in the issue nor was he told. Clearly, this was an offer Peerless Insurance felt was fair. We once again asked Michael to schedule a trial in 2008. Peter told Michael, "Call Harold Bulan, he will not answer my phone calls or letters. I want a trial."

The space on the other end of the phone remained silent.

Not only were we not being allowed a jury trial, there were other problems as defendants in the bankruptcy case. Harold Bulan continued to ignore our phone calls. Certainly as defendants in the bankruptcy case we were entitled to prove our innocence and get a trial. As defendants, we had the right to have a court appointed attorney. Assuming our court appointed attorney was Harold Bulan, we could not understand this issue. Here we were in Florida, forced out of Buffalo, we were having to put up with this nonsense long distance. Having filed bankruptcy in 2004, we were still under Harold Bulan's thumb as we had been for the past three years as if we were locked up in a steel vice. We could not get a car, rent an apartment, buy anything, until he gave us relief. Something was going on and we were not in on the issue. It had been too long, one hand did not know what the other was doing, or, worse, maybe they did.

In 2007, there were eight appearances to be held in Judge Joseph Glownia's court. Five were Compliance Conferences to make sure everything is ready for trial. The last held on June 27, 2007. The other three were cancelled. Were we informed? No.

CHAPTER 27: BUT WAIT HERE COMES 2008

On January 1, 2008, a new year was coming and a trial would be scheduled. We needed to get into the courtroom and let the citizens of the Eighth District of Western New York decide this case. We needed it done before we both died of premature old age due to intentional stress put on us by a certain few in Buffalo. Peter would continue throughout the winter to call Michael, despite being repeatedly told by the staff of Brown & Chiari that he was either out of the office, out of the office for the rest of the week, in court. The latter is the standard, so if you have the opinion your attorney is duking out your case in the name of justice, it may not be true. Usually he is having a few giggles with the law clerk holding the plumb job or filing paperwork at the courthouse to add to his file. They come up with all sorts of excuses, most of them unimaginative.

Peter continued to be patient. I was different, a vendetta had been upon us since the labor fine in 1999. Something was not right, there was a hatred going around the courthouse and stretching across the city of Buffalo. It didn't take much encouragement for Peter to continue calling Michael and the staff of Brown & Chiari. "They have to tell you what is going on, it's in the attorney's 'bill of client's rights.'" I said, continuing, "I bet Harold Bulan and Michael Drumm have been in contact with each other but neither has bothered to return your phone calls."

On April 21, 2008, I happened to be searching on the computer for various law information related to Peerless Insurance and New York State. Finding a number of lawsuits that had been levied against them, I was getting deeper into the bottomless pit of the information of the internet, I ended up in the New York State Unified Court System. In this system, there were court files available under the Freedom of Information Act under a name, index file, or the Judge. All you had to do was log on, check if you were a plaintiff or defendant, and it opened up to your case. I punched in the numbers with our names which proved fruitless.

As I continued to search, Peter once again called Michael, who surprisingly was in his office. As they made general conversation. I wrote on a piece of paper, handing it to Peter. "Ask Mike what our case number is." Looking at me as I pointed and waved for him to ask, he casually asked Michael what the number was. Paper could be heard at the other end of the line as Michael went through his paperwork. Finally, he rattled them off. "8326/2001 and 8329/2001."

Peter quipped, "How's it going Mike any news?"

"Moving right along." Michael assured him, there would be no more stalling and we were on our way.

As they chatted about the case, I went back to the computer in search for our case in the New York State Unified Court System. As Peter wrapped up his conversation with Michael, I found our case for Pro-Pak and Evans Services. That was why I could not find them before. They listed the corporation as the plaintiff and not us personally.

Scanning through the files on the computer, I was stunned to find the information set before me.

When Peter hung up the phone, I turned to inform him of the news. "Michael has not been to the courthouse on our behalf since June 27, 2007, last year. What the hell is he doing?" I was furious, but not as mad as Peter, after all they were friends, well maybe not so much. Peter gazed at the Unified Court System which told the truth of about Michael's appearances. He then picked up his phone to call Michael and ask him what he was doing.

The minute he did that my phone rang. It was Snoop. I motioned to Peter to put the phone down until I was finished. Snoop, leaving no time for formalities interjected, "Have you read the paper or seen the internet?"

"No, I haven't." explaining the fiasco with Brown & Chiari.

"Well check this out. Seventeen members of a union were arrested for racketeering and extortion charges for roughing up non-union contractors. The investigation had been going on for over five years by the FBI, the Labor Department, and the New York State police. The case was going to go before Magistrate Hugh Scott. Things are going full circle for you!"

I was astonished but not as much as Peter was. He had been a union representative for the United Steelworkers in Buffalo until Shenango closed along with Bethlehem Steel Plant. Sitting down on the couch, he looked at me.

"Do you remember the union guy that came over to me during the fire?" he asked me.

"What do you mean, that guy named Bernie?"

"Yes, the firemen were cleaning up after the fire we were still there, he came up to us and said 'I didn't know that was your building.'"

"Yes," I replied, "what about it?"

Peter continued. "He was a member of that union, I've known him for years. That union is located in the back of Evans Services building, along wooded property line by the street behind us in Hamburg."

Chills ran up my spine.

"Do you think they had anything to do with the cinderblock that had been tossed through the window?" I asked.

"Did the cinderblock come from the same source?" Peter responded.

"I don't know but, it sure is a coincidence, we should report it but first I'm going to call Michael." Michael, less than ten minutes after the conversation on the phone with Peter, had left the office.

Over the next couple of days, Peter would call Brown & Chiari, then the weekend came. Perhaps they would touch base the next week.

We decided not to report it to the various agencies involved just yet. Maybe later, as more information came out and when the sizzle went out of such big news. The investigation had taken five years and they were right in the middle of it. We were walking a tightrope without a net, as it was, and the last thing we needed was more confusion over the fire of Pro-Pak and Evans Services.

Over the weekend, I decided since Michael was so hard to reach by phone it would be more efficient to write him a letter. That way we would all be on the same page, he would have a copy and so would we. In May of 2008, I tallied up the losses with a friend who was versed in the area. Based on the 10% over the last eight years, the tally came to $12 million dollars. We calculated it conservatively based on the business fire and the original lawsuit set forth by Michael on September 12, 2001.

There was no response from Brown & Chiari or Michael. What we did not know at the time was as interesting and bizarre as the lawsuit itself. It appeared that neither Michael nor his firm not requested a fire report until May 25, 2008, eight years and ten months after the fire of August 28, 2000. It also appeared he had lost the fire report from the Sheriff's Department, despite knowing full well we had a copy and had in fact given it to him years before. His neat files were messed up; it was odd for such a neat person.

Harold Bulan himself had submitted paperwork indicating Peter and my bankruptcy of Peter was valued at $978,750.00. How you could file bankruptcy with more in assets than liabilities? Only the involved attorneys knew that one. They also combined the lawsuit of the corporations of Evans Services and Pro-Pak and added it to our personal bankruptcies.

The corporations did not go bankrupt, we did as individuals, because Peerless Insurance would not pay the corporations. This was getting to be a true cluster and the citizens of Buffalo deserved better than this. The greed and bullying of Harold Bulan based on the lawsuit, his take would be almost $200,000 the same amount as the fire damage itself way back on August 28, 2000.

Harold Bulan had not talked to us since the fraudulent 341 Meeting in 2003, when he asked only about the lawsuit. He had never answered our phone calls or letters. Never responded, to our knowledge, and according to paperwork presented by other attorneys, to any letters or phone calls submitted by them. If Harold Bulan had been fed our cases, you would have thought he would have shown a little respect for his clients, the new defendants, turning over the corrupt money for him to put in his stash. I wondered what was going on with his other cases in Federal court.

The case was getting loorier and greedier. From time to time, we wondered how this situation could have formed. What had caused people to think Peter and I were wealthy? Because of an award to a very special little girl who had lost her mother during childbirth? Peter had been named guardian, had taken it seriously to protect her while others read a newspaper article and formed without question their own opinion. It was disgusting and violent. We would continue to stay the course and get rid of the bad vibes in our lives. It just wasn't worth it to have some people around you.

CHAPTER 28: CHESS GAME STALLS

As the days of spring started turning into summer, Brown & Chiari continued to claim Michael was not available. On May 25, 2008, I sent a certified letter to Michael indicating that Peter had been trying to get ahold of him for weeks about the pending trial. We now knew according to the Unified Court System that Michael had not been to any court dates on our behalf.

We had to keep the report of the Unified Court System in our pocket. If the attorneys knew it existed, they apparently felt they were above it, and the issue did not involve the courthouse, judges, law clerks, and the attorneys representing the clients. It would be our job to stay on top of it to monitor the case as it evolved through the system. Now, we did not have to depend on the attorney's word. We could see it first hand, asking questions of the attorneys to see if they were telling the truth, while we printed E-Courts, a summary of the case docket, out on a weekly basis.

Peter received a letter from Michael dated July 30, 2008. In this letter, he mentions an attorney named Thomas Burton. The first sentence of this letter states Michael had a lengthy conversation with Mr. Burton on July 29, 2008. This was surprising since we had never heard of a Thomas Burton. He had contacted Attorney Burton about our case without our knowledge or consent. This seemed to be another ethics problems.

Rambling on in his sentences in this letter, Michael mentions a $5000 to $10,000 fee Mr. Burton would require to take over the case. In this letter, Michael only mentions the business interruption claim, not the fire damage itself. He continues to state that Mr. Burton needed a forensic economic analysis to refute the experts of Peerless Insurance. Peerless Insurance did not have an expert and Michael knew it, it was in his files. It became clear that Michael had not performed the duties we had hired him for. He was trying to weasel out of the case, eight years later.

In the letter, Michael mentions a Lawrence Lawler accounting report from October 30, 2006, not being good enough for him. Mr. Lawler is a professional who travels the country giving seminars to accountants but to Michael his report was not up to par, which he does not mention until seven months into 2008, when it was convenient for him years later.

On page two of the letter Michael states, "I'm enclosing a copy of the two 'Notice of Federal Tax Liens' shown to you at the time of deposition February 20, 2001." Peter, shaking the letter, observed Michael did not enclose the copies that were now seven years old and did not exist to begin with. You will see how this particular statement plays out when we ended up representing ourselves as defendants in Federal Court.

Michael also makes reference to the settlement that had been made earlier this year, referring to it as the offer made in December of 2007 to Evans Services and myself, and my refusal to take the offer of $45,000 or the bankruptcy trustee, Harold Bulan, on behalf of Pro-Pak. Apparently Michael once again had confused our personal bankruptcy cases and the fact that Harold Bulan either had no view on it as he had not answered any letters sent by Michael or us.

Rattling on in the letter, Michael mentions that he is not willing to continue on a contingent basis. He must have forgotten the money we gave him and the lawsuit filed in 2001 when he himself named the battleground and the letter he wrote indicating he was going to charge Peerless Insurance for payment at the end of the trial. He also forgot to mention the attorney he had reported to the ethics committee, and the money we had won and given to him.

All in all, we had given him between $12,000 and $14,000, without a contract other than the authorization we signed when he moved to Brown & Chiari. He had never sent us a bill, nor did he ever ask for payment. He mentioned once to Peter that he had to pay $30.00 to file a document at the courthouse. He never sent us an itemized bill, which we would find out later apparently was the new normal. Another ethics question regarding Brown & Chiari.

In the letter, he also wrote about preexisting debts, also not true. The debts were incurred after Peerless Insurance came after us with false claims. He proudly mentions the settlement offer he had gotten from Peerless Insurance after eight years of negotiations, that he, Peter, I, and the bankruptcy trustee Harold Bulan had turned down. The letter was full of falsehoods, childish, abusive, and untrue. Not acceptable for an attorney eight years into the case. He was going to ask the court's permission to withdraw. You see, he had a secret he did not want to get out. It seems the lawyer that had been responsible for "Kathy's Law" was using a little abuse of his own.

It would be found in paperwork as we continued our quest investigating the attorneys themselves in Buffalo and it was going to prove to be a whopper.

In actuality, Michael had contacted Thomas Burton on June 11, 2008, shortly after we wrote the letter to him in May 2008. We found the letter to Mr. Burton later in some files of the participating attorneys. The letter to Mr. Burton was far different than the letter Michael had sent us. Michael apparently had lost the Fire Investigation Report from the Erie County Sheriff's Department, Fire Investigation Unit. He mentions the fire had started from the extension cord reel referenced in Mr. Stauffer's report, the fire investigator for Peerless Insurance.

When we found these letters during our own investigation of the attorneys, we had already a copy of the fire report by Mr. Stauffer. Michael had written the Hamburg Police for a fire report instead of the Sheriff's Department. We found a letter from Hamburg Police dated in May 25, of 2008, a letter from Hamburg Police addressed to Michael, that a report did not exist because they did not have a file on the fire. Apparently, he had gotten this mixed up also.

In any case, Michael had not contacted Mr. Burton in July, it had been June. Almost six weeks earlier. We had not known about it either. Certainly this would be an ethics question Michael should answer too. Missing is any paperwork with Mr. Burton's signature. I questioned Peter, asking him if Michael had the capacity to make things up to suit his lifestyle.

"He mentions phone calls with Tom Burton but there is no correspondence to indicate there was a conversation between them. Nor did he tell you or myself that he was going to do this. This whole thing is one sided, he hasn't been in the courthouse in our behalf in eleven months, since last June 2007. He is hiding something." Adding, "Why would he tell Tom Burton he lost the Sheriff's report when he wrote the Hamburg Police Department? How many times do we have to give him the same information? Do you think there are two reports? If there are, why hasn't the other one been provided?"

Peter responded, "I don't know what he is doing."

Walking out the door to go I repeated, "He is hiding something and the other attorneys may know it. Just the amount of time involved, constant tax authorizations, almost a year without going to the courthouse, something is wrong. Give me some time I'll write him another letter, let's see how long he ignores us. He needs to take care of the business he was hired to do meanwhile I have to go back to the shop to teach a Pilates class."

Two minutes later, I arrived at the office. As I pulled up to the front door, I noticed a yellow sticker on the door. Thinking it was from one of the students, I pulled it off the glass and looked at it. It was a note from the IRS in Tampa asking me to call the number enclosed. The name Lisa Hare popped up. It seemed odd right after getting the letter from Brown & Chiari. We had never been contacted before, and had provided for over seven years' multiple tax records to Peerless Insurance through Michael.

I called the number provided asking for a scheduled a meeting to be held during the next few days. A short pause on the other end of the phone hinted to me this was not the usual request. A time was arranged to meet at my office. Hanging up the phone, I called Peter asking if he knew anything about the taxes situation. "Only the continued taxes that Peerless kept sending authorizations for." he replied. Informing him of the impending meeting to be held within the next few days, I asked him to be at the office at the requested time. "They might need some of your stuff too." I told him.

A few days later, during the early afternoon, I looked out the glass enclosed front door seeing a woman got out of the car, medium build, average height, with brown hair softly curled around her face. She had a briefcase and walked with a purpose towards the entrance. Introducing myself, I opened the door for her.

"Have a seat, nice to meet you I think!" I say to Lisa Hare.

Smiling she sat down opening her book of accounts.

"How come you haven't answered your phone?" Ms. Hare asked me.

"I don't answer my phone unless I either know the number or they leave a message."

She then told me, "Buffalo has been calling you for a few weeks."

I countered "Especially, from a Buffalo number but, it's a long story." Continuing, "If Buffalo was calling me they have not called my cell phone, I would have it on my call list." Showing her the phone, "See? Nothing."

"May I use your business phone at the desk?" she asked.

I agreed not sure what she was looking for. Lisa dialed the number as I listened. The conversation continued with the representative at the other end in Buffalo.

Within a few minutes the question came up. "Did you identify yourself?", "Do you know IRS 101?", "Yes I have her here, there was no problem." Appearing to be getting agitated, she told the person on the other end of the phone, "I left a note on the door and she called me, read the manual, I don't pick up either, who is she supposed to call?"

Placing the phone down, Lisa turned to face me. "They have been calling here and not leaving a message." Hang up phone calls from the IRS! I found it hilarious and started laughing really hard.

Ignoring me Lisa sat back in the chair, saying "I need your tax returns for 1997, 1998, 1999, and 2000."

Here we go again. I started laughing again, right as Peter entered the front door.

Introducing him to Lisa, I told him what she was looking for. He also started laughing stating, "Why don't we just keep copies of them and stash them in the nearest drawer."

By now, I was sure Lisa thought she had a couple of nut jobs on her hands. Peter affirmed we had them and he would get them for her within a couple of days. "You see, Ms. Hare, we have been in a lawsuit for eight years against Peerless Insurance for not paying for my business fire. They have continued to lie, cheat, and steal money. We lost everything – my house, business, in fact two of them. It trickled down to who ever could take a piece of us did, and they did it with a certain greed and hate."

Shaking her head Lisa headed to the front door. It was hard to tell if she had heard it before or this was a newbie for her. I suspected the latter. "See you in a few days, say next Tuesday?" I responded, "OK see you then!" wondering why everyone was so nervous about the IRS. They seemed okay me, just have your paperwork done correctly.

The following Tuesday, we met again with Peter, since they had asked for his returns also. All of the documents had been with the Brown & Chiari paperwork that had been stored in the storage unit since 2005. Handing Lisa the file of taxes, Peter said, "Brown & Chiari have the paperwork to the lawsuit against Peerless Insurance in their office. Here is their phone number, I'm sure Michael Drumm will answer the phone for you."

CHAPTER 30: PROTECTING THE CHESS GAME IN BUFFALO

Summer was turning into fall, the humidity was falling to an acceptable range along with the temperatures. On October 2, 2008, we received a formal letter, a Notice to Show Cause, from Michael telling us he was pulling out of the case. There would be a meeting, he stated, in the Judge's chambers on October 17, 2008. "You do not have to be there unless you wish to oppose our firm's withdrawal as your attorneys." This sentence alone, written by Michael, indicates Brown & Chiari were involved in this case for the duration of the lawsuit against Peerless Insurance.

Reading the letter, I pitched a fit! What did he do with all the money we gave him? Where did he show us he did anything at the courthouse except chum it up with the Judge's staff? Where are the receipts of the time and money spent? Where is the tab for the documents he supposedly filed in the courthouse? Why did he say one thing in the letters he wrote to attorneys and tell us another? Why is there no signature of his of the letter he said he wrote, without our permission, to speak of our case to Thomas Burton?

I say to Peter, "I want him to continue the case, he has been doing nothing for eight years, let you lose everything, get sick, it's almost as if he had planned it from the beginning. What is his gig anyway?" I continued, "So far he has shown nothing for the money you paid him. Based on $200 per hour where did he put in the time? We are going to get to the bottom of Michael Drumm and make him account for the time he has put in. This is our lucky break. Finally, we can meet with the Judge and let him know why it has taken so long in his courtroom."

We booked tickets that day with Southwest to get to Buffalo for our first Compliance Conference. It was on October 17, 2008 in the court of Judge Glownia. We were not sure what was ahead of us. It smelled once again of dead carp and a self-absorbed attitude. We were mad as hell and sick of Peerless Insurance, who had continued to bleed us for more money after the fire. Not only wouldn't they fulfill their end of the bargain, but they tried to try and collect more money through small claims court for not paying our monthly premiums after a year of their "bad faith." I was revolted by Peerless Insurance attorneys, their stalling tactics, sick of Brown & Chiari, sick of Goldstein, Bulan & Chiari, and especially Harold Bulan who continued to not answer our letters or phone calls for many years while he sat as the fat cat and, we suffered. Disgusting.

On October 8, 2008, we put in a complaint regarding Michael to the New York State Grievance Committee in Buffalo. As we waited for the reply, we had to get ready to fly to Buffalo go to the courthouse and state our case. This once again put strain on the budget, it had to be done. I had also learned the adage when I was a kid "If you see something and it is wrong, and you do nothing about it, then you are just as guilty yourself."

Within another week, we arrived in Buffalo on October 15, 2008. Landing early in the afternoon, it gave us time to drive around and see what had changed in the three years since we had been gone. Noticing there had been a few new clothing stores, nothing else seemed very different. The season change from summer of fall was showing in the trees along the roadway and lawns of the houses. The air crisp and clean as we relaxed with a lazy drive through the Southtowns arriving in East Aurora for a light dinner at the Globe Restaurant.

We had not let family know we were coming to Buffalo. It seemed silly to tell them about Michael and Brown & Chiari at this point. "What do we tell them?" I asked Peter. "Do we show up at their door and say by the way we are in Buffalo getting ready to go to Supreme Court and fight for our civil liberties? Do I tell them Michael screwed this case up so bad that now we are not only plaintiffs in the case against Peerless Insurance, but we are defendants in bankruptcy court? Even I don't get it!"

That morning we got up and dressed for the impending court date. I put on a long skirt, tights, sensible shoes, and a jacket. Not my usual garb but it would do for the courtroom. Peter, on the other hand, had dressed in a navy suit, prepared to duke it out with Michael. He had assembled a briefcase full of the documents counteracting Michael accusations about us. Libelous, slanderous, accusations made by our own attorney.

Peter's briefcase was filled with numerous tax authorizations that had been given to Michael and Peerless Insurance. Also, the paid taxes, quarterlies for the business, the labor fine, with the true facts of the $50,000 not $240,000 as Michael had said. He also had the letter from Michael stating he was keeping a $10,000 check in his possession for the next ten years from 2003. We need to ask Judge Glownia where the money we had paid him had gone including, another $2,000 or so he had collected from bringing another attorneys questionable acts, of the sale of Peter's house. Michael Drumm had reported this attorney to the Grievance Committee of the Eighth District, himself. The committee fined the attorney and Michael Drumm had with our permission, kept the money. So far we could account for over $12,000 of missing funds that he had taken. The lawsuit with Peerless Insurance had been taken on contingency as per Michael Drumms letters and we wanted him to tell us what he did with the money we gave him.

We had to learn to follow the money to get to the weakest link. It would take awhile but, we would find it.

Arriving early for the scheduled time, we proceeded through security, approaching the elevator which whisked us to the third floor of the courthouse. Reaching the third floor we got off the elevator, the hallway dim despite the lighting along the way. Our shoes echoed along the floor as we walked to long hallway leading to Judge Glownia's courtroom. Passing the railing, I noticed it formed a square in the center of the courthouse with small channels leading to the various Judges and courtrooms at every floor. Looking over the barrier, the stairwell was impressive, winding around the four open floors, resembling the stairs of a lighthouse, beginning and ending at the foyer of the first floor.

Continuing to the end of the hallway we found the courtroom of Judge Glownia. We sat on a dark wooden bench located outside the doors of the courtroom. While we waited for someone to show up for the meeting, the Judge's secretary came to her office next to the court. As she unlocked her door, we chatted about the impending Buffalo winters. She said she was looking forward to retirement, having worked for the Judge a number of years. It flashed in my mind she must see some really crazy stuff. Asking us for our names she disappeared behind the door to begin her day.

Within a few minutes, attorneys were beginning to show up to plead their client's case. As they milled about talking to each other, we decided to follow suit and do the same, yakking about the day and the upcoming meeting with the Judge. Within a few minutes the courtroom doors opened. They went into the courtroom and we followed walking the aisle to the second bench on the left side. As the courtroom filled with attorneys, we scanned the room looking for Michael, who was either late or a no show.

A fast pace ensued with the attorneys being called one by one, to enter a door on the right hand side of the courtroom, never to be seen again. We patiently waited for our names to be called, confident we would be heard by Judge Glownia. Suddenly, the sound of a door slamming shut brought our attention to the back of the courtroom. It was Michael, his face a brightly colored red as he nodded to us. It appeared he was surprised to see us after all. He was so used to misrepresenting himself and getting away with it, he must have expected us to follow his advice written in his letter, "You don't have to be there."

Taking a seat on the other side of the court as far away as he could, he sat empty handed, a lack of paperwork to validate his case. "He must feel very confident." I whispered to Peter who looked at me nodding his head. The friendship was ov

CHAPTER 29: CASTLING THE ROOK AND THE KING

Castling the Rook and the King is a special move in chess between the rook and the king to get a move completed between the two of them.

What came next was one of the most bizarre events, and one that will forever be burned in our memory. The door to the right side of the courtroom opened. Michael's named was called, a slight pause, then both Peter and my name were called, almost as an afterthought.

As we entered through the doorway, we were led to a small, compact office. A man with a sturdy build, a little paunchy, sat behind the desk. He introduced himself as Kurt Sajda, the Judge's law clerk. His eyes darted from Peter to Michael and then to me. As we sat before him at his cluttered desk, I was to his left, Peter in the middle and Michael sat in a chair against the far side against a wall. What the hell are you two doing here?" Kurt Sajda snarled.

"We are here to see Judge Glownia, we got this letter to be here so we are." stated Peter.

"Well he is not here and I'm going to handle this for the Judge Glownia." It was after this comment by Kurt Sajda that I became fixated on his hair. It was an extremely odd shade of orange with red streaks, outrageously sticking out of his skull as if he had pushed his finger into a light socket. He continued to affirm that he was the one to handle this situation not the judge.

The next sentence came from Michael. "You needed a forensic accountant, you owe Larry Lawler money, I talked to him."

Peter was furious. "The same Larry Lawler, a certified forensic accountant, that gave you the report in 2003 at your request? The same guy you said his report was not good enough? The same accountant that gives seminars throughout the country?"

Michael's face once again turns a peculiar red with overtones of maroon jutting from his pointy nose. He pressed back into the wall, his suit now tight against his body. Peter, escalating in anger, said, "You're the one who said we did not need one along with not needing a forensic fire investigator, you were going to put Howard DeMatties on the stand at trial. I have the letter you wrote!" Michael was pressing so hard against the wall he appeared almost flat as a pancake.

Peter was on a roll. All the years of frustration and lying by the attorneys had caught up with him. He said, "The fire was in 2000, it is now 2008, you have put people out of work, ruined my career, you have lied and worked everything to stall and not submit paperwork on time, you have lied that we owed you money to the Supreme Court."

Kurt Sajda was sitting up and taking notice as if he was going to get into trouble. Michael was now wallowing in the space around him. He appeared to be shrinking as he was considering the exit door leading to the Judge Glownia's secretary's office.

I turned back to Kurt Sajda, his paunchy face looked at us with disgust. "What do you think this is, a charity case?" he said.

Astonished by his crassness as a confident to Judge Glownia, Peter once again announced, "I paid him $10,000 which was never accounted for. He needs to finish this case. I also have a letter written to Peerless Insurance in 2001, he was billing them for all court costs and attorney's fees." Turning to Michael he asked, "What happened to the money you got from the grievance committee from that attorney that was harassing us?" Michael's face was now a blood red, which was a stark contrast against the grayish off white walls. He apparently had been double dipping also.

While Peter was questioning Michael without any answers from him, I studied the scene in the room. Kurt Sajda's face was now also red with rage, which proved to be an odd combination with his hair.

Michael then said one of the most unprofessional statements ever. "What are you worried about, you live in a carriage house."

I looked at Mr. Sajda who, along with Peter, was looking at Michael with amazement at his ridiculous comment.

That was it. I was done. I rose from my chair in attack mode, climbing over Peter to reach Michael still in his chair. Screaming at him, I said "What are you talking about? Peter's niece? What carriage house, you're a stupid jerk!"

Without an answer, Michael pulled back into the wall like a captured bird without any food or water. I was in a black rage, a place I had never been in before, a suffocating, uncontrollable anger.

"Tell your firm to get their faces and false advertising off the billboards in Buffalo, you are an embarrassment to not only them but, the law community as well. You brag you are responsible for 'Kathy's Law'. You are the most abusive person I have ever come across, let me tell you Mr. Drumm you ever give reason to even think of Peter's niece and the settlement she got, which by the way has nothing to do with this case, your behavior has been less than professional in so many ways. Peter is co-guardian, nothing else How dare you even think that a girl who lost her mother has anything to do with Peerless Insurance or any attorney other than in Surrogate's court. Peerless' refusal to pay is ridiculous. My sister was born with a brain tumor, your jackass, she suffered her whole life and died at twenty-one. You are so abusive you need an attitude tune up."

I continued to lean into his face now contorted with whatever emotion he felt. Nose-to-nose I said, "You know what Michael? Here's how it is, an attorney told me that it is attorneys like you that make it bad for the rest of them."

Apparently this made its mark. He looked at me, then at the floor. What we did not know at this point was that Michael had a secret that would involve the whole courthouse and drag in a few more Judges and attorneys as well.

Kurt Sajda stood up, asking "Mr. Drumm?"

Michael told him a real whopper this time, "I have seven red welds full of what I have worked on for this case."

I looked at him. "You are lying. If you had done your job, you would have made your firm and you some money, instead you are spending your days taking depositions. Or did you lie about that too!" leaning into him as he cringed away from me.

Kurt Sajda, with the weird hair sticking even farther straight, up stood up and got into the act. "We are done, this meeting is over, I'm going to grant Mr. Drumm the right to withdraw."

Thinking my God, where the hell is Judge Glownia and who was running the courthouse and the courtroom? Kurt Sajda? It appeared so, since we saw one document signed by the judge in 2004 and all the rest by Kurt Sajda. Snoop told us later the judge might have been at his condo in Florida.

As we entered Judge Glownia's secretary's reception area, a group of attorneys were standing in the outer area. Jumping at the opportunity, I loudly asked, "Is this how you all act? Lie steal cheat from your clients like that guy?" pointing to Michael still plopped in his chair. The complaints having spilled out from the law clerk's office into this room. They looked at me, not one of them had the guts to answer. The Judge's secretary now crying and blowing her nose.

"Sorry." I mumbled as Peter guided me out of the Judges office through the hallway leading me to the elevator.

"I'll be right back," Peter said. "I want to see if Judge Glownia is here."

I watched Peter walk back through the hallway to the Judge's courtroom. He opened the door on the left of the hallway, and as he did this I looked into the doorway on the right. Kurt Sajda his wild hair sticking up was shaking his index finger in Michael's face, and he was incensed. As Peter closed the door to come back, he bumped straight into Michael. Looking at him Peter said, "Jo Anne is pissed and once that happens there is no holding her back. You better do what's right and make amends."

Michael haughtily walked away coming towards the elevator. I was licking my chops at the thought of another little private conversation. He would be trapped like the rat he was.

He spotted me waiting for him and did an about face, and rushed past Peter to get to the stairs. It was my one-time opportunity. Running to the railing surrounding the open stairwell I commenced in a shrill loud voice, "How dare you, you piece of yesterday's garbage. Because of a lawsuit in a different case from years ago you think that Peter or I have money. I'm going to take you out, hunt you down until you squeal like a pig." "You are one of the slimiest pieces of an excuse for an attorney I have ever seen you liar!"

He picked up speed on the stairwell, and I leaned farther over the stairwell. I continued, "You are doomed you bastard, you are a liar, you steal from your clients." While I was assuring Michael he was a total jerk, I continued, "You piece of crap, how dare you say to people that Peter had lost his mind and his memory from his stroke. You bastard you are so done. Kathy's Law, really?" The remark about Peter had been made by Michael to a staff member National Fire Adjusters after Peter's medical problems.

Peter grabbed my arm to guide me back. I looked up and people had come out of their offices to see what the commotion was about. I looked up, not embarrassed, and assured the audience, "It's a wrap."

Getting on the elevator, we arrived at the vestibule. At the same time, Michael was running from the stairs on his way through a group of attorneys that had gathered in a circle in front of the elevator. My voice perhaps had been heard from the third floor, just to make sure they knew it was me, I started again "I'm going to get you, you lying piece of slime." as he ran down the steps of the courthouse and onto Delaware Avenue.

The attorneys present in the vestibule appeared to be nervous and unsettled, walking in a circle. I didn't care, as I scanned the scene looking for a familiar face. And there it was, off to the side catching the chaos, my old friend Snoop. I smiled without any more gazing through the crowd, knowing everything would be alright. Things were being covered for us in Buffalo and had been for a very long time, while we were thousands of miles away in Tampa.

Meanwhile Michael, who had complained of having murderous arthritis in his joints for years, had made a miraculous recovery. He was running up the street as if he was training for the Olympics, the arthritis forgotten, he had kicked it up. I looked at Peter laughing, "Wow, what a phony."

We left Buffalo that day not quite sure what to do. Perhaps we could go in *pro se,* representing ourselves for both Pro-Pak and Evans Services.

We would have to get cheap living quarters in Buffalo while this nightmare continued in court. The positive thing would be the ability to control the case. Brown & Chiari would have to turn over our files to us, as would Peerless Insurance attorneys. You know, to keep the playing board even and honest. It would be a risky move, fighting the legal system itself.

On October 28, 2008, we received a letter signed by Judge Glownia to allow Michael to pull out of the case. Because we were a corporation we could not represent ourselves. We had sixty days to retain new counsel, so Michael would remain our attorney until January 1, 2009, as ordered by this court. This would be the second document in eight years signed by him. The smoke and mirrors continued to make a mockery of the Judge and the court.

On October 30, 2008, we wrote Judge Glownia a letter explaining to him what had taken place in his chambers. In essence we wrote, "Sorry to have missed you since we had it in writing you would be there. Our case is eight years old and we need an attorney, we need a trial, and you yourself, Judge Glownia, asked for this case to end in a signed document in January of 2004. Nothing has been done since Michael Drumm filed suit on September 12, 2001."

I wanted to put in the letter, the attorneys have violated your order, Judge Glownia, and by the way you need to get a new law clerk. Mr. Sajda has signed so many documents on your behalf, he thinks he is the judge not you. The only reason I didn't was because I knew that the Kurt Sajda, the Confidential Law Clerk would read the judges mail first, either tell the Judge we were nuts and out of his control, or Judge Glownia didn't care.

Over the next few weeks, Peter would spend his days calling various law firms in Buffalo to retain a new attorney. One day, Peter called the Lawyer Referral Service in Buffalo, asking them if they could give him a name of an attorney in the city of Buffalo, who would sue another attorney for malpractice and misrepresentation. They gave him the name of Attorney Daniel Schoenborn, who had an office located in the Olympic Towers. Peter looked at the advertisement of the unknown firm not recognizing either attorney but it looked good in print. DeMarie & Schoenborn, "We are a boutique firm, we are small by choice; we can give you the attention you deserve."

Peter called the firm and explained the case. They scheduled a meeting for in January 2009, after the holidays. The meeting would work out timely since a previously scheduled meeting would be happening in Surrogate's Court that same week.

CHAPTER 30: CHESS CHEAT - MAKE SURE YOU HAVE THE SUN IN YOUR OPPONENTS EYES AT ALL TIMES

On November 22, 2008, Peter and I decided to write Peerless Insurance's head offices in Keene, New Hampshire. The letter was directed to CEO Michael Christiansen, who always made sure in the Peerless Insurance advertisements for his company, stated with confidence the customers where very important to him and his company he represented. Surely, he would see the true light of the situation.

It was a bold move. We stated the true facts, starting with the fire that had happened eight years before. We had not been over-insured, in fact if anything we were underinsured. The police and fire department had indicated it was an accident.

"You, Mr. Christiansen, had been for eight years paying fire adjusters fees, attorney's fees, yet the fire was for $200,000 in the middle of the afternoon. One of your adjusters has been let go by another insurance agency for questionable behavior. We have been deposed once for a statement by him, then a Deposition in 2001." Continuing in the letter we explained the whole situation to him.

We lost our house, business, we lost everything because of false information by your adjuster and the attorneys. Why were you paying everyone else all these years and not us, your clients? We paid our premiums in good faith for almost a year after the fire, then you tried to take us to small claims court for not paying premiums on a burned out structure, nor give us $25,000 emergency money for startup, or replacement for the damaged machinery. I wanted to say "Sir, you are the CEO, the umbrella for the people that keep you in business. What exactly is your problem?"

Meanwhile the IRS in Tampa called. Lisa had left a message to check back with her. We touched base and a meeting was scheduled for later in the week. On the scheduled day, I met her at the office. She appeared tired. Sitting in the now familiar spot she relayed to me what was happening. "We need to talk to your attorney, because you lost the house in New York, there was a lien on it." Aghast, it was amazing Peerless Insurance continued to ruin our lives eight years after the fire.

Giving Lisa the details of the lawsuit, the antics of Peerless Insurance and their attorneys, leading into Brown & Chiari, Michael Drumm and the recent order by Judge Glownia that Michael had been ordered to stay as counsel until January 1, 2009.

"What's his number?" she asked me.

At this point Peter walked into the Pilates shop stating, "Who's number?"

Lisa went on to tell him the new scenario of the damage Peerless Insurance had done. Giving her the number, he confirmed everything I had just told her. "OK I'll give him a call."

Later that week, we met again and Lisa had given Michael a call. He informed her he was no longer our attorney, a direct violation of Judge Glownia's order. We showed her the letter and the order from the Judge. "He is lying to you! The judge ordered us to get an attorney by January of 2009, not 2008."

She looked at us with bewilderment with what appeared to be an intentional new mess created by the law firm of Brown & Chiari in Buffalo. Peter and I now wondered how many times Michael had violated Judge Glownia's or any other Judge's order, and also questioned if the Judge's law clerk, Kurt Sajda, had in fact informed the Judge the true story of the antics going on in his office.

When the Judge had signed the order, he informed us we could not represent ourselves in his court but had to get an attorney by January 2009. Because the corporation had filed the lawsuit against Peerless Insurance not Peter or myself, Evans Services and Pro-Pak as corporations must hire an attorney to represent them in the case against Peerless Insurance, using case code CPLR321, and get an attorney. "We have until January 1, 2009, to get a new attorney," I told Lisa.

Lisa appeared to be amazed this was happening. So were we, but with one difference. We had nothing to lose at this point.

Shaking her head, Lisa said, "What a mess this case is!"

Responding, Peter told her, "We did didn't do it!" He continued to protest the attorneys for Peerless Insurance, saying they ignored their paperwork and continued to stall in front. Fax after fax, authorization after authorization, for eight years.

"We have paid a heavy price in Buffalo over false, libelous, and slanderous information put out by the attorneys," he said, "trying to keep my family matters private over another lawsuit involving a relative has spilled over to misjudgments, greed, hate over something we have no control over."

Lisa seemed to sympathize, understanding the situation we had been put into. She left the meeting, we wished each other a peaceful holiday, scheduling a meeting for some time in 2009.

On December 11, 2008, a letter came from the offices of Peerless Insurance. "So sorry to hear of your fire on August 28, 2008. We do our best to insure the fire adjusters meet our expectations." They did not read their paperwork from the customers that kept them in business. The fire had happened in 2000, not 2008. It appeared to be another stalling tactic. They were also still in violation of the Insurance Codes in New York State, and had been for over eight years. We wondered how many times the wool had been pulled over the eyes of the people in charge in Albany.

In early December 2008, Peter called Daniel Schoenborn, the prospective attorney in Buffalo, to tie into the meeting with his trip to Surrogate's court in January. Mr. Schoenborn needed the paperwork to review the details of the case of Pro-Pak and Evans Services against Peerless Insurance. We reproduced the copies we had of the lawsuit, including the supporting paperwork. There would be no more delays, no more authorizations, no more Michael Drumm, or Brown & Chiari. This case would be settled by this time next year.

The last letter of 2008 came from DeMarie & Schoenborn, from Attorney Daniel Schoenborn. In this letter he stated he had reviewed the documents, continuing it is not clear why a forensic accountant was needed, whether the $45,000 was a fair amount surrounding the debts that Peerless Insurance had created. Since Michael has the files, we need to review them, including the copies from the court of Michael's withdrawal following the complaint to the ethics board in Buffalo. He also said in the letter that he needed $500.00 from both of Peter and me to work on a contingency.

The last week of December, I checked the New York State Unified Court System. There were two meetings, one on October 17, 2008 and one on October 28, 2008, in Supreme Court. Neither date had anything to do with the lawsuit, they were all about Michael. That meant the last time we were represented in front of Judge Glownia or his law clerk by Michael it was August 1, 2007. Almost sixteen months before. Someone had been lying to us for a very long time.

CHAPTER 31: CHESS MIDDLEGAME

Peter and I decided that before any more money was handed over to an attorney, Peter needed to meet with Dan first. The meeting was to coincide with Peter attending Surrogate's Court in Buffalo in January. We would wait and see what happened after the initial meeting.

During the middle of January, Peter flew to Buffalo hoping for the usual January thaw. It would show up like clockwork reminding everyone that another blast would come from the north or west of the country but it would be over soon. This year would prove different. The frigid air from the early part of winter had left mounds of hard snow and black ice heaped along the roadways and parking lots.

Surprised, he had only brought a light leather jacket to wear for the few days he would be there. After meeting in Surrogate's Court, he headed over to DeMarie & Schoenborn's office to discuss the case of Pro-Pak and Evans Services lawsuit against Peerless Insurance. Arriving at the law firm, he was led into the conference room to wait for Attorney Daniel Schoenborn to arrive. Suddenly Dan entered the room suited up for business, standing around 6'4", filling the room with his immense form.

Peter and Dan discussed the devastation Peerless Insurance had created, losing the business, the house, along with the breach of contract. The initial lawsuit paperwork was shown to him, including the letters of Michael. He had also brought the breach of contract of Shawna Hunt and Lisa Plaster for the sale of Advanced Massage Therapy in 2005.

At this point Peter told Dan, "When I spoke to you on the phone, you told me you would sue another attorney for malpractice, I want to sue Brown & Chiari and Michael Drumm for ethics, and malpractice. Do you want me to take this one too?" Dan asked, referring to the massage therapists Shawna Hunt and Lisa Plaster who, had skipped out on the payment for Advanced Massage. "Yes" Peter replied. "They owe about $60,000 plus interest, and I'll send you the paperwork on that from Tampa."

"OK," Dan replied. "I'll be right back, let me think about this for about ten minutes." Peter thought this was an odd comment to make but having no recourse he dismissed it. Perhaps he needed to talk about this with the other member of the firm, Mr. DeMarie.

He returned to the conference room and announced, "I'll take the case, I'll send you a contract, and you both need to send me a $500.00 retainer fee for Evans Services for Jo Anne and, another $500.00 for Pro-Pak as well. When I get the retainer, I will secure the files from Brown & Chiari." Continuing, "Oh and I see no reason why you needed a forensic fire accountant either!" The deal had been made. Peter flew back to Tampa that day, leaving one foot in Buffalo and securely placing the other foot in Tampa, FL.

While Peter was in Buffalo sealing his deal, I needed to make a deal of my own. I needed a job to fund the process of the lawsuit against Peerless Insurance. Lucky found one close to my house, and with a great boss as well. I had heard through a friend a local Chiropractor was looking for a Massage Therapist for his office. I could make my own hours, make a good wage, and stay in my field which I loved.

I surprised Peter with this news when he got back from Buffalo. We needed it to sustain some type of lifestyle. It might be a while before we had our say in court, and we needed money to continue to go to Buffalo for court dates and fight for our civil rights.

Dr. Brian Morris, and his wife Suzette, welcomed me into the new office and have become a second family to me. We work, laugh, and sometimes cry together. We understand each other and the needs of the patients. His patients are like family, as they are to me. It's a wonderful combination of work and play for both the staff and the patients as they progress through the tribulations of the innovative health care system.

Peter then relayed the scenario that had happened in Dan's office including the ten minutes he had left the room. "Do you think he made a phone call?" I asked.

On January 29, 2009, a letter was sent to us by Dan asking for the contract between Advanced Massage Therapy and Advanced Massage Therapy of Western New York owned by Shawna Hunt and Lisa Plaster. We sent the contract, along with the payment schedule to Buffalo, as I yakked away at Peter.

"Thank God I don't have to help any more therapists so they can get money from the government and then screw me into the ground." I said. The loosely used term of 'spiritual,' a favorite saying of the therapists, came into the conversation as we both laughed at the falseness of it all.

I continued, "Remember the one who was claiming unemployment while she was working for us?"

Laughing, Peter interjected, "How many people get fined by the labor department in Buffalo and then call them for inaccuracies with the unemployment ethics of their sub-contractors filing for unemployment on our computer?"

I returned with my statement, "How about the one that stole the massage chair and the sheets? I could have lost my business over these classic idiots, or wait, I did through the other ones. "adding "This kills me New York State pays for these people to go to school they require them to have a guarantee of a place to work, I the business owner give them that, then when I complain to the state about the quality and questionable actions of the therapists the State of New York tells us "That's your problem."

Arriving at the post office, we gathered the paperwork and sent it to Dan via certified mail. This was move that we would use for many more times, it would need the signature of the receiving party.

On February 23, 2009, the Unified Court System showed a removal of the stay of suspension, placed by Kurt Sajda and/or Judge Glownia on October 28, 2008. The case was to continue in front of Judge Glownia with Dan representing Pro-Pak and Evans Services against Peerless

Insurance. Brown & Chiari had gone up in smoke. It was during this time that Dan called Peter.

"Do you have any files in Florida?" he asked Peter, adding, "I have been going through the paperwork of the two red welds of Michael Drumm, they are a mess, and none of it is in order."

Peter retaliated, "Michael Drumm told Kurt Sajda and us in Judge Glownia's office last October that he had seven red welds, not two!"

"I've got two." Dan stated quietly.

Peter answered, "I will send you what we think is important, the rest I can tell you over the phone so we can keep open communication. I have everything you need or I can put together any files you are missing or lost signed by Michael Drumm."

Continuing, Peter told Dan, "This is strange, Michael is a very neat person. For you to get files that are not arranged correctly, or missing indicates that the files were purged." There was no response at the other end of the phone. Within a few seconds the conversation had ended.

Hanging up the phone, Peter turned to me to inform me that there were either four red welds missing or Michael was lying to Judge Glownia's law clerk about the size of his file. Looking with amazement to Peter I asked, "Aren't you glad you used Magic Jack last December before we signed the contract with Dan?" Peter then eyeballed the stack of paperwork we had gotten from Brown & Chiari. "I wonder if they knew they were sending the files to us?" "Probably."

Peter and I had been to one of the local tourist areas a few months before this last event. He lifted a small item off the display hooks and started to read it. Without a word he had gone to the cashier to pay for it. Wondering what it was he told me as we were waiting in line. The object could be used on your phone with any area code that was available throughout the country.

"Why do you need that?" I had asked.

"You never know when we might need it."

As it turned out, the man with the so called loss of memory due to strokes was smarter than most of us. Peter's memory would be intact through this whole ugly scenario. We had called Brown & Chiari asking for the files to be faxed to a local Buffalo area code with a made up number. For the better part of the day the paperwork was faxed to us from Brown & Chiari via Magic Jack. We thought we had captured the whole case so we could review it.

On February 28, 2009, a letter came in the mail showing Peerless Insurance had retained Attorney Katherine Fijal of Hurwitz & Fine. She had been an attorney at Lustig & Brown until they suddenly closed their offices in Buffalo a while back. It appeared she was taking over the case from Attorney David Sleight who had perhaps gone out on his own after collecting his fees from Peerless Insurance. Peerless Insurance was now on their fourth attorney in their quest to not pay us and had violated so many codes in New York State it was truly an embarrassment.

The paperwork would show up on E-Courts on May 5, 2009. So far, Peerless Insurance had gone through four attorneys, we had gone through two. They had continued to stall and postpone paperwork until the last minute every month for over nine years. Right under Judge Glownia's nose.

On April 14, 2009, a Compliance Conference was held. Peerless Insurance needed more time to become familiar with the case. The Judge granted the new attorney more time.

On July 27, 2009, there was another Compliance Conference. This is the first time a trial was mentioned, according to the New York State Unified Court System. We were relieved that it appeared our new attorney knew what to do in the courthouse. Dan was asking for a trial.

On July 28, 2009, exactly one month before the ninth anniversary of the fire, there was a final Compliance Conference. This was the final meeting between the attorneys and the Judge's law clerk.

On August 27, 2009, there was a meeting between the attorneys and Judge Glownia. It involved alternate dispute resolution. It looked as if we were going to try mediation with a Thomas P. Notaro, the court appointed mediator, before going to trial.

The next day, August 28, 2009, nine years, 469 weeks, and over 3000 days since the fire, a meeting was held between Judge Glownia and Thomas P. Notaro to discuss the case. They met again on September 16, then on October 9, and the last on December 16, 2009. The next day, on December 17, 2009, there was a Compliance Conference held in Judge Glownia's chambers. Mr. Notaro was not at this meeting.

In 2009, there were nine meetings scheduled and nine meetings held. There were no cancellations, delays, or excuses. Things were looking up from the old days with Attorney Michael Drumm. We wanted to go to trial and get it over with once and for all. Peerless Insurance had held us in a grip with their staff, attorneys, and fire adjusters for over nine years.

There had been at least sixteen adjournments, some lasting for the better part of a year, before 2009. There had been no shows and delays making a mockery of the court that the citizens of Western New York were paying for with their taxes.

Nine years and not one accusation, not one hesitation on our part. We wondered again how often this was going on in an already depressed area. Who was running the show in Western New York? The attorneys? It was a problem for sure and we were not going to let it go for one minute. As Peerless Insurance continued to fight until the end of each year with delays, we became more intense and involved with the situation that had been created for us. While they had the money to continue violating every insurance code available, we had the determination to make it right.

While the lawyers were laid back in the case, we had started to collect paperwork and documents, with Snoop's help.

We would continue to watch the Supreme Court Appearance Detail on the internet almost daily, keeping the information between Peter and myself.

CHAPTER 32: CLASH OF THE KINGS

In March of 2010, a raid was conducted on a horse farm in a suburb of Buffalo. We heard of the invasion from a number of sources in Buffalo, including Snoopy. Once we were informed of the case, we read about it in the paper and on the internet. It had taken over the city with the media taking the lead and informing the public of the inside scoop, or so they thought. Observing that case on E-Courts, also we could keep tabs on it with the antics of the Supreme Court.

It looked as if the horse abuse case would be going before Judge Glownia's court as well. We continued to stay quiet to not disturb the course of action for that case or ours. We were coming to the top of the courtroom calendar according to E-Courts. If we kept mum, we would go to trial very soon, before this new case that had hit the media across New York State with a frenzy.

As it turned out, this case would be a bizarre as ours before Judge Glownia. There would be pickets by animal rights groups, drama between the participants of the case, relatives involved, an alleged affair, and the media seemed to salivate on the issue. While the voices of gossip were made on either side of the wooden horse fence, we watched precariously standing on the top of the wobbly railing, hoping not to fall and crash to the ground.

On April 19, 2010, Peter was reading the Buffalo paper that had continued to be sent to us in Florida. He still enjoyed reading it daily while drinking his coffee. As he scanned the news from Buffalo, he came across an article of five people pursuing an opening of the Water Authority in Buffalo. The part-time position paid $22,500 yearly for a three-year term. Scanning the names, he noticed the name of John V. Elmore, a local attorney from the Brown & Chiari law firm, a former prosecutor, state trooper, and recently the chairman of the Eighth Judicial District Grievance Committee. This was the same committee that we had put in the grievance against Michael in 2008.

Peter reflected back to the conversation he had had with Michael after he had put in the grievance against the other attorney for harassing during a house sale. "I'll never have a grievance put against me, I have a friend that would take care of it for me." he had said. Peter, happy to get money for the harassment, had given the award collected to Michael to be used towards our lawsuit. Was this the friend he was talking about? It seemed a little too close for comfort for us. Had something happened when we put in the grievance against the law firm of Brown & Chiari and Michael? We would keep quiet about this also for now. It would not do much good to put in a grievance against the Eighth Judicial Grievance Committee itself.

We followed the animal abuse case with everyone else. As we now checked our case, along with the new case, before Judge Glownia on the New York State Unified Court System, it appeared to mimic our case with court delays, adjournments, what appeared to be stalling. It was also taking on a personality of its own, while our case became stagnant with the last court date in July of 2010, it appeared everything had to stop to make way for the fury of this case to continue.

I counted my blessings every day throughout this year for the great job I had with Morris Chiropractic. It had become my second home. We would laugh along with the patients of my ongoing frustration of antics of Buffalo.

Peter was trapped living in substandard conditions while Buffalo took its time with nonsense. More than once I told him, "Hang tight, they want you dead and out of the way, we will win this one way or another." and "Don't forget the conversation we had with the attorney when he referred to Buffalo Supreme Court as 'Kangaroo Court.' Remember? He said 'We may all hate each other outside of the courthouse here, but when we get into a Judge's courtroom we act like ladies and gentlemen, and show respect for the Judge.'"

I continued, saying, "The Judge should project respect for the courtroom and the reverence, unless he isn't there to do it, and has left everything up to the Confidential Court Clerk to either hold conferences, meetings, or adjournments, sign documents dealing with a lawsuit, that is his job," adding, "Just my opinion, I'm not an attorney."

On March 8, 2011 Judge Joseph R. Glownia transferred our case to Judge Deborah Chimes within a few days we spotted it on ECourts. Peter called Dan and demanded a trial. This had gone on long enough.

Soon, the early part of summer in Florida was followed by the hot, humid rainy days throughout the next few months. It was a small price to pay, only lasting three or four months a year.

On July 28, 2010, we received an email from Dan Schoenborn. The trial had been set for September 11, 2011. The email continued, "Additionally the defense noted they have never had both of your depositions. When can you be here in Buffalo in September? Try and get me several dates that would work for you."

Peter called Dan immediately to tell him if the trial was set for September 11, 2011, it would be an odd time to start a trial since it was a Saturday. Dan apologized and said he would check into it. Peter also told Dan that a deposition had taken place at Lustig and Brown on February 23, 2001. Dan responded that it appeared Attorney Katherine Fijal was missing the deposition, and she had never received it from the previous attorney, David Sleight.

Peter gave dates for the following September of 2010. We could be available anytime from the middle of September to the end of the month because we had to wait for our social security checks to pay for the trip. Peerless Insurance by now had one month short of ten years to prepare for the trial date, and would be granted another year to get their act together. This would be the second deposition and the third statement to be given to Peerless Insurance, the wicked child of Liberty Mutual.

We remained calm and steadfast in our commitment to not only go to trial but to fight for all the clients who had gotten screwed over by Peerless Insurance or any other insurance company that had come their way. It was time to fight back and we had the ever growing documents in our possession to prove it.

On September 13, 2010, we flew to Buffalo to give our second deposition for Peerless Insurance and their attorney, Katherine Fijal, of

Hurwitz & Fine, the following Wednesday. We were as prepared as the first statement given to Gary Gable in October of 2000, and attorney David Sleight in February of 2002. We did not think about the deposition, the questions, or anything else. We knew what we had stated all along had been the truth. We also noticed there was an escalation of lies being told about us along with the slanderous gossip in Buffalo. Snoopy had been keeping a vague tab on things going on without being noticed.

Arriving at the Buffalo airport in the early afternoon, the weather was sublime. The bright blue of the sky, the crispness of an early fall was in the air. Soon after we rented a car, checked into a hotel.

Hopping back into the car, we decided to take a ride out to Angola to visits the cemetery where Peter's mother, sister, and father were buried. As we traveled the slow route, we passed through Hamburg along Lake Erie. The water was calm, just before the brutal storms of winter would once again ice over the immense water. Traveling Route 5, the trees along the lake were starting to change. The starkness of the pine trees mixed with the red and yellow of the trees was stunning.

Stopping at a local florist in Derby, we bought flowers for the gravesite of his family members. Arriving at the cemetery, we continued down the sloping hill of the Presbyterian Church to pay our respects to his family. As we stood in the quiet, sunny day it was as if time stood still. So much had been lost by this family, so much had been given. Leaving there, we headed to the home Peter had owned along Lake Erie. It looked as if it had been remodeled and updated. The gazebo had been left along with the detached garage.

Looking at Peter I said, "We should have kept that house, you owned it outright, Peerless Insurance would not have hurt us in any way."

Affirming my comment, he replied, "They would have gotten us anyway. The attorneys and a few other people of Buffalo think I have a lot of money remember?"

Answering his comment, I announced with a statement that sounded like as question, "Greedy bunch, huh?"

We left the area and meandered our way to Orchard Park where we had bought the house together. Driving through the town, the leaves on the trees a little redder, brighter than in Hamburg and Angola. We were in the middle of the snow belt of Western New York, it generally got colder faster and longer.

Driving through the village, we checked out where the therapist was working, according to Snoopy. Heading up Jewett Holmwood Road, we pulled into our old neighborhood. Arriving at the house we had yanked from us six years before it looked the same the woods covering it brilliantly along three sides.

As we sat in the car peering out the window, I noticed the flagpole that had flown over Lake Erie was still located off to the left of the house. Peter suddenly yelped, "I forgot to get the copper plate from the flagpole you had gotten me for my birthday."

We stared at that flagpole as if it was the most important thing in the world. Just one more entity that had been destroyed by Peerless Insurance and their lies. My eyes shifted to the woods to the right of the house remembering the men I had seen sitting on the ground the day Peter got home from the hospital after open heart surgery. I had forgotten to say anything to Peter that day, so many other things were going on.

My memories floated back to the day Peter had come home from the hospital in Buffalo. The house had been filled with flowers and plants delivered from friends wishing him a happy recovery. I had gone to the back bedroom to get extra pillows and blankets for Peter as he sat in the recliner in the living room. I looked out the bedroom window and there were men were sitting at the edge of the woods staring at the house, as if they were stalking. I remembered the man with the subpoena who had knocked on the front door that day, then running to his car and peeling off. I looked at the woods from the car remembering it for the first time.

Coming back to reality I eyed Peter and I mumbled, "It's a wonder we did not die from living here. Peerless Insurance, their attorneys, and the henchmen that followed us around after the labor fine and the fire." I was ready to leave Buffalo for the final time. Peter drove the car heading to a restaurant in East Aurora for a light dinner and a drink.

The next day we drove around the city, then had a reunion dinner with Snoop that night in Lewiston, about an hour away from Buffalo. It appeared the horse abuse case was quiet with a number of adjournments throughout the last couple of months. However, the media around the case was having a field day with the hi jinx of the animal abuse case. I wanted to let the media know what was going on with the manipulation of our case during the same time period but we had a trial coming up the following year in September of 2011 and had to keep quiet.

CHAPTER 33: THE CHESS MEETING - AN INVITE-ONLY EVENT

The next morning, we woke up to a dark gloomy day in Buffalo. We stopped at the small restaurant for a light breakfast, then headed out for the second deposition that Peerless Insurance had insisted on. We needed to get the truth out to Katherine Fijal and Peerless Insurance. We knew a court reporter would be present, as they had in the deposition of 2002. We knew we had to get our words out in a concise manner so we would have a copy to add to our ever increasing paperwork.

Pulling into the parking lot to the opposite corner to the Brisbane Building, we headed off to meet with Dan. The three of us then walked over to Hurwitz & Fine to meet with Ms. Fijal. As we patiently waited Dan's cell phone rang. "Where are you?" asked Ms. Fijal. Apparently there was a mix up. Dan had forgotten to tell her he had moved from the Convention Tower to the Brisbane Building. She and the court reporter were at his old office. After a short conversation, it was settled they would now walk over to her office for the deposition to commence.

This was not getting off to a good start. While we waited for the rest of the cast of characters to show up, Peter asked Dan what Katherine Fijal was like. "Depends what side of the bed she gets up on." He replied.

Soon she arrived with the court reporter in tow. Appearing cordial enough, I thought fleetingly of Dan's remark, wondering if she knew this is what other attorneys thought of her.

As we all sat at the conference table to repeat once more the same questions we were already asked. Apparently Katherine Fijal had to make some billing hours up. Peerless Insurance was more than willing to pay her instead of us. The next few hours were filled up with the attorney eating up the billing minutes. Peter would be going first.

At 10:19 a.m., the proceedings began with the usual questions. "What is your history?", "Where do you live?", "Do you work?", Peter repeated the answers he gave to the same questions from the deposition of 2001, and the same statement to Gary Gable, who thought he owned Peerless Insurance in 2000.

While he was going through the motions with Ms. Attorney Fijal, I purposely removed myself from hearing anything from the deposition. I wanted it to be clean and pristine. As I looked out the window of the high-rise, I noticed the clouds and the wind had picked up, as if it was going to snow. We needed to get out of Dodge right after this to avoid any delays getting back to Tampa.

At 10:20 a.m., Katherine Fijal asked Peter "Did you review anything for today?" Peter replied, "Yes I read a little bit." My head fired back into the room. What was there to review other than the first statement and deposition which Katherine Fijal claimed she did not have? She had slipped up, and was moving on to the next question. I could not get Dan's attention; he was looking at his paperwork. Even he had a copy of the original deposition, so why didn't Ms. Fijal? I made a mental note to get to the bottom of the latest lie when there was a break in the deposition from Peter to me.

A little later, Ms. Fijal asked, "Tell me about the Consent Judgment, but I really don't need to know it you explained it under oath in 2001." I could not believe I was hearing this crap. I looked at Dan and then Katherine Fijal. Someone had lied to us and they were getting sloppy. Either Ms. Fijal had lied to Dan, or Dan had lied to us. I wanted to jump over the table to confront him. Instead, I let the court reporter she had hired to take the words down as she continued. Nice and Neat.

At 11:33 a.m., Ms. Fijal asked, "You filed bankruptcy under your name correct?"

Peter replied "Yes."

"Was there no bankruptcy filed for Evans Services?"

"No."

"None for Pro-Pak?"

"No." Peter said again.

"There was a bankruptcy for both you and Jo Anne?" she asked. "Personal?"

Peter replied yes and we continued on with the fiasco, knowing Katherine Fijal had lied, costing us more money for travel to a fake deposition put forth as a stalling tactic by Peerless Insurance.

At 11:39 a.m., Ms. Fijal asked, "The damage done to the building, the amount of $488,000 how did that figure come about?"

"Dennis Gaughan claimed some of the assets of the lawsuit against Peerless. The figures from NFA were around $260,000, before we went bankrupt." Peter replied.

At 11:40 a.m., Dan asked, "How did Dennis Gaughan come up with $488,000?"

Ms. Fijal, taking the cue, chirps in "Yeah, how did that happen?"

Peter answered, "Mike Drumm came up with the original lawsuit of $980,000 in business loss, maybe Dennis added to it."

Ms. Fijal stated, "You owe taxes in 2003 for $67,000."

"Impossible. I didn't have a business or an income in 2003." Peter replied.

At this point there was dead silence and Ms. Fijal requested to go off the record. Our suggestion for you the reader is, if you are caught in a deposition, is make sure you request before you start to not to ever go off the record. This way all statements and conversations will be recorded. It is your right to request this. This will keep both you and the attorney for the opposition focused, and more inclined to tell the truth.

At 11:58 a.m., eighteen minutes later we went back on record. Dan looked at Peter, saying "If you give me the taxes, Katherine and I have something to work with. We can discuss it."

Ms. Fijal pulls out her briefcase to show Peter a document with the title "Responses to Interrogatories." It was a document found in Michael's red weld but not by Peter or myself. It appeared there was another file roaming loosely around Buffalo. She continued, "Have you seen this?"

Peter responded "No I haven't."

Fijal continues "This is Michael Drumm's answer to interrogatories and you should have signed it."

Peter responded "I have never seen it." He also knew he would have kept anything with his signature. He was known as "Pete the Packrat," and had kept all the paperwork from this case. Apparently Michael had forgotten to give us a copy for us to sign.

At 12:00 p.m., Ms. Fijal continues, "There are liens against you from Envior-Care, Key Bank, SPS Temporaries, and Erie County Industrial Development Agency." She herself had been the attorney for the latter case. She should have known it was Peerless Insurance digging its nails into our very soul to destroy us. Instead, Pete eyeballed her. "Peerless should have picked up for Envior-Care. They cleaned up after the fire. Key Bank was for the machinery lost, SPS Temporaries, was for the Wal-Mart job. Erie County Industrial was for the rent I owed because Peerless did not pay anyone until much later and they never paid us."

Peter said, "I took out a special policy when I leased the machinery from Key Bank, Jo Anne signed it. Peerless did not pay that either."

Ms. Fijal replied, "No one tried to collect?"

Peter told her, "No it went to Michael Drumm."

"This is ten years later and no one has a suit against you?" Not waiting for an answer, perhaps she figured it out, she continued, "Do you know the basis of these tax liens?"

"No, I do not."

"As you sit here today you do not know of any tax liens?"

"No."

She didn't continue the deposition. She knew they did not exist. They had been in her files since 2001.

By 12:15 p.m., Peter was done with his deposition.

I was ready to spill the apple cart. Ms. Fijal had referred to the depositions she said did not have from 2002. Dan had emailed us on August 28, the anniversary of the fire, when he told us the trial had been set but Katherine Fijal did not have the previous deposition. It would be my turn and I told Dan she did in fact have the original deposition, having referred to it a number of times.

There was not going to be a break. I was called next. Mine would go fast and furious. I suspected Ms. Fijal wanted it to end.

At 12:20 p.m., she started with slightly different questions, followed by, "The Examination of Oath - did you review it?"

I wanted to scream at her, to yell, *"What the hell is going on in this room. We had spent thousands of dollars to fly here, over the years we had assembled countless paperwork Michael had either lost or purged. Thousands of hours copying, buying ink, paper, shipping it to Buffalo, to help you get this lawsuit settled and you right here, right now, are referring to a deposition you say you do not have. You are just another lying attorney working for the devil."*

Instead I said "No."

Katherine Fijal took me back to my marriage, divorce, children, jobs, education until reaching the sale of Advanced Massage Therapy. "They didn't pay you?" she asked?

"They started to, it was like pulling teeth to get $600.00 a month from them." I replied.

At 12:27 p.m., Ms. Fijal again went off the record to discuss the massage therapists. Dan explained he had filed a claim against the therapists the suit itself had not yet been filed.

At 12:28 p.m., she asked me, "Do you have tax liens?"

"No."

"Do you have any involvement with Evans Services?"

"No, I own the building."

"Why do you own the building?"

"In case anything happened to Peter, I could sell it."

Katherine Fijal was bouncing around this deposition as if she was trying to water ski for the first time. She asked how long Peter and I had been together. Telling her since 1992 she remarked, "Sometimes it happens." Dan interjected and said, "Yes it does, yes it does." This room was getting weirder and more bizarre. If Peerless Insurance wanted to pay for this nonsense let them. It wasn't as if I didn't warn Michael Christenson, the CEO for the company in 2008.

At 12:38 p.m., she asked, "Tell me about the labor fine." She was jumping all over the place, and it was interesting to hear an attorney from Peerless Insurance refer to it as a "labor fine" when attorney David Sleight in the deposition in 2001 had thrown my words against the wall for not calling it a consent judgment.

At 12:40 p.m., she apparently caught herself and asked, "Do you know why you had to sign the consent judgment? You personally?"

"No." It was becoming increasingly clear Ms. Fijal was confused.

"You owned the building?" she asked.

"Yes."

"Who paid the mortgage?"

"Peter."

At 12:49 p.m., she asked, "Tell me about Mary Coleman."

I responded "Mary Coleman works for the labor department for the State of New York."

"Why would Mary Coleman come to your business at Advanced Massage and tell you, you need a time clock for Evans Services?"

I knew but, I would not bring it up here, Snoopy was too close to the situation, possibly in danger. Besides it was none of her business. I answered "I don't know."

By 12:53 p.m., the saga of Mary Coleman and the State Labor Department was done. I was sick of both of them and whoever had sent her in.

At 12:54 p.m. she said, "Tell me about the tax liens."

"There are none."

Fijal responded "J.K. Harris has disclosed some documents to us stating you had IRS liens against you." She was showing me some document as I stated "I have never seen this."

"I got this from J.K. Harris, it was in their files do you know anything about this?"

"No."

What I did not know was Ms. Fijal's previous firm, Brown & Lustig, had sent Michael a letter. In this letter, it states that J. K. Harris & Co. had never heard of us and they had no dealings with us. She was lying with the deposition being transcribed by a neutral party.

Another document was handed to me by Ms. Fijal. I read it out loud for everyone in the room to hear ending it with the statement, "This is interesting as I continued to read from the alleged letter, 'If you want us to suspend collections of the penalty while you suit is pending in court,' what suit? This letter is from 1999."

Attorney Fijal stated, "I don't know what it's for. It does not say Evans Services or Advanced Massage," continuing, "I don't get it."

Dan interjects, "No cover letter?"

"No." as Ms. Fijal stated it was in their file a pile of stuff from J.K. Harris.

Dan cautiously asked, "Was this file shared with Mike Drumm?"

Ms. Fijal replied, "That's standard procedure, come in everyone gets a copy." Something smelled stinky in the room, I wondered if we all noticed it. A lot of lying was going on and Ms. Fijal was the leader.

At 1:02 p.m., Ms. Fijal brings up the deposition of 2001. The deposition she said she did not have.

At 1:03 p.m., Ms. Fijal proudly holds up two copies of exhibits from the depositions of 2001. I looked at her, saying, "The copies are duplicates Ms. Fijal."

"They are?"

"Yes and they are from New York State, not the IRS."

Her answer was amazing to hear. She said, "Maybe we got them faxed."

At 1:04 p.m., she said, "Tell me about the IRS in Tampa, Lisa Hare, and your personal bankruptcy."

The chain of events would take about twelve minutes to complete as I included the hang up phone calls, the quartiles paid by Peter for the business, the loss of the house, copies of the taxes once again being turned over to the IRS in Tampa. As the time went on, it was becoming apparent in the room, files belonging to us had been purged. There were too many missing pieces that we had replaced over the years.

At 1:16 p.m., she stated, "I do not have a copy of your personal bankruptcy, do you have a listing of them?" Personal being the key word here. The lawsuit against Peerless Insurance had nothing to do with the personal bankruptcy other than the fact they caused it through non-payment and all the violation of the insurance codes in New York.

At 1:22 p.m., she asked, "Have they extinguished the bankruptcy?

I thought to myself for a minute, deciphering attorney's terms they used for questioning. "Yes, they have." and I explained the bankruptcy was closed on Peter and myself. Harold Busan the trustee presented it himself to the court and it had been signed off by Federal Judge Carl Bucki and Federal Judge Michael Kaplan in 2006.

"You lost the house prior to the bankruptcy right?"

"No, after."

At 1:25 p.m., I'm telling Ms. Fijal I want the IRS to push hard in this case. I had given the address and the phone number myself of Peerless Insurance to the IRS. She looked at me and appeared shocked at the news. I found this behavior funny when I found my letter to Michael Christenson in her files a couple of years later.

At 1:33 p.m., Ms. Fijal handed me a letter. As I looked at it, I noticed the letterhead. "What has piqued your interest?" she asked.

I answered, "This is a statement that Key Bank was going into Advanced Massage Therapy for payment of the machinery that Peerless Insurance was supposed to pick up."

This was not the answer she was looking for. I continued, "Peter went over to the bank and talked to the manager, who told him the monies were taken out of Advanced Massage to pay for the damage to the machinery after the fire." She ignored my testimony and moved on to anything she would want to hear.

"What are these bills? SPS?"

This was becoming repetitive, "The company Peter used for the Wal Mart job. Peerless didn't pay them either they cleaned up after the fire. Peter told you that. "

"Peter testified to that?"

Bored, I was thinking pay attention to your own questions. Instead, I said, "Yes he did. This morning."

"How many hours do you work at the chiropractors?"

"Three to nine hours." Thinking, thanks to Peerless Insurance and the goon squad, the attorneys and Gary Gable.

That ended the deposition. We parted ways with Ms. Fijal appearing confused and tired. We did not tell her what she needed to hear to void the lawsuit against Peerless Insurance. As we left the offices of Hurwitz & Fine, we had once more fulfilled our end of the bargain. The same questions and the same answers as the deposition of 2001, except for the blurb about Michael Drumm.

If the lawsuit held up to the day it was filed on September 12, 2001, at the nine percent interest. Peerless Insurance owed us a pile of money to pay for damages - not only the building, business interruption, machinery, lost wages, health problems due to their negligence, false advertising, violation of the insurance codes in New York State, it kept going and going. My wish to put them out of business would certainly put a dent in their illegal practices if not destroy them. It would be okay. It would all come out in the trial. It might be somewhat interesting for the citizens of Buffalo to hear about the trial, there had been an ever growing cast of characters that might be called into the courtroom and our attorney, Daniel Schoenborn, would be the king of the chess game plowing his way through to the other side and capture the whole crew.

We walked the small hallway to the elevator, riding from the sixth floor to reach the foyer. Walking the few short blocks, I noticed it was getting colder, the winds had picked up, the late stages of fall were coming and soon winter would be upon the area. I turned to Dan to ask what he thought of the deposition. His six foot plus frame was bent over, almost eyeball to eyeball with me. Startled, I noticed he was wringing his hands at a furious pace, rubbing and folding them, as we walked towards the Brisbane Building. He was a nervous wreck, his suit a rumpled mess, I wondered what the hell was going on with him now.

We got to the foyer in the Brisbane Building he was still folding, twisting, and wringing his hands. Not as if he was suffering from arthritis, like Michael. It was something else. We had done everything over the years Peerless Insurance had asked us to do. Asking him again what he thought, he brushed me off saying he had to make some phone calls. Ahhhh ... I thought he noticed Ms. Fijal had lied about not having the previous deposition from 2001.

I started to ask him if he had noticed Ms. Fijal had the deposition in 2001. Dan was pulling, lengthening his fingers, rolling his fists, digging into his other palm, hand-over-hand as he cut me off. "You did great today, I can't talk you about it right now we will wait for the deposition to come back." Continuing to the elevator, he left us stranded in the foyer of the Brisbane Building. He turned and said, "I have to make some phone calls. I will get back to you in a couple of weeks." With that, he disappeared into the elevator. He had to make some urgent phone calls, he was too busy answer the only question we had for him.

I started to get a queasy feeling like I had with Michael. The last meeting in Judge Glownia's court had been July 28, 2010, two months before the deposition we had just attended.

We had a trial scheduled for September 13, 2011, we had better not make any noise protesting to Dan about Ms. Fijal's slip-up. We could discuss it when we got closer to trial. Certainly he had noticed the lies - why else would he be wringing his hands, bent over as if he was protecting something close to him? It was odd, but it was less than a year to trial. I let it go that is while inside the Brisbane Building.

We left the building and had gotten into the car before I mentioned it to Peter. "What's with Dan wringing his hands?" Peter then told me Dan spent a lot of time in Arizona and maybe he had arthritis. "Now?" I asked. "Winter hasn't even started yet, it's windy not cold."

Peter told me to forget about it, then interjecting, "We have less than a year before trial in Judge Glownia's Courtroom. Don't make waves."

We were running neck to neck along the justice tribunal with the animal abuse case mess and we knew to keep our mouths shut. We were reaching high up in Judge Glownia's courtroom to be heard. Just one case ahead of us.

The rest of that year we waited for Dan Schoenborn to guide us to the trial that would be happening in September of 2011.

March 8, 2011, while we were reviewing the E-courts calender, it showed that Judge Joseph Glownia turned our case over to Judge Deborah Chimes who appeared to have a lighter caseload. Peter called Daniel Schoenborn, who told him Judge Glownia's caseload was to heavy and he needed relief. When asked if this would impair our case going to trial, there was a suspended silence on the other end of the conversation. "Let me get back to you on that." interjected Dan.

A few days later Peter emailed Dan informing him that he had reviewed Judge Chimes case load and it appeared she had a sufficient amount of days open to continue the trial scheduled for September 13, 2011. It was a while before we got a response, but when we did it was exciting to hear.

Dan Schoenborn called Peter to tell him a representative from Peerless Insurance was going to fly in to Buffalo and make an offer for a settlement on our case. "Can you be here on September 21st to meet in Judge Chimes office?" Peter confirmed the date and not only would we be there but, we would bring all the paperwork with us to show Peerless representative the mistakes they had made.

Meanwhile, the participating attorneys had cancelled the trial for September 13, 2011 and were willing to settle with us instead. It looked like I was going to get an early birthday present. Finally, all our hard work would pay off. After sitting in Judge Glownias court for over ten years, we were finally making headway in Judge Chimes.

We rented a car to take us on the long ride to Buffalo. Loading the trunk with a dolly and all the paperwork we had accumulated since the year of the labor fine, we headed out to finally get justice in the Eighth District of Western New York. Checking into a hotel the first night, I insisted that we bring all the paperwork using the dolly, with us into the room. It was all the evidence we had and we needed to show it to the representative from Peerless Insurance.

The next day we arrived in Buffalo and checked into a hotel on the outskirts of town. This time Peter convinced me the paperwork in the trunk of the car would be safe since he had parked next to the front door of the hotel. We were feeling pretty good since we knew we would be treated with courtesy and respect the following day in Judge Chimes court.

Getting up the next day, we felt refreshed and confident that we would finally be heard. Walking to the car, I popped the truck. Yes everything was there filed nice and neat, ready to present to the representative from Peerless Insurance.

Driving into Buffalo, we noticed the bronze Buffalo statues perched on the slight hill reminding us where we had once lived. Smiling, I glanced at Peter reminding him I had passed them the day of the fire so long ago. "Things will be different now." I remarked in an off-hand way. Little did we know what we would be walking into that day with the Confidential Clerk to the Judge, Jill Toholski.

We entered the parking close to DeMarie and Schoenborn's office. Loading up the dolly with the documents, two depositions, emails, letters from all the attorneys, machinery invoices, improvements to the building, the billing and payments made to the once thriving business. The boxes of evidence filled the dolly to the top handle. Strapping the bungie cords to stabilize the towering files, we headed to Dan's office.

After a few precarious mishaps over the uneven concrete sidewalk, we arrived at the main foyer. Riding the elevator to his office, we rolled the dolly into reception room. A woman welcomed us saying Dan would be with us in a moment. "I hope that's not for me!" as she rolled her eyes. Laughing Peter told her "No, we are meeting with the representative from Peerless Insurance and he may want to look over the paperwork."

At that instant Dan walked into the office. Greeting us and pointing his finger to the pile of paperwork he said, "What's that?" Peter reminded him he had told him we would be bringing the paperwork, that was why we drove instead of flying. Dan grabbed his index finger pulling on it, "You don't need that."

"Why?" Peter asked "I told you I was bringing and you agreed."

Dan retorted "If we need it we can come back and get it." Pulling and twisting his finger.

"I don't want to leave it here." I protested. "It will be fine." he stated, believing no one will touch it. Taking a mental photograph, we left it with reservations.

We then left his office and headed to Judge Deborah Chimes office to meet with the representative. Entering the correct floor, Dan told us he would be back in a few minutes he wanted to talk to the Judge Chimes Confidential Law Clerk, Jill Toholski.

A few minutes went by, then a few more, as we watched people walk through the area of the foyer. Finally, tired of looking, I turned to Peter "How long do you think he has been gone?" Peter looked at his watch "We have been here 47 minutes. I looked at my watch when we went sat down and he went into the judge's office."

A few minutes later, Dan came out of the room and told us to follow him. We entered the room of the outer office of the Judge, pulling up three chairs to a desk. Peter was on my left and Dan Schoenborn on my right. Soon after Jill Toholski entered the room and sat at the desk. Introducing herself she stated "Peerless Insurance will offer you $200,000 not one dime more." Peter and I looked at each other then turned to her at the same time saying "We want a trial!"

"Well you're not getting one, the judge wants this off her docket and gone!"

Peter looked at her and said "What? We want a trial!"

What followed next was some of the crudest information we had ever received from Buffalo. Jill Toholski stated "No one cares about you or your trial in this town, if you had a trial they would be looking out the window wishing they did not have to hear this crap."

"Where is the representative from Peerless?" Peter chimed in. "The representative from Peerless Insurance is Katherine Fijal." Jill Toholski fired back. I didn't wait for Peters answer to her remark.

Plaintiff to Defendant

I got up from my chair "Crap? You are a front man for a Judge and you call this crap!" I exploded. "You have not only insulted every person in this town, who by the way contributes to your paycheck but, then you insult the very people you work for? How dare you think you are that important! I call it useless!" then I added "Who is paying you, really?"

She stood up "This meeting is over with."

"Go ahead." I said, you have enticed me to write a book about the garbage going on behind the scenes in this town?"

She sat down. "Take the $200,000 and go away."

"No."

"Take it." she repeated.

I looked at her, seeing for the first time the corruption in the courthouse. "No, you will give us a trial." Peter interjected "You lied to us about the representative from Peerless Insurance? And you let them do it? You are supposed to be neutral, not working for Katherine Fijal, Peerless Insurance attorney!"

We got up from the chairs to go to the door. She beat us to the door. "Take the money or you will regret it."

Tears overflowed my eyes and rolled down my cheek "No, you had better give us a trial." Leaving the area Dan was following us. I turned and looked back at him, I observed his hands. Here we go again, pulling, twisting, and rubbing his hands over and over. Oh God, I thought here we go. Peter chimed in "Let us discuss this, give us two weeks and we will let you know." I looked at him with disbelief at his actions of falling into place with the attorneys clearly, after all we had been through in the courthouse he knew something was amiss.

Leaving the room first myself, then Peter, and lastly Dan Schoenborn, Peter winked at me. He had another plan. For that matter, so did I, it was time to write the book and not just think about it in a reluctant diary.

We walked to Dan Schoenborn's office pretty much fed up with the court system in the Eighth District of New York State. Taking the elevator, we grabbed our paperwork on the dolly. Dan turned to us looking odd in so many ways, he said "Think about the offer, you will never get anymore. Call me within two weeks or all the offers will be off the table and, we will have to schedule a trial again."

"OK, we will think about it." Peter said knowing full well we would not. Things had gotten so tainted with falsehoods, we knew we had to take it to the end.

We left that day in September turning what had once again been a nightmare into something that was going to be fun. We were going to see our friends in Tennessee for a little visit.

As we rocketed along the highway heading to Gatlinburg, we discussed the information we had. Writing a book would be a first for both of us. The changes in the foliage had been catching our eye. While the leaves in Buffalo had been changing to the various hues of color indicating an early winter was on its way, it had barely altered as we continued to drive south.

What had ended in disappointment and another hit to the financials' turned into pleasure. We had a definite plan of finishing the case, writing a nonfiction book, and getting the word out if we survived it.

Vivian had become a close friend of ours in the mid 90's. I had just started my business as a Massage Therapist in Orchard Park. Vivian had her massage business in West Palm Beach. One day early in the afternoon, a man came bursting into the office yelling "I want a massage!" Looking up from my desk, I saw a man in his early sixties. He continued "I picked this place because my Massage Therapist in West Palm has her business with the same name as yours. I can have her in the winter and you in the summer if you are any good!" His name was Dan. He came every week that summer, leaving around Labor Day. Vivian would see him during winter. It was a great deal all around.

Every year, Vivian and I would talk on the phone when the seasons would start to change and our mutual client was getting ready to come back to Orchard Park for the summer. Dan would then spend the hundred days of summer telling me to leave the area and hook up with Vivian. "You guys would make a killing, and do half the work. You both have guys that could take the business farther for you, and you could just run the massage business." It always sounded great, but that was when we had two businesses and a family around. It would not have been feasible.

Vivian moved in on the massage business as the profession became more acceptable. Having written a book about the massage insurance billing for Florida, she had been working closely with insurance companies to provide coverage for people involved in auto accidents and work injuries. What had started as a manual for Florida, soon swept the country and became the lifeline for insurance billing for the massage profession. John, her husband, did the marketing and Vivian would be the presenter.

Arriving in Gatlinburg, Tennessee, late the next day, we rode up the hill to their home. Pulling into the driveway, we were greeted with hugs and kisses all around, John and Vivian ushered us into the house. "You are done with Buffalo right?" I looked at her trying to keep up a good front.

"Sadly not yet, we will be having a trial. We have been told by our attorney Dan Schoenborn, probably next year." I said as I relayed the latest Peerless Insurance story. "There was no representative from Peerless Insurance, it was the opposing attorney, Katherine Fijal." Continuing, "It was probably illegal but, they just keep pushing, and we don't know why."

Vivian, all ears because she was familiar with the various insurance companies, yelped, "Peerless who are they? I never heard of them."

"Who knows." I replied. "They seem to be the brainchild of Liberty Mutual and they have very deep pockets." adding, "Let's have some fun."

We goofed around that weekend, including calling our mutual friend and massage client Dan, who by now had moved permanently to Florida.

Within minutes, he had us laughing hard, something Peter and I hadn't done for a long time. Dan continued the mantra "Why don't you get together now, it's not too late, you would make a killing, listen to me, you should have done it years ago!" Continuing to giggle, I told Dan, "Listen, Peerless Insurance and their friends would be more than happy if there was a little killing going on, after all they have been paying their attorneys to keep us at bay for over eleven years."

A few days later, we left Gatlinburg driving through the Smoky Mountains until reaching Georgia, where we turned off to another route to make our way back to Tampa. It had been a good trip. We had made headway in Buffalo discovering Jill Tohowski had not had a representative from Peerless Insurance - it had been Katherine Fijal instead. Nothing impartial had been observed at the so called meeting. Jill Tohoski however, had inspired me to write a book about the court system in the Eighth District of New York. We had gained a new strength to continue because of her blessing and taunts.

Arriving back in Tampa, we relaxed. We knew we would reject the offer, but we would make the involved attorneys and the law clerk wait the two weeks. We wanted a trial, we wanted the people of Buffalo to make the judgment on this case, not some law clerk.

Two weeks to the day, Peter called Dan. "We are not going to take the offer, we have lost too much over the years due to Peerless Insurance neglect, bad faith, and stalling tactics. Where was the representative from Peerless?"

When Dan affirmed it had in fact been attorney Katherine Fijal, Peter told Dan it had been a low blow by Peerless Insurance. He asked Dan if he knew beforehand that had been Katherine Fijal.

After a suspended silence, Dan answered with a statement "I was told a representative from Peerless would be there." Continuing, "I have to go, I have to make a few phone calls."

Peter hung up the phone while I went to the computer to look up the activity of our case on the Unified Court System. It said that on August 18, there had been an adjournment. The next date had been September 21, and had been called a Settlement Conference. This had been the meeting with Judge Chimes law clerk, Dan Schoenborn, Peter, and myself. Attorney Fijal had been waiting in another room for our signature on her paperwork to be submitted to Peerless Insurance.

CHAPTER 34: A DEAL IS CUT TO ELEMIATE THE ROOKS ON THE CHESSBOARD

On October 24, 2011, Dan called Peter asking if he had any paperwork that Michael had submitted to Judge Glownia. Peter told him he had sent it to him in 2009 with the original paperwork which replaced the missing papers of the messed up files from Brown & Chiari. Thankfully we had all the original paperwork in our possession.

Peter pulled out the original paperwork and the order signed by Judge Glownia. Filling out the cover fax sheet, it would be coming from Dolittle & Seymour. The time is posted to the right upper side at 1:08 of the fax with a note from Peter.

"Dan, I don't know if I sent you this notice of motion to preclude, so I'm sending it now via fax. As far as I know, it was not answered at the time. Pete."

It contained paperwork dated December 11, 2003, signed by Michael. It was filed with Judge Glownia and it appeared to be a relief demand with the grounds of "willful failure to respond to discovery demands CPLR Code 3126." It was signed by Michael Drumm.

On November 2, 2011, I wrote a letter to Dan about the rumors we had been told over the years about the labor fine that had transferred to the Federal Labor Board. I included in the letter implications regarding the parties involved. As the years went by, I had felt sorry for them in an odd kind of way. They had wasted their lives over so much useless hate. I was glad my home was now in Tampa. If Dan put the letter in his files, we never found it. Good thing we kept the original with the certified receipt.

That very same day, Dan wrote an email to Peter. "You were going to get me a copy of the documents from the government indicating they were not proceeding in some of the liens or claims." Apparently, he had not read the letter and paperwork we had sent him a number of weeks beforehand. That day, we sent him another letter with the same information as we had given him before. There were no liens against us other than the labor fine. While we waited for Dan to take care of the matter, we waited patiently for some action to be taken of the violation of the CPLR Code 3126 by Peerless Insurance and their attorneys in December of 2003 and the order signed by Judge Glownia in January of 2004.

Apparently, the attorneys for Peerless Insurance had been refusing to comply with discovery or Judge Glownia's order since at least 2003, if not before. Dan would surely take the matter up with Judge Chimes and Ms. Fijal.

On April 2, 2012, Dan sent a letter of new demands made by Ms. Fijal. It had to do with the now 12-year-old discovery that Peerless Insurance was completing. Dan had sent a number of pages including a note stating to us, "I want you to pay the most attention to demand Number 8, Number 12, and Number 20. "

We looked at the attached pages. It was an Order for Preclusion. Apparently, Peerless Insurance was asking for still more information in their discovery which they had for ten years.

Number 8: "Provide the P.O. Box number for Evans Services, Pro Pak, Peter Kirisits, and Jo Anne Gleason." Ridiculous... but we had them ... all the way back to 1996 until we got forced out of Buffalo. We had them for a reason. Checks for work done by Peter's company and mine had to be delivered to an office not and open mailbox. Since the offices did not have a secure mailbox we had P.O. Boxes. Not so unusual for a company.

Number 12: "Include the bankruptcy filing for Evans Services, Pro-Pak Industries, Peter Kirisits, and Jo Anne Gleason." Once again we had to explain to Dan that Pro-Pak and Evans Services did not go bankrupt. The lawsuit against Peerless Insurance was Pro-Pak and Evans Services suing for breach of contract by Peerless Insurance. If Katherine Fijal or Dan Schoenborn still did not know this, it would be amazing. Peter and I had filed personal bankruptcy, because Peerless Insurance had held us with a vice until we lost everything including the building and his business. Number 12 would prove to be a big deal within a few months, we just didn't know it yet.

Number 20: "The Plaintiffs are in possession of a computer that was taken out of the building on the day of the fire. Either provide us copies of the files on the computer or make available to the attorneys for Peerless Insurance."

Immediately, Peter called Dan. "I sent you the files and disks, we have more, give them to Katherine Fijal." adding "How many times do we have to tell Peerless Insurance attorneys. We filed personal bankruptcy because Peerless Insurance did not pay us, they paid us nothing!" A slight pause came from Peter, "Yes we have all the P.O. Box numbers." Apparently, Dan told Peter that Peerless Insurance was stalling, and added "Let her come down there to look through the files on your computer."

On April 25, 2012, a letter came from an associate of Dan. "Enclosed are tax authorizations for you to sign for Peerless counsel and us to go through." I turned to Peter amazed, "Isn't this at least the ninth time we have signed authorizations?" Not waiting for an answer I added, "They have all our taxes and have had them almost ten years."

On April 26, 2012, an email came from Dan Schoenborn. "The court has scheduled your case for January. We are finishing up discovery. I'm still concerned about the liens, maybe you should get in touch with the IRS or any other claimant that wrote you about before."

Our concern was growing. Why would he be asking for information we had sent to him by certified mail first years before, then months before, then weeks before.

On May 22, 2012, Ms. Fijal sent Dan a letter. It was passed to us. In this letter, there were five questions asked of Dan to have us provide.

Number 1: Track the improvements made to the property and the loss of business.

Number 2: Contractors, payroll services, and costs of running the business.

Number 3: We need tax authorizations 2000 through 2002.

Number 4: Startup costs after the fire.

Number 5: Your clients provided transcripts of the phone messages left by the IRS. Please provide the dates the messages are left.

Number 6: Provide tax authorizations for 2000 through 2002.

There were no profits, we had no machinery to work with. Peerless had, by 2002, ruined the business with intention, and had done it for profit. Their profit. The only thing that had been not been provided to Peerless Insurance was the dates of the messages left by the IRS. It crossed our minds, perhaps we would be bringing my phone with the messages to trial. I had saved the messages and the phone; they had followed me from phone to phone since 2008. Perhaps Ms. Fijal should call Michael to get the dates.

On May 15, 2012, we again signed authorizations for Peerless Insurance. Apparently, Ms. Fijal had written the IRS and she got an answer from them. "The cost for information would be $115.00 per page. Adding, the years you are asking for have been purged; the records only go back for ten years."

We did not know this letter existed during 2012. We would find it later, with a lot more paperwork, in all of the attorney's hand with their letterheads, or addressed to them.

On September 12, 2012, a Note of Issue was filed by Dan. He called us that day saying, "Your trial has been scheduled for January 14, 2013. I will be picking the jury on the 10th and the 11th." Continuing, he stated, "I do not want you in the courthouse when the jury is picked, but you can come up early and we will discuss things over the weekend." This was the second time he had refused us entry to the courthouse.

Also on September 12, 2012, Ms. Fijal filed a Special Term of Note of Issue. They needed relief, they were not ready for trial.

On September 27, 2012, Dan called us stating the trial had again been continued to be set for January 14, 2013. That day I made plane reservations with Southwest Airlines. Finally, we would be able to state our case before the Supreme Court with Judge Deborah Chimes presiding.

On October 9, 2012, a pretrial conference held. We did not believe for one minute what Jill Toholski had said about the citizens of Buffalo. They did not need someone like that representing a Supreme Court Judge either. We would hand the lawsuit over to the jury for them to decide.

On October 24, 2012, Dan sent Peter an email. One year to the day he had asked for the Court Order to be sent to him regarding Judge Glownia. The email said:

Peter,

After you sent me some Bankruptcy documents we did some further checking at the court, and found that Joanne [sic] has a similar document as you. The problem now is that I now have an obligation to report the settlement offer to the Bankruptcy Trustee [Harold P. Bulan] I have no choice. If I ignored the Order I would be violating a Court Order and would be getting myself in trouble. The claim is neither yours nor Joannes, [sic] it is the trustees. I will write the trustee on Thursday [either the next day or another Thursday] and advise on the status. I have no choice. If you care to speak with him that is your business. I will copy you and Joanne on my letter. I'm sorry I have no choice. Dan

Peter called Dan to ask what he was doing. You see, the statute of limitations had run out by 3 years and 13 days to sue Michael Drumm, the champion attorney of Brown & Chiari.

Dan also was not following up on the lawsuit against the massage therapists for violation of the sales contract. Nor was he looking into Michael violating a Court Order signed by Judge Joseph Glownia, way back in 2004.

Daniel Schoenborn had resigned from our contract to continue our case to trial in January of 2013. He had a better offer coming in. Did we know it at the time? No, but when we found out all hell would break loose. The corruption of the lawsuit had spread across the Eighth District as if a blizzard was coming into the area without the snow. It was hidden in the back rooms of the attorney's offices of the Eighth District of

Western New York. It would soon turn in a frenzy of corruption, lies, and a payoff.

After reading this email, Peter and I both called Harold Bulan's law office. He was unavailable, we were told. This was a continuance of the many phone calls we had made to him over the years. What we did not know was he had made a huge mess of the bankruptcy. He had never returned or answered our many phone calls since 2003. We had no paperwork of the mess he had made, but he would be forced into giving it to us very soon.

On November 1, 2012, Dan sent a letter to Judge Chimes with more lies and libel:

Dear Justice Chimes,

As you know these actions are set to begin with jury selection on January 10, 2013. You may not know that neither I, nor my office, were the original attorneys on either action. I have been recently supplied with documentation from the Bankruptcy Court that reveals Harold P. Bulan Esq. still maintains control over these actions although the individuals involved have been discharged in bankruptcy. I now have a clear obligation to report the status of negotiations to Mr. Bulan, as well as the upcoming trial. Obviously, I do not know what his position is but as soon as I find out, I will advise.

Very truly yours,

Daniel L. Schoenborn

Cc/Katherine Final

Guess what! We didn't know he wrote the letter to Judge Chimes. The deal was almost done and he was now part of the corruption of the lawsuit. We would find it later hidden in some paperwork.

We had been led to slaughter by the attorneys and now had none.

Dan had also lied to the Judge Chimes about us. He had known about the bankruptcy and the cast of characters of Brown & Chiari and the lawsuit case, since he and Peter met in January of 2009. He did know about the bankruptcy. We had the paperwork to document it: a letter from him dated December 14, 2011, where he wrote, "I may need the bankruptcy paperwork in the future but, hold off for now." He was now in bed with the rest of the "Bullies from Buffalo."

We would find both letters from both attorneys to Judge Deborah Chimes later in the ever-growing files of the various attorneys. They got too confident and then sloppy. They forgot to clean up their mess. The chess game was now turning into a lying, cheating game of the attorneys. We had to find the hole in the cheating chess game and remove the thieves.

On November 9, 2012, an affidavit, also known as a sworn statement, was supplied by Ms. Fijal. The document is full of innuendos, with abstract and downright libelous writing. 110 accusations, through twenty-six pages. It had become a free for all in the courthouse of Buffalo.

On November 13, 2012, Ms. Fijal wrote more libelous misstatements, lies another 17 pages long. At the end of the second letter, she had apparently gotten bored or careless, she signed the document for the courthouse as "Katherine Fijal, Esq., Attorneys for the defendant, Erie Insurance Company." Bizarre to say the least, along with more lies down the road from her.

It was hard to believe Katherine Fijal had made so many misstatements in writing. Peerless Insurance and their attorneys had put us through hell, along with Michael Drumm of Brown & Chiari. The constant letters to each other and to the Supreme Court Judges were a tall tale full of libel, to say the least. The worst was the constant statement of the labor fine for $240,000 not the true figure of $33,623.57. That had become stagnant in the paperwork of Michael Fitzgerald, choir boy for the Department of Labor for now thirteen years.

It started to feel like a Ponzi scheme in the chess game, all the way across the board, and it was spreading a blood red substance laced with green across the black and white face of the game.

However, the attorneys had gotten sloppy. They had forgotten to pay attention to the "Freedom of Information Act" that had been instigated in 1966. Also, there were a few ethics questions involving Michael Drumm and Brown & Chiari. We had now switched fully from plaintiff to defendant in the Eighth District of the Courthouse's of Buffalo without our knowledge. Attorneys Michael Drumm, of Brown & Chiari, and

Katherine Fijal, the attorney for Peerless Insurance, had forced us into bankruptcy. Attorney Daniel Schoenborn's job was to make sure we stayed there.

We continued to check E-Courts of New York State on a daily basis.

On December 11, 2012, a pretrial conference was held with Supreme Court Judge Deborah Chimes. It appeared the lawsuit was continuing without a hitch, we had only a few weeks to go, as we continued to try and reach Dan Schoenborn and Harold P. Bulan without success.

On December 13, 2012, Peter called Dan, who finally answered his messages. He and Peter discussed an upcoming meeting to be held in Bankruptcy Court in January of 2013. Dan informed Peter he was not going to go to the meeting because he was not invited. Peter then told Dan, "Since Bulan will not answer my phone calls, you need to invite yourself, and set the paperwork straight." Peter started to hang up the phone looking dejected.

I jumped up from the chair. "Hand me the phone." I was furious.

"I'll write the Federal Court Judges Bucki and Kaplan and then Harold Bulan, telling them what happened to us." Dan told me."Do what you think you should do."

The all too familiar click of the phone had started again.

That day we wrote Judge Carl Bucki, Judge Michael Kaplan, and the head of all the Judges in the Eighth District of Western New York, Chief Justice William Skretney. In the letters, we included our paperwork way back to the fire of 2000, and outlined everything that happened since then.

The letters were sent certified mail the next day from U.S. Post Office. We were assured by the staff that someone had to sign for the incoming mail.

It was that easy. All we had to do was continue the civil lawsuit and Harold P. Bulan would get his 20% off the top of the lawsuit, like he had wanted in 2003. Time was now running out for him to claim anything in Bankruptcy Court. The bankruptcy was reaching ten years old and he wanted his money. As usual, our letter to him went unanswered, as did the phone calls.

In 2012, there were eight conferences scheduled three were cancelled.

On January 3, 2013, Peter called Dan Schoenborn. He told us Judge Chimes had been switched off our Supreme Court case and sent to Chautauqua, New York, to continue her judgeship there. Our new judge would be Supreme Court Judge James H. Dillon. The third judge in thirteen years.

Dan continued, telling Peter, "There is going to be a meeting with Judge Bucki about your bankruptcy, you can't come, he will not let you into the meeting it is just with us."

Surprised by Dan's statement, Peter asked, "You're going to be there?"

Dan mumbled something about the weather, and reminded Peter once again he could not come to the meeting.

Peter responded "I'm coming to that meeting with Judge Bucki and so is Jo Anne."

Dan protested, "You can't, he will not allow it. If you come up, he will not let you into the courtroom, if he does let you in the courtroom, he will not let you say anything."

"What courtroom?" Peter announced, "You said you were having a meeting!"

Suddenly another click of the phone. Where did he learn that from? I wondered.

There was no mention of a meeting with my bankruptcy judge, Judge Michael Kaplan. Peter hung up the phone.

"We can't get into the meeting or courtroom to say anything." Peter told me.

Looking at him, I was amazed. "This is the United States, what do you mean? We couldn't say anything in Supreme Court and we are now defendants and we can't speak here either, in Federal Court? It's Federal Court and it crosses all the states, not just Buffalo, New York and especially the escapades in the Eighth District of Buffalo!"

You see, Dan could not have us show in in Buffalo for the so called meeting, it would spoil his secret and make him look bad in front of Judge Bucki and then Judge Kaplan. We just didn't know it yet.

On January 6, 2013, we cancelled our plane flight tickets three days before we had been scheduled to go to Supreme Court trial and pick a jury on January 9 2013 and go to trial on January 14, 2013. A few weeks later, on January 17, 2013, there was a meeting scheduled between Judge Deborah Chimes and Judge James Dillon. They would meet later, after she supposedly went to the Southern Tier to settle in after her transfer from Buffalo to another courthouse.

On January 28, 2013, a fax was sent to Dan from Attorney Fijal.

Dear Mr. Schoenborn,

  Please be advised that Peerless summary judgment motion in the above referenced matter which was scheduled for January 30, 2013 before the Honorable James Dillon has been adjourned without date pending receipt of all settlement papers. Please do not hesitate to contact me if you have any questions.

Very truly yours

Katherine A. Fijal

The attorney for Peerless Insurance had done what Peerless Insurance had paid her to do and it had cost them plenty. However, not as much as if we had gone to the scheduled trial date. The citizens of Buffalo would have decided the innocence or guilt of the parties - not any attorney, law clerk, or insurance company.

We now knew we would carry the corruption of the attorneys on our backs until we found out the true story. We would not give up until we found out without a doubt what the hell was going on in Buffalo and who part of the plan. It would take another year of harassment from Peerless Insurance, with the devious intentions of the various attorneys involved trying to cover their tracks. Or so they thought.

I was grateful I had a wonderful job at Morris Chiropractic to get out of the horrible dark, cramped quarters with boxes piled to the ceiling in every room. The situation was getting so deep with the paperwork the actual living space had been diminished once again by a number of feet.

The space for living and walking had almost turned into a tunnel effect, broken only by a few pieces of furniture to either sit in or go to sleep.

Peerless Insurance had forced us to live below the poverty line, in a hovel with their paperwork, while the greedy attorneys grabbed for the spoils of their thievery.

Peter would continue to think and dwell on the case, looking for clues in the paperwork of Michael Drumm and Daniel Schoenborn. I was furious we had not had the opportunity to enjoy the benefits of our hard work in Buffalo and had literally be tossed out like yesterday's garbage from the area.

CHAPTER 35: INVISIBLE CHESS MOVES

In March of 2013, the weather in Florida had felt unusually hot and humid. I had been driving a Plymouth Neon for five years after my Volks had mysteriously caught fire that fateful day. By now the air conditioning had been gone for a year, the gearshift had fallen off and I had to drive it with a screwdriver inserted into the panel to get it going. A new car was out of the question, or so I thought.

One Saturday, Peter and I rode around looking for a car that could be bought on a tight budget. Visiting the various deanships I was told, "You can have it for $350.00 a month."

"No I can't. I had to file bankruptcy because Peerless Insurance did not pay for my fire at my business."

"Who are they?" we would hear.

"The evil child of Liberty Mutual."

"Good to know." they would reply.

The conversation would continue, "If you filed in 2003 and this is 2013 you should be out of it by now. It only lasts ten years."

One dealer told us, "I got out of Buffalo, my timing was better than yours."

Surprised to hear this statement, we wondered what had made him leave. We got in our car and pulled out from his dealership starting to drive back the dreadful house. Peter suggested we go to the Volkswagen dealership in Tampa instead to give us a reprieve. I went along with it thinking, I could at least look at the new cars for 2013.

Driving into the parking lot, we cruised the line of new Beetles. Scanning the line, they jumped out to me waiting to be called up. Silver, blue, black, school bus yellow, white, and red. Stopping at the white was one with a black top, it winked at me begging to be taken out for a drive.

Within seconds a saleswoman approached us. "Let's see what we can do." as once again I had to mention that Peerless Insurance had forced me into personal bankruptcy. "Come inside we will talk to my boss, maybe it will work for you."

Dragging my sorry butt into the showroom for more humiliation, I once again relayed my story. He turned to me, saying "Take it home for the evening and bring it back in the morning, you can lease it." Driving it home that night, I felt a weight being lifted off my shoulders for the first time since August 27, 2000, the day before the fire.

Returning to the dealership the next day, he got into the financials. "It looks like you have a lien against you for $67,000." We were shocked, and did not know where this was coming from. Peter mentioned the release from the IRS to the dealer and to me.

"I have a release from the IRS - got it in 2009." I proudly announced to the manager.

"Go see your accountant and make sure, then I will give you the car. For that matter take the levy and car with you to the accountant."

On March 25, 2013, I met with my accountant. Relaying my "Release of Levy" from the girl at the IRS, he picked up the phone. "Let me call the IRS for you, I will straighten this out." He seemed to know the employee at the IRS, chatting and making small talk, while my file was pulled. "You have never had a levy against you. Show this to the dealer and he will give you the car. By the way it fits you perfect." I hugged him knowing it was good living and working in Tampa. They acted like ladies and gentlemen.

It was mine, all mine. Well kind of, the lease was for the next three years. I would then buy it outright. The day I leased that car was the day our lives started to change. That same day, we tried to call Dan to once again tell him we did not have liens against us. We were told he was in court, or at least somewhere in the courthouse. Instead of calling us back he sent the following fax.

March 26, 2013

Dear Peter and Joanne

I received the message about your car. Unfortunately, all inquiries, regarding liens, and creditors, and particularly the government tax issues should be directed to Mr. Bulan, the bankruptcy trustee, as he should have what claims are to be satisfied with the settlement. The mailing address for Mr. Bulan is 14 Lafayette Square 1440, Buffalo, New York 14203 and his telephone number is 716 838-4300. It was our understanding from you that there were no outstanding tax liens.

Very truly yours,

Daniel Schoenborn.

I emailed a note back to Dan telling him once again I did not owe any liens. We then sent a letter and telephoned Harold Bulan. Neither one answered our email, phone call, or certified letter. They were right in the middle of doing unethical dirty business to cash in on the payoffs.

It was another fine example of excellent lawyering in Buffalo. Dan had finished the deal he started with Michael Drumm of Brown & Chiari in January of 2009. The secret was getting bigger with more people involved. It would be hard to contain it and within a short time it would start to ooze out the blood money once again across the chessboard. They made a fatal mistake, they thought we were stupid, and that they were above the laws they represented.

On May 17, 2013, I received a letter from Dan.

I have been advised that the battery belonging to you is still in the possession of defense counsel [Peerless Insurance Attorney Katherine Fijal]. There [sic] office is located at 1300 Liberty Building, Buffalo, New York 14202.

Very truly yours

Daniel Schoenborn.

We had been dropped like the hot potato and they still did not have it right. It was not a battery; it was a battery charger that Gary Gable had stolen from the property while we were on vacation in 2000. It weighed over a hundred pounds. After thirteen years, Peerless Insurance had decided to give it back. I just hoped Ms. Fijal didn't try and sell it. That would include a charge of receiving stolen property and then selling it for profit. Any attorney would tell you that is against the law, a punishable crime by an attorney which may result in her losing her license and it would not sit well before a judge.

After thirteen years of harassment, we had no need for the battery charger.

Peter called Dan, who had remained our attorney to keep us at bay. His staff answered the phone. Peter relayed the message to them to have Peerless Insurance send a check for $400.00 to cover the loss of the battery charger. We never heard back from him or Ms. Fijal, there was another plan going on. The attorneys were using an old tactic to separate, conquer, and divide.

On July 8, 2013, Peter was sitting in the dark dingy living room surrounded by the boxes and items from the house in Orchard Park that did not fit into storage. As he pondered the thoughts in his head, he had a light bulb go off. "I wonder if there are transcripts to your case and mine too. I'm going to call the Buffalo Courthouse today and see if they can steer me in the right direction."

I turned to him, saying "good idea."

Surprised he had thought of this, we would go behind the attorneys involved and see if the court could figure out what they were doing. Reaching for my purse, I said "I have to go back to work, call me if you hear anything."

A few minutes later Peter called. "I called the Courthouse in Buffalo, they have been looking for us for over five years!" I told them all the attorneys knew where we were. I also told them we had called Dennis Gaughan to tell him we were moving, he was the only one that knew other than the utility companies and the bank. "His secretary told me she would pass it on to him!" Exasperated, Peter continued on, "How come when we changed the address from the house in Orchard Park to Florida, we did not get one thing from the courthouse in Buffalo?"

"Every piece of mail that would have come to Orchard Park came to the house here, everything except from the Bankruptcy Court!"

Peter was furious, "The woman told me today I should have notified them in writing. She told me my bankruptcy attorney should have told me to do that."

When I told him I had notified Dennis Gaughan and had written Harold Bulan, she asked me if we had ever lived in Las Vegas, Cleveland, Cincinnati or North Carolina. When I told her no, we moved from Buffalo to Tampa, she said she was going to write me a letter.

That day, I got onto the websites Spokeo, Intellieus, People Search and every popular search locater I could fine. There was not one match for Peter's or my last name that coordinated with anything other the New York and Florida. As I finished searching the internet, I told Peter, "Someone is pulling some more crap behind our backs. There is a secret among the attorneys we just don't know it yet."

That same day, I wrote Judge Skretney, the Chief Federal Judge of the United States for the Eighth District of Western New York. In this letter, I asked him to intervene since we had started as plaintiffs and ended up as defendants in his Eighth District. I suggested to him something was amiss in the courthouses of Buffalo, maybe he should either check it out himself or send someone in to do it.

A letter came back dated July 18, 2013. It came from the Bankruptcy Court of the Eighth District. In this letter, we were informed that Judge Bucki and Judge Kaplan could not read our letters. They have to remain neutral. It also said, "Fill out the enclosed form and we will file your address with the bankruptcy system, we will show you how to get the transcripts regarding the case before Judge Kaplan on January 9, 2013 and Judge Carl Bucki on January 14, 2013. You have to file a Note of Adversary proceedings to clearly identify each case. You need to call your attorney Harold Bulan or Daniel Schoenborn. This letter will remain on the court docket. Dennis Gaughan and Harold Bulan will receive email notifications. We have your current address."

I asked Peter "What is a Note of Adversary?"

He did not know either so, I looked it up. According to the site on the internet under "laws", it said it was a misdeed of one or more parties in a financial arrangement.

"Well just another day in the neighborhood, we have been trying to fight this for years, what is the cover-up? What is Schoenborn doing hooked to Harold Bulan's hip? It has to go back years with either a misdeed by Peerless Insurance or one of the attorneys or both!" I exclaimed.

We called Dan, who clearly had something to do with the bankruptcy. Harold Bulan and Dennis Gaughan were also called. None called us back, not even the attorney who had pulled out of our case the previous month, after the Statute of Limitation had run out on suing Michael. The same attorney who had told us not to come to the "meeting" of Judge Bucki. Dennis Gaughan, the attorney with so many friends, who had referred to Harold Bulan as "His Majesty." We also called Harold Bulan, who was holding on to his bad habit of not returning our calls. But then he might not have been in Buffalo, he was probably in his condo in West Palm while his rooks in the chess game handled his work for him.

In July of 2013, we sent for the transcripts of the so called meeting with the two Federal Judges, Judge Bucki, and Judge Kaplan. What really happened at the meeting was clearly different than what we had been told.

The meetings were held the same day we were to appear as plaintiffs in Supreme Court - first for picking a jury and then for a trial against Peerless Insurance. The same time Dan told us not to come.

While we waited for the transcripts to arrive in my computer mailbox, I thought it might be a good time to check E-Courts to see if anything new was going on.

On January 3, 2013, there was a meeting scheduled in Judge Chimes court regarding our case. We were to be in trial within the next week. The meeting was adjourned. On January 17, 2013, there was a meeting between Judge Chimes and Judge Dillon. They were once again changing Judges with our case. Looking further, there appeared to be another meeting between the two Judges on March 14, 2013.

The meeting indicated our lawsuit against Peerless Insurance had been settled before trial, without our knowledge.

Buffalo needed a panel of Judges to audit the cases presented in the courtrooms each year. Just to make sure things were done right. The panels of retired judges did exist in other parts of the country and it was voluntary. The judges from the Eighth District had chosen not to be advised or have any auditors check their cases once a year.

E- Courts had done its job for us. It had recorded every movement that was entered about our case for the past thirteen years. The lies of the participating attorneys were now out in the open. It would be our job to fill in the smoke and mirrors of the lawsuit against Peerless Insurance to bring this case to justice.

CHAPTER 36: CHANGES IN THE LEADERSHIP OF THE GAME

We had studied the moves of the opponents in this chess game for many years. Based on the moves of the rivals, we would continue to make our attempts for a fair day in court the best way we could. There was a hidden double dealing game going on in the game since the first attorney, Michael Drumm, had to make a mess of the lawsuit. It was probably a good thing Brown & Chiari used him for mostly depositions, as he had told Peter when he signed the contract to work for them.

The chess game had changed within the courts, and we would not be able to follow it on a daily basis. The trustee, Harold Bulan, had made sure of it. It appeared the only way we would be able to get back in the chess game would be to start following the bankruptcy case on Pacer.

Pacer is a service that provides online access to the United States Appellate Court and bankruptcy records and documents. It is a restricted government website for official Pacer users that have to be registered. Looking at the site, it appeared you had to be an attorney, creditor, or a creditor's authorized agent. That left us out - tilting off the chessboard. We could not plan our next move without seeing the moves of our new opponents.

It had been a long afternoon waiting for the results from the courtrooms of Judges Bucki and Kaplan. I called Snoop and mentioned the current festivities in the courthouse with the attorneys. I was then informed that the only way you can get the proceedings from Pacer was to get in and out as fast as you can. "Do it fast so no one will take a look at the movements."

"Impossible. I'm not that savvy, we will have to wait until we got the transcripts from the two Federal Judges courtrooms." I said, adding,

"They can't have any more 'meetings' without our knowledge it will be caught by the transcripts and documents of the courthouse."

Laughing, I continued to tell Snoop, "The attorneys had us living all over the United States. Funny huh?" There was no laughing on the other end of the conversation.

As I continued the dialog, "All the attorneys knew it too, not only did Peter talk to Daniel Schoenborn from Florida, but he sent stuff here. Harold Bulan had to know, but you see they are hiding something we just have to find it."

I continued, telling Buffalo Snoop we would see what the transcripts held for both Peter and me after the check cleared for the release of the secret meeting.

I woke up the next day to the surprise of my life. Our attorney, Daniel Schoenborn, and Morris Horwitz had appeared in court together and, they had appeared before Judge Michael Kaplan with tall tales from the dirty back rooms of the attorney's offices, and they lied to a Federal Court Judge.

CHAPTER 37: 3 QUEENS TRICK

Once again, Harold Bulan along with Dan and Morris Horwitz, had mixed the civil lawsuit with our personal bankruptcy. Harold Bulan had changed it himself with help from his two friends.

JO ANNE GLEASON TRANSCRIPTS

Before Federal Judge Michael Kaplan

January 9, 2013, 10:00 a.m.

Page 1

Line 2: "Morris Horwitz appearing for Harold Bulan Your Honor." Harold Bulan had sent in a fellow attorney from his firm to take care of the dirty work. We had never heard of this guy and it is the first time he is mentioned in any paperwork.

Paragraph 3: "Daniel Shoenborn, special counsel for Harold Bulan trustee." What a surprise! Dan had switched the chessboard around and was getting rewarded for his efforts in the corrupted case. It had been his job to keep us of the courtroom so he could reap his stolen goods.

Page 2

On Line 4, we learned Harold Bulan had recently taken his name off the partnership and put Morris Horwitz's name on it. The bankruptcy had been closed in 2005. We had received letters to the effect when we still lived in Orchard Park, New York. Harold Bulan had reopened the case in November of 2012, just after the Statute of Limitations for suing Brown & Chiari had run out, and two weeks before the trial in Supreme Court. He smelled money, and he wanted the package wrapped so tight, so the agenda could be kept. His newly appointed administrator, Daniel Schoenborn, would now be rewarded for keeping the secret between the ever growing number of attorneys, and they were now involving two Federal Judges.

Line 6: "This is Mr. Bulan's application for $200,000. It requires a hearing the 14th of January in a companion case."

Line 11: Judge Kaplan states, "OK I received a letter that had been written to Judge Bucki by Peter and JoAnne Gleason. I couldn't understand the letter. It's says I implore you to consider the continuance and schedule this trial, but there is no trial."

Morris Horwitz ignores the Judge along with Schoenborn who was probably rubbing his hands over and over.

Line 20: Morris Horwitz states, "I asked Mr. Schoenborn if he was available this morning so..."

Line 24: "In case they were here?"

Line 25: Horwitz again ignores the Federal Judge, saying, "So he could advise the court on this."

Page 3

Line 6: Judge Kaplan asked, "Is Mr. Kirisits or Ms. Gleason here?" [I imagined Dan Schoenborn now bent over wring and pulling on his hands]

Line 7: Dan answers, "No they are in Florida." He goes on to describe the corporation lawsuit in Supreme Court, not the personal bankruptcy.

Line 11: Judge Kaplan asks if they are "mooted by the settlement." Bulan had stopped the Supreme Court case of the two companies we had owned against Peerless Insurance, and had brought them into our personal bankruptcies.

Line 12: "Right," Dan answers. Dan is telling the Judge he had done his cover-up and wanted to get paid.

Line 15: Big "thank you's" by all the three participants.

PETERS TRANSCRIPT

Before Federal Judge Carl Bucki

January 14, 2013

Page 2

Line 2: "Morris Horwitz appearing for Harold Bulan trustee."

Line 4: Morris Horwitz tells Judge Bucki that "Last Wednesday Judge Kaplan approved this order."

Line 5: Morris Horwitz started to mess up, he should have done his homework but who would he ask, Harold Bulan? Morris Horwitz had failed the course entirely.

Line 7: Morris Horwitz is telling Judge Bucki inaccurate information about us including us being married. He goes on to state we were co-owners in a business, also false. He then boasts and lies to Judge Bucki telling him Peter and I will get $70,000 in the settlement each. Dan is taking a third, who by the way did not even show up for this hearing before Judge Bucki. Morris Horwitz continues, telling Judge Bucki "Dan Schoenborn has virtually no expense in this case."

He had a different job he had done for the past three years for the cast of characters.

Lines 21 to 22: Morris Horwitz mentions a "Subject of Summary Judgment a motion by defense counsel [Katherine Fijal and Peerless Insurance]." He is talking about Peerless Insurance once again filing another motion to stop the Supreme Court trial, or at least stall it again.

We later found in attorney Katherine Fijal's file this Summary had not been written until January 28, 2013, two weeks after this court date in Federal Court, and had never shown up in E-Courts. Very sloppy lies while the transcripts recorded their statements for us.

Page 3

Lines 6 to 8: Judge Bucki states, "It's hard for the court to determine whether its opposition or not. But no further opposition this morning." What he was talking about is anyone's guess. There was no question the attorney was lying to this Judge also

Lines 9 to 14: Morris Horwitz is talking about Dan and states, "These clients are seldom happy with the results of the settlement." He fails again to mention to the Judge the lawsuit in Supreme Court had been going on for thirteen years.

Lines 24 to Page 4, Line 4: Morris Horwitz is relaying to the Judge from the letter from Dan, "The building and property were not well taken care of or maintained." Dan never had the case until nine years after the fire and he had never entered the building. Thankfully we had kept the invoices and improvements for over $70,000 from before the fire of August 28, 2000. He was lying to a Federal Judge.

Page 4

Line 3: Morris Horwitz continues misleading Judge Bucki with a vengeance "The place was full of paper." In reality, the warehouse was empty. Dan had the photos and the fire report from Erie County Fire Investigation unit. The building was empty and he knew it.

Line 4: Morris Horwitz continues with his libelous statements. "There was a fire investigation." In fact, there were fire marshals at the scene with a written report from them indicating the fire had started from a short in the cord for the electric forklift.

Line 8: Morris Horwitz states, "The lawsuit was for $300,000." He is once again lying to a Federal Court Judge, this guy was so full of self importance and his pitiful lawyering it was mortifying to read.

Line 10: He mentions a Summary Judgment for $200,000 that did not exist nor would it until two weeks later in the month. We found this in yet another attorney's file that was in our possession.

This was another transcript for a hearing that lasted a little over a minute in Federal Court. . Daniel Schoenborn was so busy administrating the next chess move outside of the courthouse he decided he could be a no show for this hearing. He had wrapped the package tight, or so he thought. He was going to collect a lot of blood money from other people's backs and had no shame about it.

I realized after reading the corrupt transcripts, I should have mentioned it to Snoopy who would have gone to these so called meetings as an observer and caught it.

This same day, I started to write my memories of various conversations and the reluctant diary flooded my head. I started putting files together and writing. I would write to show what could happen if you are surrounded by corruption of attorneys protecting each other at your cost. You were an afterthought. It had become a free for all in Buffalo and we had been the prey. All the letters, emails, documents submitted to the courts, everything, was written in their hand. It seemed like a federal offense started by the attorneys themselves. I smiled to myself, thinking maybe they would try and sue us. It would prove great for book sales.

That night, pulling out my throw away phone from the closet, I called Snoop in Buffalo relaying the new idea of a tell all book. We had nothing to lose Peerless Insurance had taken it all, what was left was minimal and thirteen years later. We had nothing to lose but, life itself. Peerless and the attorneys and the back room deals created for themselves had affected the quality of life there also.

Buffalo Snoop replied "You are going to need some help from Florida, someone who knows the ropes, I can only do so much from here, you can go around the craziness of your case in this town and work it from Tampa." Little did I know what Snoopy had in mind for us in Tampa. It would prove to be a lifeline.

If we could find someone in Tampa that was as clean and virtuous as Buffalo Snoop, it would prove valuable to all the participants. We knew Snoop would finally be on the way out of this scenario. The mission had been accomplished, or most of it, regarding the budding cast of participating characters who had joined forces to produce as much confusion in the Buffalo Supreme and Federal courthouse's as possible. Buffalo Snoop had done what had been promised, and it was getting too weird and close up and personal for my close friend to continue.

TRAPPING THE PIECES ON THE CHESSBOARD

Everything remained on hold until we got to summer of 2013. The word had gotten out that we had ordered the transcripts and no one could make a move again without our knowledge. As one week turned into two, we had to do something. Peter and I looked at each other. "Hey! we still have plane tickets from last September we cancelled for the trial that was supposed to happen when they had these meetings. Let's cash them in and have a little vacation in Buffalo and do some snooping around ourselves you know breeze in and out. We have to use them by September 27th so, let's just go now!"

Scheduling the flight for August 19,2013, a Monday both Supreme and Federal Court would be open for business. I would be losing time at

Morris Chiropractic but, it had to be done. Dr Brian and Sue along with the patients knew there was a problem with the transcripts from the Federal Courthouse. "Get that damn case out of Buffalo!" I would hear daily as I grumbled about the court system in the Eighth District of Western New York.

August 16, 2013 was a Friday. As late in the afternoon as he could Peter made the phone call to Dan Schoenborns office of DeMarie and Schoenborn. Speaking with one of the staff Peter continued "We will be in Buffalo for a vacation and will be picking up our paperwork on Monday." The staff member of Dan Schoenborns office to him "The files will be ready." There was no mention of Dan being in the office that Friday or the following Monday. If he had been there he would have remembered something in his files he forgot to purge.

On that same Friday I again called the Snoop in Buffalo. This time I was using another throw-a-way phone when we had conversations. We made plans to meet again in Williamsville, the time to be determined.

Apparently there was some new information we needed to know, it was to hot to be said over the phone.

Packing for the trip over the weekend we knew we would be arriving in Buffalo by late afternoon. We had to rent a car and get over the DeMarie and Schoenborn pick up the paperwork before they closed for the day.

That Monday the weather was a stunner in Tampa Bay and it would also prove to be the same in Buffalo without the humidity. Timing would be crucial and we had to make accurate scheduling to get every document out of Supreme Court Federal Court making a big deal out of it. Arriving in Buffalo midafternoon we had brought the same dolly and we had used to bring our paperwork to Dan's office when we were told a representative from Peerless Insurance was going to meet with us in Supreme Court Justice Deborah Chimes office. At the last minute Peter grabbed an empty suitcase in case we needed it.

Dragging the dolly behind us we arrived at the auto rental outlet and headed downtown to the Brisbane Building to Schoenborn's office. Getting out of the car we looked at each other smiled, which in our world meant don't say anything until we get back in the car. As we arrived at the offices of DeMarie and Schoenborn the female staff member greeted us then disappeared to get the files from the back room.

We could not determine if he was there or not, the hairs around my neckline were raising which usually meant a sign or something out of the ordinary. If he was there, he was too "chicken" to come out and face the situation before him. For that matter he might be out of town as he always was for one reason or another, spending most of his winters in Arizona away from his clients in Buffalo. This was a Monday in August. I dismissed it, he did not matter anymore, we had a new goal to meet. Get the truth.

Soon the girl brought out the paperwork we had come for. As she entered the main reception room we loaded it on the dolly she handed me a piece of paper. "Here you need to sign this." Placing the paperwork on the dolly I signed the order. Replying to her I handed it back to her "You need to also sign it and give me a copy please." She then left the area to prepare the copy of the paperwork. As she reentered the reception area she announced "I bet you are surprised this is over with, you could have a bonfire with all this paperwork!" "Not quite I whispered to myself as we attached the bungee cords around the top of the paperwork to the dolly.

We wished each other well in the future as we tried to walk casually out of the office of Dan Schoenberg for the last time. Once out of her sight we ran for the elevator, only to walk causally once again through the main lobby of the Brisbane Building.

We continued the casual walk to the parking lot opposite Dan Schoenborns' office, hairs on my head once again raised instinct telling me we were being watched. By whom I did not know, neither of us said a word not did we turn to look up to DeMarie and Schoenborns office window.

We had learned over the last 13 years to never let them see you stressed. Peerless Insurance themselves had taught us. During the next year we would learn many more ways Peerless Insurance and their representatives would be deceitful to their own clients. What we did not know was that the dolly contained all the information from all the cast of characters as far back as 1999. All the law firms, Peerless

Insurance paperwork and all the corruption. If we had known that day we would have been scared stiff for our safety in Buffalo, New York.

As we loaded the paperwork into the trunk and backseat of the car, we then pulled out of the lot heading to the nearest UPS to get the stuff out of town.

Entering the facility in Amherst we spent $150.00 to get Daniel Schoenborns paperwork out of town and into Tampa. We would bring the rest back in the carryon suitcase when we left leaving it in the hotel room when we were not there. My instinct continued to tell me we were being watched and had been since we left Dan Schoenborns office. The only other one that knew we were in Buffalo was Snoop.

As we left the UPS I punched in the numbers on the throw away phone. Snoop "What happened?" I told my friend we had gotten all the paperwork out of Buffalo. "Good idea, now tomorrow go to the Federal Courthouse and get the paperwork then walk to the Supreme Courthouse a block or so away and get all that paperwork." "The paperwork from the Feds should not cost that much but the paperwork from the Supreme Courthouse will be expensive, that case is so old it has mold on it."

Before I could ask why, click the phone went dead. We learned not to ask Snoop anything, we did as we were told and it always proved right.

Calling it a day we headed over to the Globe restaurant in East Aurora. As we arrived at the quaint restaurant, nothing had changed the décor was the same, midcentury casual. We were greeted with a warm welcome as we entered the main dining area filled with tables and chairs. Sitting down we opted for a fish fry and a few well deserved vodkas, we were happy no one we had knew had come in for a bite to eat on a Monday. We were in a different mode than when we had been part of the Buffalo community and had been for a very long time. The foul smelling child of Liberty Mutual, and, the approved cast of characters involved in the chess scam were participating to benefit themselves.

After a delicious meal we drove to our former house in Orchard Park. As we slowly passed the house we felt sad and beat up from the past 13 years fighting for our rights. We had put so much money into two businesses and the house only to lose it over a few lying attorneys who had no shame. We continued to look at the house that held so much love and fun, so much sadness and trauma in the end.

As I looked past the flagpole we had brought from Peter's house on Lake Erie, I saw the wister a I had planted to cover up the shed. It was the same height it was when had bought it years before. Laughing it was amazing to see it had held on throughout the harsh Buffalo winters.

Still parked in front of the house the mood changed in the car as we wondered out loud what Peerless Insurance had to gain over this and why? Why had they continued to accept and cash our monthly insurance coverage if they had no intention of paying us, then try and take us to small claims court for non-payment. What a crappy insurance company they had been for us.

We had to take the corruption of the case to the end. It had to be done. The chess game was starting to look like a Ponzi scheme taking from one person and giving to another.

We said our final goodbye to our sweet house that had so many memories. A house filled with love of family especially around Christmas. The four foot nutcrackers mouths filled with coins and dollar bills for the smallest grandchildren to grab after Peter put money in for them to take home. The oldest would grab first, Peter filling up the mouths again for the little ones to take a turn. Other memories of when my beautiful twins would visit rocking Nick in the hammock chair as he watched the leaves from the Sycamore flowing in the wind. Peter cuddling with his girlfriend little Brooke so content, as I snapped away with the camera.

Pulling back to the reality of why we were in Buffalo. After telling Buffalo Snoop we were in town, we both felt as if we were on high alert as Peter confessed he also felt as if we were being watched.

We pulled away from the house for the last time starting a conversation on the facts going back to the hotel.

Morris Horwitz and Dan Schoenborn had tried to close our case without telling us and had lied to the Federal Judges as per the transcripts from January of 2013. Daniel Schoenborn had told us not to come to the meeting in January of 2013.

None of the pieces fit on the chess board and there were to many, nothing lined up or fit right.

It looked like we would be forced to take it to the end of the judicial system that appeared to be rotting from the central heartbeat of the courthouses itself.

We checked into our room as I turned to Peter and told him the good news. "I can't let the rest of the paperwork stay in the car we have to bring it up to the room." Rolling his eyes, he dragged the first load of paperwork up to the room as I kept watch over the rest in the car making note of license plates on cars pulling into the lot.

That night we had a good night's sleep. The first in thirteen years. It helped that we knew what we had to do the next day. Get the paperwork from the Federal and Supreme Court today finish what we came for and get out of dodge by the end of the next day.

The next morning was bright and cheery in Buffalo with mild temperatures telling the citizens it was getting close to the end of Summer. We used fishing line to cross over the closet where the paperwork was stored from the night before. We the tied up the entrance door to the room leaving the Do not disturb sign on the hotel room door.

After stopping for coffee at the small restaurant in the hotel we headed for our next mission passing the bronze buffalos on the side of the hill, we headed along the mainline into the city. Parking the car in the covered lot in the city.

Heading to the Federal Court building we entered through the foyer to the security gates. Spilling my phone, keys and money into the plastic container, followed by Peter doing the same we exchanged pleasantries with the guards. "Where do we find files relating to a case in federal court?" We asked. After telling us the correct floor that would lead us to the room that held the computers we entered the elevator.

Entering the small room with a woman behind a desk with glass covering the area, she directed us to the nearby computers. She was pleasant and seemed to enjoy her job with the public. "What is your case Number?" she asked. Telling her our separate numbers dealing with the court she remarked "That's and old case I'll show you what to do." As she walked over to the computer she punched in numbers that took us to our paperwork. Peter and I then sat at individual computers until we found the false addresses sent to us. As we went through the paperwork that had been entered it was true the court had us living everywhere but, where we did live in Tampa, Fl. Squealing with the excitement of finally seeing the inaccurate information entered by an unknown person in Buffalo I went through my file contained in the computer. Turning to Peter I asked "Finding anything?" "Oh I'm finding plenty and we have to get all these copies." Smiling at me.

Getting up we returned to the girl behind the desk the sequence of each case and the paperwork we needed to be copied. "That is going to be expensive, you have over." She stated "How much?" "About $50.00 and it has to be a money order or a check adding "It looks like you have over 450 copies to be made at ten cents apiece it will be $50.00 I will call you later with the exact amount." "Sold." Peter chimed in when can we pick them up?" "Tomorrow if we work at it, if not the next day." Peter charming her "We have to catch a flight out of Buffalo by tomorrow afternoon, is there anything we can do to speed it up?" "I will try as hard as I can to get it to you by tomorrow morning. I'll call you as soon as they are done, just give me your phone number then, I can call you with the exact amount of the bill." the woman countered.

Perfect! we exchanged numbers and wished each other a fine day.

The next job was to get the paperwork out of the Supreme Court. Located a short distance away and close to where we had parked the car we started walking along the street to the building to get the paperwork. As we walked up the stairs to enter the foyer, we once again were met with security. Piling our stuff once more in the plastic container we entered the Supreme Courthouse. Another security guard was stationed just inside the doorway to the left. Stopping Peter asked him where the files would be kept for a case in courts. The man turned to his left, pointing towards the room at the end of the hallway. "You will find everything right there."

Halfway down the aisle to the room I looked at Peter "Why does everything seem so familiar here?" Laughing Peter responded "This is the bottom floor of where you took Michael Drumm out as he was running the marathon down the stairs from Judge Glownia's courtroom reception area on the upper floor. "That guy gives me the creeps." I responded.

Peter humored me as I continued my one-way conversation. Entering the receiving area of the room at the end of the hall. There was a man who had walked up ahead of us to apparently turn in some paperwork. The woman was busy apparently finishing filing from the previous person who had just walked away.

Why I did this I will never know but, I turned to Peter within ear shot of the man in front of us and said "I hope we are in the right spot." The man dressed in professional attire with a nice looking tie, turned to me and said "What are you looking for?" Peter said "We are looking for paperwork to our trial in Supreme Court. "What year is it?" "2001, it was a business fire." Peter responded. "That case is really old? who are the attorneys?" "Brown & Chiari." "What are they doing with your case they are personal injury attorneys!" Peter started to give him the short version of our tales from Buffalo as, the woman was starting to wait for the paperwork to be turned in from the man who was apparently an attorney.

The man slipped his paperwork in the space below the protective glass, then turning back to us he said "Maybe I can help you, why don't we talk next week." Peter answered we don't live here anymore we live in Tampa, and we will be leaving tomorrow" The man turned to the walk to the elevators wishing us good luck.

We were next up. "How can I help you." The woman politely said. "Peter had turned into the spokesman. We are her to pick up our paperwork from the court." "Case number?" she asked. Peter knew it by heart 8326/2001 and 8329/2001. "Are you kidding that case is really old, you will have to go the basement of the building to retrieve it." "Where is that?" The woman directed us along the same path past the foyer. "Take the stairs to the basement and you can talk to the gentleman behind the desk."

As we started the errand to the Supreme Court Basement the man we had been talking to was sitting with his paperwork on a bench along the elevator. As we looked to him we waved and continued walking. Suddenly he was before us "I sue other attorneys and you may have a case!" "Tell me what happened!" Peter turned to him and started the scenario back to 1999 and the labor fine, then the fire then the bankruptcy. "Who is you trustee?" appearing inquisitive. Peter answered "Harold Bulan." "I don't know him, I know some of them but, not him." Adding "I have a condo in Deerfield Beach right next to West Palm, I'm going to be there within a few months. Here is my card if you wish to speak with me maybe we can meet in my condo." Peter took his card thanking him as the man rushed back to the elevator where he had left his paperwork.

   We continued to walk the stairwell stepping down the shallow stairs to the underbelly of the Supreme Courthouse. A large u-shaped counter was surrounding the large room holding all the files from all the cases held in the Supreme Court. As we walked up to the counter a tall thin balding older man was holding the controls to the room. "Can I help you?" "Yes we are looking for our case from a lawsuit against Peerless Insurance. "Do you have the case Number?" Peter rattled off the numbers and wrote it on a piece of paper at the same time. "That case is very old to be here. Are you sure they are the right numbers?" Peter then stated that it was and they were attached to Evans Services and Pro-Pak Industries. "Wait a minute I'll look it up." He walked to the back of the large area only to disappear within the files of the courthouse.

A few minutes later he came back "Well I found it, and it is going to cost you a lot of money to get it." Adding, "I always tell people if you have a case in this courthouse make sure you get copies of every piece of documents your attorneys submits. It eliminates a mess like this." "The paperwork has to be pulled copied and you can pick it up next week." Peter explained to the man "We live in Tampa can you send it?" "Now you are talking more money that will be at least $300.00. I can't even figure it out yet because I don't know the postal fees. I'll call you when we get it together." Peter wrote down his phone number and gave it to the man. Taking the paper with the number the man looked at Peter. "I have never seen such a mess in a long time if ever. Good Luck."

   Leaving the Supreme Courthouse, we felt as if we were getting closer to the secret and we were. As we walked out of the building, breathing in the fresh air. Peter said "Let's go to a place where I know the attorneys go for lunch." Surprised, I followed him a couple of blocks until we reached a tiny restaurant. He opened the door and it was as if we stepped back in time. The small room was filled with a few tables and chairs. Men in suits were sitting at tables having a bite to eat and some coffee.

We sat down at a table next to the wall and observed the room. Suddenly a figure came into the doorway letting the door slam shut. As we looked up he kept a slow lazy gaze on us as he passed the table sitting in the back of the room. I looked at him, then at Peter who was watching him also.

A waitress came to the table handing us old menus and asked if we wanted coffee. I needed some and so did Peter. As she left with our lunch order and brought back the coffee, she said "Your lunch will be with you in a minute." I scoured the room in front of me and Peter was facing the man who had just walked in. Soon our lunch was set before us, biting into the sandwich I looked up towards the door of the restaurant opening again. Oh my God It's Snoop!

My hand reached to Peter's as Snoop dressed in black and white swished by us, only to sit with a few gentlemen in the back of the room. The man who had come in earlier that was so interested in us forgot about looking at Snoop. Peter eyeballing the lone figure sitting at the table was still watching us.

Leaving the restaurant, I suddenly got the brilliant idea of calling an attorney who I held in high regard. Answering his phone, I told him I needed an attorney for a business fire we had experienced. "Do you have an attorney?" I responded "Well that's a long story, Brown & Chiari were our attorneys." What the hell are they doing with your case they are personal injury!" I started to defend ourselves and mentioned we had Dan Schoenborn after them. "I have heard of him. "he said. A pause on the end of the line then paper rustling. "Here is a number call this guy he is good." "Kisses!" I said. He called me nuts and hung up. That's how that went, as usual, jabs to each other all in good fun. Plus good news, someone in the law profession had heard of Dan Schoenborn.

As we headed back to the city to return to the hotel room, we would pick up more documents and ship them to Tampa since we still had too much to put in the carryon. Peter's phone rang, it was the clerk from the Federal Courthouse "Your paperwork is ready you can pick it up tomorrow morning and the charge at ten cents apiece is fifty dollars" Thanking her Peter assured her we would be there early the next day.

I called the attorney that had been suggested to me. Luckily he could take us and would meet us the next day at noon. He was located near the airport we felt blessed we could do it on our flight out at 3:00 p.m.

We then went back to the UPS outlet and shipped more documents out of Buffalo.

Driving away from UPS we decided to bypass dinner and just go back to the hotel. Watching the local TV channels, Buffalo seemed distant and faded as the newscaster carried on about the news of the day around the Western New York area.

Soon bored I headed to the ice machine located in the main dining area of the hotel. Walking along the rows of rooms I noticed an alcove at the end of the hall. Thinking it might be an ice machine I entered the small area only to find out nothing was there. As I continued along I noticed another alcove entering it I found an ice machine as I was filling the bucket by something jabbed me in the back. Turning around I was swearing like a sailor. Looking at me was Buffalo Snoop. "What the hell are you doing?" I yelped. "Watching you today, idiot. What were you doing today eating at that place?"

I reminded Snoop that Peter was there also and he had suggested it. "Well watch it, they know you are here get the hell out of here before you get hurt!" "Oh Yah" I retorted "Tell them to sod off I'm sick of the 'they' stupid's. Tell them to man up and face what we are going to put before them!"

Snoop grabbed my ice bucket and shoved a box in it. "Go back to your room and stay there." "Remember the conversation we had that was too involved to tell you on the phone?" "Yes' I replied. "The attorney's bit of more than they could chew, they are protecting themselves within the Supreme Courthouse. not sure if they had the ability to see it through to the end, things are happening here and you will now use this." pointing to the box.

Pushing me aside Buffalo Snoop charged down the hall turned left and was out of my sight. Without missing a beat or bothering to look in the box, I did as I was told and went back to the hotel unit.

Entering the room Peter looked at me "What is the matter? Your face is all red." "I just ran into Snoop, twice in one day is too much." Peter peered into the ice bucket "A box?" as he reached into the cubes. Pulling it out it contained a new throw away phone and a new number. "Snoop told me to stay in the room they know we are here."

Peter turning the phone in his hands "Well that's what we do we stay in the room until we pick up the paperwork from the Federal Courthouse tomorrow morning. Meet with the attorney at 12:00 turn in the car and we are out of here."

The next day, we gathered our remaining paperwork from Dan Schoenborn's office, shoving them into the carry-on luggage with the few clothes we had brought along for the trip. We headed over to the fourth attorney for a meeting before flying out of Buffalo to go to our home in Tampa.

Pulling into the parking lot within minutes to the airport, the office appeared to be a little seedy. Entering the cluttered and dingy first floor, we climbed the stairs to the reception area of his office. The room was filled along the walls and to the ceiling with paperwork and files. Not like the office of Michael Drumm. It was then I realized we had never seen the office of Dan Schoenborn, just the conference room and the front reception area. Suddenly, it came to me that perhaps he did not have the clientele that he had given the persona of having. Especially if he spent most of his time wringing his hands and bent over or spending his winters in Arizona while his clients waited for his return to Buffalo.

I went on to better thoughts than Dan Schoenborn and Michael Drumm. Surely there had to be a good attorney, other than my friend, in this town. Someone who would have the knowledge of years of experience in the law field. As we entered the office, the secretary led us to another medium sized room indicating we could sit in one of the nearby chairs. We could hear an attorney's voice but it was muffled and in a deep conversation apparently on the phone.

I looked for an outlet along the wall to plug in my tablet to get a good charge before we got on the flight back to Tampa. Finding one, I set the soon to be out of juice tablet on the table to charge for the flight home. It had become a valuable tool in the process of get-togethers in Buffalo. Inconspicuous, it looked as if it was just another toy and could be kept in my purse or my pocket. The new technology had certainly been beneficial to us along our excursions to Buffalo.

Within minutes a slender built older man entered the room. Introducing himself, he seemed knowledgeable and well spoken. He asked us the length of the case and what year it was filed. Peter told him the case was filed September 12, 2001 a lawsuit against Peerless Insurance for bad faith.

"That case is old; why didn't you call me before?"

Peter told him the case had been with Messerendino, Celniker & Estoff, a law firm that specialized in corporate cases. The attorney replied, "Yes they were good but they do not do it anymore."

It was then Peter told him we had moved with the attorney from that firm to another.

"Who were your attorneys?" he asked us.

Peter told him Michael Drumm of Brown & Chiari until we had filed a grievance against Michael Drumm for being incompetent.

"What the hell are they doing with your case, they are personal injury attorneys!"

Peter then told him neither James Brown nor Donald Chiari had ever said a word to us while we were in their offices in Lancaster, adding it was never indicated what their specialty was on any letterhead or documents sent to us by Michael Drumm. I asked, why would Michael Drumm have us move to a firm that does not specialize in corporation law? It was followed by the usual pause without an answer. I laughed to myself with the craziness of it all in Buffalo. Apparently we would be writing a book exposing the "Big Guns."

"Who was your last attorney?" he asked.

"Dan Schoenborn." Peter answered.

"Never heard of him, who is he with?"

"DeMarie & Schoenborn," Peter said.

The attorney retorted "Yeah, I heard of DeMarie, not the other guy."

I started to amuse myself with the thoughts of anyone in Buffalo never hearing of Daniel Schoenborn, he must have kept a very low profile, with his attorney boutique law firm. Buffalo was not that big a town and the attorneys we knew, all had knowledge of the other attorneys in town.

The consultation would take a couple of hours and he was gracious enough to not charge us. We told him at this time we had ordered all the paperwork from the courthouse the day before, and had already gotten the paperwork available from the Federal Courthouse. He seemed startled we had done this, nonetheless he did not ask us what had made us go to the Supreme and Federal courthouse. I suppose he didn't care; it would be his call to review it.

He then told us to make copies of the Supreme Court paperwork and send them to him. He would then review it for $200.00 an hour and make his decision. We were to also send him a check, money order, anything except cash, for $2000.00. "I want the money first and send me the paperwork with it." Peter looked once more at me crestfallen. I chirped "I have it, I will make out a money order Saturday and get it to you."

Continuing, he told us, "If I take this case it will be $8,000.00 to $10,000.00 for a forensic fire adjuster to go through the building."

Peter interjected that it was thirteen years later and had been converted to another business. Peter also told him that both Dan Schoenborn and Michael Drumm had written to us insisting we did not need a forensic fire adjuster and Peerless Insurance did not have one either. "I don't care what those guys said, this is what I say, this thing is a mess. It will cost $50,000 to bring it to trial too, so be ready, I know you have money!" looking at me.

I found this hilarious, laughing inside my expensive self. It must have been the $20.00 running suit I had bought on sale, or perhaps it was the Pandora bracelet my daughter had given me that I wore everywhere, especially to the courthouse. It kept me grounded and knowing she was with me all the way, even if she was not aware of what was going on with us.

Or perhaps the attorney had done a little investigating of his own on the internet about Peter and the previous court case involving his niece.

Peter looked at me again with a doleful look on his face, as if it was going to be pulled out of the air. I looked at the attorney and stated again, "Ok I can get it." Thankful once again for Morris Chiropractic and the patients that were funding our quest for justice in the various courthouses in Buffalo.

It was time to catch a flight back to our home and friends in Tampa. As we got up from our chairs, I walked over to the nearby table to pull the plug to the tablet out of the wall outlet. The attorney looked at me with shock, he hadn't noticed what was in plain sight. The tablet had been charging and he looked at it as if he had been taped on one of the apps. I still have that old tablet and have gone through two more. Best invention ever made, so many uses through the apps. We parted ways at that time to drive to the airport and catch our ticket out of Buffalo.

As we reached the Buffalo International Airport, we returned the car and walked the short distance to the airport entrance. Within an hour we would be catching Southwest Airlines for a direct flight back to Tampa Bay. The time would pass quickly on the plane. We had to review the past four days and enter it on the tablet, in case we wrote a book so we would have notes to refer too.

Arriving in Tampa that late Thursday night, we pulled up to the house. We had to remove the rigging of the traps we had learned to install in case anyone entered the house while we were gone. The fire of the Volkswagen a few years back and the illicit affairs of Peerless Insurance and their attorneys had forced us to live with caution all the times.

This horrible place we had been involuntarily placed to live in was nothing more than a jail with substandard living conditions. Mold was forming on the ceiling and the owner had refused to fix it. "Too busy." they said. I would look at Peter and ask him if they wanted us out of the picture too. It was an unfeeling, cold, dark place somewhat like a cave. However, we could hole up from the world, eat, sleep, and continue to go through the files always looking for something new.

In our opinion, the Buffalo attorneys involved in our Supreme and Federal court case starting in 2000 wanted us dead and out of the picture. Just hearing them not only lie with the verbal word but, write it as well to us and then the two Federal Judges indicated they felt they were more important than their clients, the judges and the people that they were representing and continued to keep a soon to be exposed vital secret to themselves.

I went to work the next day grateful to have something normal in my life. The questions came to me all day from the patients and staff. "How did it go? This is so wrong; it is not right. What the hell is the matter with the courts in that town?" They knew, and so did we, that the chessboard had cracks in it and the pieces were not fitting. The King and Queen were going to fall if they were not careful.

That Saturday I sent a money order for $2000.00 to the attorney, along with the paperwork for his review.

CHAPTER 38: HERE COMES ONE OF THE CHEATS

The following Monday, we received the rest of the files from DeMarie & Schoenborn's office. I had worked that day until midafternoon, arriving home sooner than usual. Peter informed me he was going to the grocery store for some items for dinner.

While he was gone, I looked at an opened cardboard box and peered inside the box containing the files. I looked casually and then something caught my eye. Reaching in to see what the paperwork consisted of, it was a shocking surprise to find that Katherine Fijal, the defense attorney for Peerless Insurance had her files mixed in with Dan Schoenborn's.

In fact, hers were neatly stacked next to his - as if someone from De Marie & Schoenborn or Katherine Fijal herself had filed them next to each other. It appeared to be her defense file to be used for the trial that was scheduled to start the previous January of 2013, just before Harold Bulan and 'Henchman Horwitz' made his illicit move to Judge Bucki and Judge Kaplan. I called Peter.

"Get here as fast as you can, we have Katherine Fijal's file and it shows where she has been lying to all the Supreme Court Judges for years. We have her file for the Supreme Court trial in a box!"

Her defense file contained a stack with two holes along the top of the paperwork. As I continued to look through it, the box held the depositions from 2011, or pieces of it, that would prove beneficial to Peerless Insurance in the trial. She had decimated some of the deposition regarding the statements we had made, inserting with her handwriting and notes what she felt would help her case. Included was the labor fine for $240,000, not the $33,000 and change we owed after paying the previous $15,000.

Peter pulled in the driveway and entered the house. Handing him the paperwork I had just found, he started to go through it while I continued on with the second batch of Ms. Fijal's paperwork. It was then we saw the taxes dating back to 1997. Peerless Insurance attorneys had received them in 2001 from Messerdino, Celniker & Estoff according to the letterhead. She had them all along, but had continued to stall with Peerless Insurance's permission until 2012, asking repeatedly for us to sign tax authorizations for submission, until the IRS told her to either pay for it or knock it off.

She was a spiteful, libelous, insidious liar, no wonder she looked so tired at the deposition we had in 2010. She had been screwing people around for over ten years, with Peerless Insurance's approval. Michael Drumm, Dan Schoenborn, and Katherine Fijal had formed an alliance. Peerless Insurance was paying the bills and had the deep pockets to harm their own clients with intention. The greed, jealousy, and hate had now taken a back seat to the cover-up by the attorneys in Buffalo.

These attorneys were too much, they believed their own narcissistic advertisements where they thought they were so special. They were actually nothing more than subcontractors to the people that hired them: you and me. The attitude of being the best attorney ever didn't even come close to a few others well known in the community and the country for being great. These guys were the real deal; while local devious attorneys were just an embarrassment to society.

As I continued through Peerless Insurance attorneys file. I found the libelous letter from Katherine Fijal to Judge Deborah Chimes. It was then we started to look for the letter we had written to Judge Chimes for Dan Schoenborn to hand to her. It was missing from his files and the Supreme Court files we had gotten out of Buffalo. Apparently, Judge Chimes had never received it, only Katherine Fijal, representing Peerless Insurance had gotten her letter into Judge Deborah Chimes. It seemed odd, very odd.

I went to one of Daniel Schoenborn's files along the walls of the crowded house. Looking along the side of the boxes of our files where we had written what was inside, I found it and the certified mailing receipt attached to it. It was our original letter to Judge Chimes, showing the date I sent it, shortly after we had received Katherine Fijal's libelous letter to Judge Deborah Chimes. The letter defending ourselves against Ms. Fijal's crap had never been given to the Judge Chimes by Daniel Schoenborn, he had destroyed it. We continued to look through all the files and discovered the missing letter to Judge Chimes was never sent. Nor was it found in the Supreme courthouse files but, more about that later.

Continuing to look through Katherine Fijal's file, we also found the original deposition from 2001 that she said she did not have in 2010. We knew she was lying then, because she had slipped up, in the deposition we went to and this confirmed it.

Now we had the proof of all the slanderous and libelous lyingand it was in Peerless Insurance original attorneys file of Brown & Lustig. Had she also lied about her cronies not giving the file to her? Apparently yes, to stall a few more months in the Supreme Courthouse at our expense and with Peerless Insurance's blessing. It was a deadly game they were playing. On top of that, they were making a mockery of all the Judges in the Eighth District of Western New York.

CHAPTER 39: BAD CONDUCT OF THE PLAYERS IN THE CHESSGAME

As we continued to look through the documents that had been altered by Katherine Fijal, we wondered how Daniel Schoenborn had been named administrator of our case in the personal bankruptcy. It didn't add up, he had resigned as our attorney two weeks before the scheduled trial date of January 9, 2013, before Judge Chimes or Judge Dillon. It was hard to decipher, also Judge Chimes and Judge Dillon had a meeting on January 3, 2013. Six days before the Supreme Court Trial.

January 9, 2013, the day Dan was to pick a jury, he had a better offer coming in. Morris Horwitz of Harold Bulan's law firm had invited him to show up to the so called meeting before Federal Judge Michael Kaplan.

Apparently, Dan lied to us over the Christmas Holidays about Federal Judge Michael Kaplan and Federal Judge Carl Bucki. "They do not want to see of you." he had said. Now I wondered why he had made this statement. Was there more going on in bankruptcy court than we knew? And what the hell was going on in Supreme Court at the same time?

Had Harold Bulan, of Bulan Goldstein & Chiari, tainted the case to hide something? Collusion among the attorneys? Ethics question? Conflict of interest? Protection of Michael Drumm of Brown & Chiari firm?

Morris Horwitz, the new partner of Horwitz, Goldstein & Chiari, had apparently taken over our case for Harold Bulan. He had stated in the transcripts that he called Dan into the arena because he was familiar with the case. In the same transcript, he also ignored Judge Kaplan when he asked a question twice ... and the Judge let it ride, not insisting Mr. Morris Horwitz show the respect that a Federal Judge should have.

Dan knew at the time, and kept quiet, that the expenses incurred in the bankruptcy case had been business expenses to do with the civil case in Supreme Court. We had discussed it many times over the phone and before the deposition with Ms. Fijal. It was documented by their own questions in the deposition and in letters.

I wondered if Dan had passed one of the many qualifying exams and even had the qualifications to be representing anyone Federal Court.

We were home in the comforting arms of Tampa, Florida. A totally different set of values. We would continue to figure this out from 1,500 miles away and we would need help. We now had in our possession all the files from Peerless Insurance, including the letters, depositions, and authorizations they sent over the years, from as far back as 2000. All of the attorney's files ranging from the first attorney, Lawrence Rubin, to attorneys David Sleight and Maurice Sykes, and lastly Katherine Fijal, attorney for Hurwitz & Fine. They were all attorneys for Peerless Insurance. The other files contained all the papers, depositions and letters from Michael Drumm and Daniel Schoenborn. Lastly, we had the transcripts from Federal Court in January 2013. Most important we had the E-Courts documents showing every meeting in Supreme Court with every Judge from Glownia, Chimes to Dillon.

It was now September of 2013 and we felt we had good things happening to us, especially since I leased the Volkswagen from Brandon Volkswagen in Tampa. Unbelievably, we had more in our favor. We had Tampa for security, we had three phone numbers, one for Tampa, the other for Buffalo, another for West Palm Beach, given to us by the attorney in front of the elevator in the Supreme Court building. We had an ever increasing number of contacts in Tampa Bay, and a decreasing amount in Buffalo. We wanted them to think we had just fallen off the fence and slunk away into the swamps of Alligator Alley.

The first thing on the agenda was to wait and see what my $2,000.00 had bought in Buffalo. The fourth attorney would look over the files and give us a report. We had to be as meticulous as possible while teaching ourselves how to continue to work the chess game.

The cast of characters was now over twenty people - most from the law field. While we waited for the attorney to forge through the files, we had to make a plan of our own. The following weekend we went to Costco and picked up three-inch-wide notebooks and plastic inserts to put in them. We then pulled all the files out and categorized them by person and law firm. We then went to the dates located in the letters, depositions and hateful mail from Peerless Insurance and broke it down again by date and year.

It was tedious and costly. We had to be meticulous as possible. We were teaching ourselves how the attorneys handled their affairs. It was like looking for a needle in a haystack, but you didn't know what the needle looked like. It had to be somewherein the immense files we had not run across before, something that would tie in with the Supreme Court lawsuit.

We did not know how much time we had, but we knew it would probably prove futile to hire an attorney from Buffalo, and at the price they had indicated they wanted was out of our price range. Peerless Insurance had made sure of that with the continued bullying over the years.

We were in personal bankruptcy because Michael Drumm and Harold Bulan had bungled the case with their greedy, hateful selves. I had been told the previous week in the hallway of the motel by Snoop that Harold Bulan the Trustee was not my friend and would do anything to get money out of it just for himself. "Looking to retire." Snoop had indicated, and the employees in the Federal Courthouse knew it. "Stay safe and watch your back."

"To what extent had the hoax been done?" I asked Snoop.

"Probably Years, and that's just your case." Snoop replied, as the spotted white and black hair and the pudgy body of Snoopy slunk away into an unknown place.

We had to find out. I wondered if Peerless Insurance had continued to railroad their way across the rest of the New England states as they had in New York.

Meanwhile, it took the new attorney six weeks to go through the paperwork. We received a letter from him stating he had taken longer than expected and needed another $2,900 to make up for the cost of his time. Then he would need between $15,000 and $50,000 to take the case to court, and by the way you owe $240,000 to the Department of Labor.

It was a grandiose letter with all the wrong facts in them. If this guy had used ten hours to get nothing but the wrong facts, he was overpaid and would be getting no more money from us. I felt like asking for a refund based on libelous statements.

Peter picked up the phone and called him. The attorney couldn't be happier.

"Great letter I wrote wasn't it? It took me a long time to get it together!" probably puffing out his chest with pride at the other end of the phone.

Peter, not impressed with his self- authoring of miss information informed him not only had he gotten all of the facts wrong but, the labor fine was for $33,000 not the $240,000. There was silence on the other end of the phone. He had sent the letter to us to add to our file of proof of the ongoing incompetence. And it was in his handwriting. Dumbass.

Peter hung up the phone exasperated. "Do any of the attorneys in Buffalo actually read their paperwork or do they just look for keywords on the first page!"

We did not send this guy any additional money since we had already paid $2000.00 for the wrong inaccurate information, and it was a verbal quote not an itemized bill. He still has the paperwork to this day for his scrapbook. He can keep it, but better not share it with anyone without our knowledge or permission, we already went through that with Michael and Thomas Burton, whoever he was.

I made a call to Snoop. Relaying the information, the attorney had given us all the wrong information. "This guy says we owed $240,000 for the labor fine, tax liens, and all the rest of this crap."

Snoop growled, "You owe $33,000 and some change, let me make a phone call and get this straightened out."

I didn't ask and Snoop did not tell to who the phone call was made to.

The next move was to get to the talked about meeting with the attorney we had met in the hallway of the Supreme Court building. Calling him the meeting in West Palm Beach. Setting up the meeting, we would be driving over in December while he was fixing up his place.

Leaving a few weeks later, we once again gathered up the paperwork to show him the details of the lawsuit. After a four-hour drive weaving in and out of traffic we managed to arrive in Deerfield Beach in one piece. It had a small town feel to it, beautifully kept, surreal compared to Interstate 95 of bumper to bumper traffic within its borders.

Checking into a local hotel we made a phone call to the attorney to solidify the meeting for the next morning, followed by a small dinner, then to the room for a good night's sleep.

The next morning, we headed to his condo in West Palm Beach for the meeting. As we pulled into the gated area, he was standing outside, pressing a button to let us in. As I started to head out from the driver's side, Peter informed me he was going to keep the paperwork in the trunk of the car, just in case the attorney mentioned anything odd. As we sat with the attorney in his condo, he seemed nice enough, speaking of family values and his wife. Soon we started to discuss the case and he wrote down the information and asking questions.

"I just left my firm and I'm working as a solo attorney. I need a sure thing because I'm going into retirement and this case is a real mess. By the way who is the bankruptcy trustee?" he asked us.

"Harold Bulan." Peter replied.

The attorney turned and pointed "He has a place right down the street from here, I know him!"

Up came the hairs along my hairline. We had known Harold Bulan had lived in Florida for a while but kept quiet about it. We continued to carry on the conversation, talking of general stuff, the weather, the winds of West Palm, and his family. We knew we had to let him go, to close to the rest of the cast of characters. As we got into the car he said, "Sorry you had to come so far...but I can't help you, I'm a solo firm." adding "Is that a new Volkswagen?"

"Yes, the day I got this car, things started to turn around in Buffalo for us. You know, more and more information." patting the trunk of the car where the paperwork was still intact.

We said our goodbyes and headed back to Tampa. As we headed out to the interstate, I asked Peter, "Did he say anything in Buffalo when we were standing in front of the elevator about Harold Bulan?"

Peter laughed, "So you caught it too, he said he did not know him." I laughed. It was getting close, we just did not have the latest move on the chessboard yet. Soon the holidays would be upon us, the courts would be having short days with a skeleton staff. This year would prove no different.

PART IV

CHAPTER 40: 937 WEEKS

Still in Peerless Insurance's vice, would celebrate the holidays with our friends, along with my Aunt Pat and "her boys", as she liked to call them. They were about ten years younger than me, and we had a lot of catching up to do from the years that had been lost since living in Buffalo, New York.

The New Year of 2014 came upon us, it had been a great holiday visiting relatives. The conversation never stopped, my fabulous Aunt Pat now in her 90's was never at a loss for conversation, sharp as a knife, holding court while my cousin Jan cooked his way through the afternoon filled with laughter and, of course, the latest antics of the attorneys in Buffalo. This included the up-to-date trip to West Palm Beach describing how the hairs rose on my head again.

"You need to write this down and get it out!" Jan would exclaim "This stuff is crazy and bizarre!"

I countered "I don't know how."

"Just write it down, let it fly, and publish it!"

Glenn chimed in "Just do it, it's not like there aren't writers and artists in this family!"

It felt like a dare, then a triple dare. The first dare had been Supreme Court Judge Deborah Chimes law clerk, Jill Toholoski, admitting I would make more money if I wrote a book. My family had said it, cousin's, friend's, patients, and now the latest was coming from people who were important to me.

We had everything including but, not all the paperwork from the bankruptcy court. That would come later in the year since they could not continue without our knowledge. We had never been part of the backroom deals in Buffalo. We did not know the ending to the book yet, even though the bad boys from Buffalo thought we were forever gone. It would be cumbersome undertaking and we were not getting any younger. Peerless Insurance had made sure we had turned from Plaintiffs to Defendants and it had taken fourteen years to cover the still unknown secret or two being held in the dirty hands of the attorneys. I started to write, putting all the files, notes and letters into a sequence. No mistakes - just the facts of the corruption and laziness of the participants.

One Saturday morning during the first week of January 2014, my throw-away phone rang. Knowing who it was I picked it up. "What's going on?"

Snoop responded, "I'm over here in St. Petersburg. Come and meet with me. I have someone I want you to get together with, a friend of mine."

Answering with surprise, "We will meet with you but, we just heard there are some people there in from Buffalo, not a great idea to meet in public. I will drive the Volks over. I'll be there in about an hour and a half. Meanwhile you go to Philthy Phil's and stand upstairs at the railing with the tables and chairs. I'll call you before we get there, I will circle twice then you will know it is us, especially in the Volkswagen. You get in whatever car you have and follow me to the food market around the corner."

Snoop retorted, "You are spooked aren't you?"

I answered, "No, just careful, especially in the St. Petersburg area, I don't need the drama or previous people in my life. We have had to act like this for over fourteen years while these idiots with sub-standard values continue to harass us.

"We are not sure who Peerless Insurance is carrying and who they aren't. They continue to dig into their bottomless deep pockets and use their money for devious ways trying to break us."

Snoop guffawing with apparently an audience of one nearby "Alright you made your point."

Click.

Driving over to the beach, we had the Volkswagen top down. Tampa Bay would be beautiful that year throughout the winter, spring and, early summer until the hot humid days of July and August set in. As we neared the street in front of Philthy Phil's, we looked up and there was Snoop, who immediately walked away from the railing. We drove around the block again and a car with New York State plates pulled up behind us. Nothing unusual, there are a lot of New Yorkers that flock to the beaches stretching along the Tampa Bay in the winter.

There was no need to stop at the grocery store. We would head over to the cemetery where members of my family had found their final resting place. Weaving through the snow bird traffic we pulled into Memorial Gardens, passing the site of the family parcels and continuing to the end of the road. Located behind an arbor, we walked the curved brick path until we reached the fountain. No one would see us here.

"What are we doing here?" asked Snoop as the silent partner stood by. Snoop, with folded arms, walked up to the fountain and the benches surrounding it. Turning, looking at both Peter and myself, Snoop said, "Original, very original."

I felt nervous not knowing who the new person was standing nearby but, who had apparently had heard about to our escapades in the Nickel City. Snoopy, catching my attitude, laughed and introduced the person to Peter and myself.

"Settle down, this is your new contact, Tampa Bay Snoopy, a trusted soul mate for you, my friends."

Once again, Buffalo Snoop asked why we were meeting here. I replied this was a special place where no one but the employees of Memorial Gardens would see us and they would think nothing of it if they did. Relaying the story to the two of them I told them the bizarre set of events.

"I had to buy this plot to protect myself from a destructive person in Buffalo," adding," I have no intention of being buried here, I plan on selling it, but it might save my body from being donated to a place against my wishes."

Buffalo Snoop looked at me with amazement. "What the hell are you talking about!"

I continued with my disturbing story of abuse of the elderly. My mother resided in a nursing home in Buffalo, against my wishes, we were here. When she died, they had refused to release her body to the embalmer, who she had paid years ago for her body to be cremated. The man had representing the funeral home called me in Florida with the news that the head of the nursing home and his wife refused to release the body."

Buffalo Snoop mouth open pleaded with me to continue.

"The poor mortician had to fight tooth and nail to get the body of my mother out of the nursing home, to the cremation process, while these two narcissistic jerks continued to show their false importance. The Power of Attorney they had talked themselves into with my mother, they both had forgotten that the title of Power of Attorney dies and expires with death of the person. My mother knew this and never let it be known to the idiots involved.

"My mother, she was smart, she let this idiot be her Power of Attorney and let me remain as the Executor of the Estate. When she died, this person and her attorneys gave me such a hard time I had to call a dear friend who was an attorney to explain the situation.

"When they did not believe him either, my attorney called me back and had me call the attorney for the nursing home in Buffalo. When the nursing home attorney she didn't answer she let my calls go to messages. It was my chance to tell her in no uncertain terms, what the plan would be as the one-way conversation continued. I finished telling her that my mother had made plans in the early seventies to be buried here with her sister, my sister, and the rest of the family. I would be damned to let a ninety-four-year-old lady be hanging from a meat hook or in a vault as per the power of attorney's wishes.

"My last words to them were, 'If you do not know this law of not only New York State but, other states as well, I suggest you go and have lunch with one of your law cronies and they will keep you informed of elder law and the legal dying process. If you continue to ignore my mother's wishes, and myself as the Executor of the Estate, you will find yourself in the biggest lawsuit of your life and so will the two jackasses that are telling you these lies.' Then my turn came up. 'Click,' I hung up the phone."

"Who does that crap over a dead body?" Asked Tampa Snoop.

"You would be surprised. Where do you think the statement 'over my dead body' comes from? I still have the paperwork from the seventies, eighties, and nineties just to keep everything intact." I concluded, "Now let's get down to business about Buffalo, the attorneys and Peerless Insurance Company."

The introductions continued with a deep conversation of the antics of Peerless Insurance and the attorneys. I looked at Tampa Snoop adding, "I'm happy to meet you in so many ways, you probably think we are crazy, but these last fourteen years with Peerless Insurance and the attorneys in Buffalo has been nothing short of hell on Earth. We know they are covering up something and we don't know what adding, "They thought for years Peter had money, he is just a co-guardian for his niece." A hand was held up in front of my face indicating for me to stop.

"I know all about it, there is more to be found out. Peter and you both have to take this to the end to make it work. You now have me to help you and, I have my ways of getting into things from here." We stood there staring at Tampa Snoop.

Buffalo Snoop was bent over cackling like a crazy person, thinking it was the funniest thing ever.

Tampa Snoop continued, "We will do what has to be done from here, this crap would never happen in this town, no one would put up with it, there has to be more to the story and we will wait it out. You will use a different phone to call me, another throw-away. We will use the same system you used in Buffalo. we can meet at different areas and in different ways."

 A piece of chalk was removed from a pocket along with a water bottle. "Come with me." Tampa Snoop said. We walked a short distance back down the paved walkway towards the parked cars. As we reached a mid-sized rock, Tampa Snoop wrote down a phone number, I copied it to a piece of paper that Buffalo Snoop had handed to me. As soon as I finished, the bottle of water was poured over it and it was washed away with a rag.

"You need to go through all the paperwork from the bankruptcy court you picked up in Buffalo. I hear you are pretty good at picking stuff out, Peter." Tampa Snoop was now the new handler.

"Go through it until you become familiar with the dealings of the Federal Court house." Continuing, "Be careful on the internet too, and stay away from anything to do with Pacer, you can't afford it and you might be able to be tracked, it's for the attorneys and members of the court."

The chain of events was getting weirder and weirder. What had started out as a business fire in 2000 had taken us to the depths of places you never knew existed. A $200,000 fire is not a huge deal. We had to find out the real issue.

Tampa Snoop looked at me "How old are you anyway?"

"I'm going to be seventy and Peter is going to be seventy-five."

"This is disgusting." Tampa Bay Snoop said. I wasn't sure if the comment was about our age or the length of the case.

Walking away from us, they got into the undescriptive car with the New York plates, we got into the Volks, turned around and headed back through the long driveway of the cemetery, ending a visit to the area where I had been forced to buy the burial site so I would not end up on a meat hook or in a vault in Buffalo. It had proved a useful day, but also a day not out of the ordinary. A car with New York plates, visiting our plot we had no intention of going too, a visit to see a family member who had passed on. No one would even give it a second thought.

We were getting close. We could feel in in our bones. We now had help from Buffalo and Tampa.

We found it challenging that a defendant apparently could not have a judge read a letter written to them, but the same judge could hear an attorney commit slander and libel in the courtroom. To our benefit, we now knew we had to order every transcript in Federal Court dealing with our case.

We would continue to wait for letters coming from the Federal Court to notify us of appearance's that had been scheduled. The attorneys could no longer schedule court dates without notifying us, since we had sent the correct address by certified mail to the bankruptcy court. The rules of court had to be followed by everyone including the judges.

While waiting for the letters of appearance for Federal Court, we would collect and read every piece of paperwork the attorneys had submitted to the Supreme and Federal Court in Buffalo. The paperwork from Supreme Court would take longer to arrive than had been anticipated, but it would hold even more information than we had suspected. The case would be corrupt from the beginning 14 years before.

We would continue to live a quiet life to save money, feeling we were being watched in Florida. I had been very skittish since my old Volkswagen had blown a few years before. I would no longer take the dogs for walks through the nearby park, go out at night by myself, or do much of anything. We had to lay low for the time being, waiting for the next move out of Buffalo.

As the weeks went by, we would discuss what we should be doing in retirement instead of this crap. As we dreamed the fantasy life, we thought it would include resting, traveling, boating, or other forms of entertainment. However, somehow we were picked to do this job, not sure why or by whom, and we would continue the path set before us.

Peter would read the newspaper sent from Buffalo every day. The town was becoming foreign to both of us. Every so often, some weird thing would happen to one of the citizens and it would never be followed up by another news story. The exodus was continuing out of the city to other parts of the country. It had been a good move for us, except for the ongoing lawsuit, keeping us hostage

One day, Peter started to look through the bankruptcy papers we had gotten a few months before.

We had thought the paperwork from the Supreme Court would have been delivered before the New Year, but there had been a delay. We did not have the $300.00 to pay for it. We would have to work ourselves backwards from the bankruptcy court to Supreme Court to avoid more delays. In the meantime, we would gather the money together to pay for the Supreme Court paperwork that had been copied in the guts of the courthouse the previous August.

CHAPTER 41: HOW MANY PIECES ARE ON THE CHESS BOARD?

As Peter reviewed the bankruptcy paperwork, it noted a 341 Hearing had occurred on August 10, 2004. Not knowing what a 341 Hearing was, he looked it up on the internet, he phoned me, and explained it to me. It was supposed to be a meeting with your bankruptcy attorney, the trustee, creditors, and you, the debtor, to go over the bills that had led you into the bankruptcy world.

I thought for a moment. My review of the date took me back to the courtroom that day in August of 2004 the day we met the trustee, Harold Bulan. He had been sitting behind an elevated desk, while Peter and I had taken our turn on the cutting block.

I started my rant about Harold Bulan over the phone to Peter. "We never had a meeting with him or our creditors, he never asked us what we owed, and I will tell you right now the whole thing is a con game. The only thing Harold Bulan ever said to either of us was 'You have a lawsuit and I'm talking 20% off the top when you get to the trial.'" My anger was real now about the sleaziness of it all. "Even the greedy trustee knew we had a winner for a lawsuit against Peerless Insurance. And he never answered any of our certified letters or phone calls for over nine years! What was the deal with that?"

I then asked Peter if he had any meeting with Harold Bulan that he could remember outside of that day of August 10, 2004. "Never" he replied.

Peter continued "The only thing I can tell you about Harold Bulan, is that Michael Drumm told me Harold Bulan could be beneficial and help us, because of the closeness of the attorney firms, and he was also after the 20 percent of the lawsuit."

The hairs raising again on my head, I asked Peter, "Do you have any proof of correspondence between Harold Bulan and Michael Drumm?"

"Yes, I do and it's in the files at the storage place."

I then asked Peter, "Does the paperwork show the letterhead of the two firms?"

Peter informed me he had it for Brown & Chiari and Michael Drumm with letters addressed to Harold Bulan of Bulan, Goldstein & Chiari. He would look for the letterhead from Harold Bulan's firm later in the day. I told him to wait until we went through all the bankruptcy files we had received from the Federal Courthouse. If Harold Bulan was working as a trustee for the Federal Bankruptcy court, it would be in that paperwork, not of Bulan, Goldstein & Chiari.

I chimed in, "Hey Peter, not bad for a guy Michael Drumm mocked out for having five strokes and a lack of memory. Maybe Michael should take some lessons from stroke victims, he might learn a little compassion for others and follow the procedures of Kathys Law himself."

Peter, ignoring me, interjected, "I know we have paperwork written by Michael to Harold at Bulan, Goldstein & Chiari."

"Do you think that Michael and Harold were holding information and avoiding any paperwork going through the Federal Courthouse? "adding "I mean Morris Horwitz either lied to the federal judge about the amount of the lawsuit or Michael Drumm set them all up." "listen the lawsuit was for $988,000 in Michael Drumm's paperwork yet Horwitz told the judge it was for $200,000, where is the other money? You know the $688,000 follow the money Peter and you will find the greed."

Peter responded, "They were definitely talking to each other about our case, it's in the paperwork we have in storage." adding, "If Harold had written to us as the bankruptcy trustee representing Bulan, Goldstein, & Chiari it would be it would have been in Michael Drumm's file also."

"I see you in a couple of hours when I get home." hanging up the phone.

When I arrived at the house a few hours later, the conversation ensued about the personal bankruptcy of both of us, and of the supposed 341 Hearing on August 10, 2003. Peter and I looked over some of the paperwork from the bankruptcy court and discussed the proceedings that had actually happened instead of the smoke and mirrors presented in the paperwork provided by the attorneys within the Federal Courthouse.

The next morning Peter pulled all of the bankruptcy papers. He then put them into two: piles one in his name the other in mine. The other paperwork sent to the various phoney addresses would be dealt with later after the bungling job of this mess had been straightened out. When he was finished it came down the following:

PETER'S BANKRUPTCY

June 6, 2005: Peter's bankruptcy case was now closed.

June 15, 2005: The TRUSTEE'S REPORT OF NO DISTRIBUTION to Judge Carl Bucki was filed by Harold Bulan stating he made a diligent inquiry into the estate, financial affairs of the estate, the duties had been fully administered, except what was exempt. [exempt being the crucial word]The trustee requested to be discharged from any further duties as trustee.

June 21, 2005: Judge Carl Bucki for Peter's case stated the trustee has performed all duties and the trustee requests to be discharged from any further duties as trustee. IT IS ORDERED the case is approved and the case is now closed.

July 20, 2005: The trustee was paid from our funds. [The first payment was made to Harold Bulan]

February 9, 2010: A refund/credit of $155.00 was paid to Dennis Gaughan by the Financial Department. The transaction number was 889859.

February 09, 2012: Harold Bulan now of Bulan, Chiari & Illecki, LLP, had reopened the case. You see, Harold Bulan wanted to retire and close every case that was still on the docket. He wanted to take our case to the graveyard before he died. It looked like Judge Bucki was in agreement even though they had closed the case almost seven years before. In our opinion, Mr. Bulan had to protect Brown & Chiari. Daniel Schoenborn also had the paperwork and was holding all the cards. The secret and the payoff would be for protecting Michael Drumm of Brown

& Chiari and himself. Reading this we would be continued to be left in the dark until the Summer of 2014

JOANNE'S BANKRUPTCY

August 10, 2004: The laughable 341 Hearing was held with Harold Bulan

August 24, 2004: Harold Bulan applies to be Trustee for the bankruptcy, after the embarrassing phony 341 Hearing that was a sham.

October 13, 2004: Harold Bulan files a Statement of Intent to sell ownership of Advanced Massage Therapy, which was not part of the bankruptcy was Evans Services another corporation owned by me. Again, none of the corporations had filed for bankruptcy, not Evans Services nor Pro-Pak. It was personal and Harold Bulan was continuing to make a mess.

May 12, 2005: Harold Bulan files a Motion for Non-Abandonment of Interest of the business fire loss. He appeared to be mixing up the personal bankruptcy with the corporations.

June 6, 2006: A letter was sent, stating "The US trustee has reviewed the final account; the certification and estate have been closed. The MOU [memorandum of understanding] has been filed April 1, 1999. [perhaps the labor fine] and has no objection to the Trustee's certification that the estate has been fully administered and is ready to close."

June 23, 2006: The bankruptcy is closed. The trustee is paid. The second payment to Harold Bulan.

December 4, 2012 A motion is made to reopen the bankruptcy by Harold Bulan. The fee of $260.00 is deferred. [by the court]

December 4, 2012: Application is presented to employ Harold Bulan.

December 4, 2012: No objection by the federal court.

December 6, 2012: Order granting application of Harold Bulan

December 7, 2012: Notice of Appointment of Harold Bulan in reopened case.

December 13, 2012: Certification of Notice is sent to Peter Kirisits of 3 Pine Terrace Orchard Park, N.Y.

December 17, 2012: Application to employ Daniel Schoenborn as Special Counsel to the trustee.

December 17, 2012: Peter and I sent the letter to Judge Bucki, Judge Kaplan, and Chief Judge William Skretney. In this letter, we asked the Judges to release the case from bankruptcy court and put it back in Supreme Court. Judge Kaplan suggests in the transcripts that he was reading Judge Bucki's letter. He did not mention he had gotten one also sent certified mail.

So the Judges do read their mail and attorneys do lie to them.

January 13, 2013: A change of address is noted for me in the federal courthouse paperwork. This was beyond odd as I did not fill it out and I did not send it nor did I get notified of it. Someone within the court system had gotten into our file and changed my address before I even knew they had the 'meeting'. With that done we continued to not receive any documents or Certificates of Services (letters informing me there was a court hearing). I do not know who put in the change of address, if there is access to it I'm not aware of it.

It was another violation of Federal Law to commit this crime. Someone had gone into the paperwork and changed our address without our knowledge. Whomever it was appeared to be filing a false document in our names, without our knowledge in the Federal Courthouse. It narrowed down the number of people that could be possible involved. It had to be someone directly involved with the case, or indirectly, but who had access to our file. This was the last of the address change that was submitted by someone from the Federal court. There would be no addresses changes again. We had stopped it in the summer of 2013.

During this time period, Certificates of Service flying all over Buffalo to the different attorneys. We would never receive one until May of 2014. Over a year later. They needed time to get it right and protect the goal of keeping us out of the Supreme and Federal courtrooms, and almost succeeded

We started to wonder what was going on within the offices of the Federal courthouse and who had introduced the patty-cake game into the chessboard. It had to be someone who had access to the files. We would be told by the Clerk of Court of the Federal Court that the access to our files were yet to be opened to the "Freedom of Information Act" passed on July 4, 1966. The Clerk had told us in the Summer of 2013, "Your case is not opened to the public yet, although it will be on September 13, 2013."

What we did not know was we should not have lost our house either, it was exempt, as was the machinery and equipment related to Evans Services and Pro-Pak. Harold Bulan had also managed to collect some money from Advanced Massage Therapy, probably kept it all for himself.

Dennis Gaughan, Harold Bulan, Morris Horwitz, and Daniel Schoenborn knew this also. If they did not shame on them. They had to be so lazy and used to doing it their way they constantly messed up. We wondered how many other people they had done this to, how many left Buffalo because of their bungling. We wondered about the Judges Carl Bucki and Michael Kaplan. What the hell was going on in Buffalo that they were fighting us so hard?

It was mind boggling to wonder why Michael Drumm referred us to Dennis Gaughan, other than the statement that he was the Hamburg Town Attorney at the time and could help him in the courtroom if he appeared before him. Why would Michael refer us to Dennis Gaughan, who referred to Harold Bulan as "Your Majesty".

The "Cast of Characters" had to know they had ruined us financially, emotionally, physically. They had to know our poor quality of life by being denied a trial that had been scheduled twice. The constant lying of the attorneys had to stop and we would prove it by the end of summer of 2014.

We had to lay low throughout 2013 and five months into 2014. We had other things to do while we waited for the next court date in bankruptcy court.

Apparently, when we ordered the transcripts we had raised some eyebrows.

From January of 2013 to May of 2014, we did not know what was going on. One year and four months it took to fit the pieces together. Arrangements were being made in the back rooms of Buffalo attorney's office, without our knowledge. The phone calls we made, the letters written, and the faxes sent would not be answered by Daniel

Schoenborn, Harold Bulan, or Morris Horwitz. It seemed that they were guilty of not only ethics violations but perhaps some illegal activities as well.

Peter, by ordering the first of the transcripts, had thrown a wrench into the machinery. It was like a speeding car going along the highway without water in the radiator. It was as if we looked at the gage of the car to see if it was going to blow up, then gunning the pedal to make it to the nearest facility to get water.

Having gotten used to the enormous pressure from Peerless Insurance, we had learned to spin tightly around the circle of characters, keeping them as close together as possible, as if they were all standing on a dime. If one fell off they would all go down and scatter into many broken pieces; the egos, self-importance, self-respect, everything would be gone, fighting it out in Federal Court with the transcriber typing away and perhaps the audio going at the same time. You knew to keep it honest.

As 2014 came into our lives, it had now been fourteen years of abuse by Peerless Insurance and the people that had led the chase, insisting that we live in misery. This appeared to be a group of miserable, ungracious, insidious folks who knew what had happened to us, including wrong information about Peter's wealth, choosing instead to take the cowardly way out. That would be their choice, we would ignore them and continue to struggle for our civil rights as citizens in this country. What had happened in 1999 had followed us to 2014 as they laughed at us and we continued our pursuit.

Periodically, I would meet with Tampa Snoop getting updates about the situation in Buffalo. There was movment going on in Buffalo and it would turn up soon in Tampa.

As winter turned in early spring, the weather in Tampa was magnificent. One day, I texted Tampa Snoop to meet me at Circles in Apollo Beach for a late lunch or early dinner.

We arrived at the same time coming from two different directions. Getting out of our respective cars, we walked through the door to reach the hostess, who led us to the back porch overlooking the marina. Circles is known for their great mounds of shrimp loaded on a platter served hot or cold. Ordering the latter with the capresse salad it would be enough to share, enjoy the latest news while we overlooked the brilliance of the water while the various boats rocked gently back and forth at the marina.

As our conversation drifted, we reached the topic of the Federal Court case of both Peter and myself. I told Tampa Snoop we hadn't heard a thing since Peter ordered the transcripts almost eight months before. We had decided to lay low for the past year while we waited for Harold Bulan to make his next move. Legally, he would have to send us notices to our address - not the five hundred phony addresses that had been provided to the Federal Courts by an unknown person.

Tampa Snoop agreeing with the latest move and mentioned, "You were told by Judge Dillon's law clerk that the Judge was not familiar with your case right?"

"Yes, he left a message on my cell phone." I replied.

"Do you still have it?"

"I may, and if I do it would be with the phone that has the messages from the IRS when we had Dan Schoenborn."

"Did you know that Judge Dillon, without Judge Chimes, made a motion on January 30, 2013, sixteen days after the so called meeting with the Judges in Federal Court with Morris Horwitz?"

"No." I said.

Tampa Snoopy continued, "Why did Judge Dillon and Judge Chimes have a meeting on March 14, of 2013?"

"I did not know that." I answered.

I explained to Tampa Snoopy that Judge James Dillon was the third judge to be scheduled to handle our case against Peerless Insurance in Supreme Court. Whether he had anything to do with keeping the secret between Dan Schoenborn and the other cast of characters, I did not know and only the Judge himself would be able to answer that.

Tampa Snoop continued, "The meetings between Judge Chimes and Judge Dillon, there was another meeting on January 17, 2013 that was also adjourned. Were you informed?"

"No."

Snoop had snooped, "So you had no idea that Judge Chimes and Judge Dillon had a meeting on January 17, 2013, three days after meeting in Judge Bucki's court?"

"No, by that time we had no attorney, Dan had gotten a better offer from Harold Bulan by then. I would not have a reason to check on Judge Dillon or Chimes."

Snoop once again came back with, "So no one ever told you?"

"No." I said. "We found out in July 2013 seven months after Harold Bulan brought Dan Schoenborn into his fold of attorneys. It was found in the transcripts we sent for in July of 2013, with Judge Kaplan."

"Do you have any paperwork indicating Dan Schoenborn was working for Harold Bulan?" Snoop asked.

"No, all we have is an email from Dan telling us to refer all questions to Harold Bulan, when I was buying the Volkswagen last March."

"Do you have a copy of the email from Dan Schoenborn?"

"Yes, we have kept all paperwork, emails, letters, statement to Gary Gable, two depositions, taxes everything from 1999 to 2014." I answered, adding, "Sometimes we had to ask for it, for example, the transcripts but we have everything including stuff I haven't gone through yet, mostly in Dan Schoenborn's file."

"Why didn't you go through his?"

"Because we suspected the files were purged at Brown & Chiari law firm, and we were the ones that recreated the missing files and sent them up to DeMarie & Schoenborn."

Snoop looked at me with reflection, before asking, "You have every bit of paperwork since 1999?"

Smiling, I said, "We have paperwork all the way back to 1997 and before."

"Tell me about Michael Fitzgerald."

I continued the story to Snoop, explaining, "Well, he charged us and another business with a labor fine, they left town, which in turn caused endless damage to people's lives all because of a time clock neither Mary Coleman or he never checked to see if it was in. Peter told me he had a short stature and at the time had a mullet. We were set up."

Laughing, Snoop said, "Oh business by day, party by night huh?"

Not familiar with the meaning of the hairstyle, Snoop informed me of the flair of the hairstyle while we laughed like hell while chomping on the shrimp.

Soon we were back to business. "Adding together the facts and the dates, here it is: you were told by Dan Schoenborn not to come to the so called meeting on January 9, 2013, in front of Judge Kaplan. You were also told by Dan Schoenborn that Judge Joseph Glownia on March 8, 2011, had switched your case to Judge Deborah Chimes right?"

"Yes." I replied.

"Then you got switched again as you were once more close to trial right?"

"Yes, Dan told us Deborah Chimes got switched to Chautauqua, New York, and we were going to go to Judge Dillon and the trial would be a long way off. Harold Bulan stepped in to stop the Supreme Court case and put it into Federal Court."

Snoop asked "Why?"

"I don't know."

"Yeah, we don't act like that here."

Looking out towards the marina I ignored the comment as I noticed a figure walking along the dock. "Wow!" I exclaimed.

"What do you see?" Snoop asked.

"I can't believe this but, the guy walking along the dock sure as hell looks like Judge Glownia to me! I've seen pictures of him in the Buffalo paper and I think he has a place around here."

Snoop looked out following my gaze to the marina. Turning back to me Tampa Snoop said "Tell me more."

Laughing I said, "Look at E-Courts and see how many times we have been cancelled in his courtroom, sometimes it would be almost a year before we got back in." adding, "I should look at his calendar on the E-Courts site now and see if there is a pattern with him, he has been very controversial since we were in his courtroom along with the horse abuse case."

As we continued to observe the look alike walking leisurely along the path, we made plans to meet in the future. Next time it would be somewhere else, a different time, a different place. "Look through all the paperwork from Supreme Court and Federal Court while you are waiting for the next move from Buffalo. If you find anything interesting set it aside for your future use." Snoop advised. Leaving the restaurant, we parted ways once again, our cars headed in two different directions.

Meanwhile, we would sit and wait for the Certificate of Service to arrive from Harold Bulan's office.

Within a few days following lunch with Snoopy, Peter and I once again went through the paperwork. This time picking the Federal Court papers we found three interesting things.

December 7, 2012: a Notice of Appointment of Harold Bulan reopening the case. A month before the Supreme Court case was going to trial January 9, 2013 to pick a jury.

December 13, 2012: A Certification of Notice was sent to Peter at 3 Pine Terrace Orchard Park, New York. It was sent to the wrong address. We did not get it.

December 17, 2012: An application to employ Dan Schoenborn our Supreme Court attorney as Special Counsel to the Trustee, Harold Bulan. He had to be picked, he was keeper of the secret. It looked as if the attorneys were trying to settle our case without our knowledge. Not being allowed at a meeting is one thing, not being allowed into a formal court setting is another. It was grounds for malpractice, not for one attorney but now for two.

The questions started coming. Had Dan been at the first meeting with Peter in January of 2009 left the room to make a phone call to Brown &

Plaintiff to Defendant

Chiari, advising them Peter was in his office, and looking for a lawsuit against them for malpractice? It appeared so and only he and Michael Drumm could answer the question. Dan had drained more money from our coffers by insisting we go to Buffalo twice, once for a second deposition in 2011, stating the first was lost, and then again in 2012 to meet with the phoney representative from Peerless Insurance, which turned out to be their own attorney Katherine Fijal.

It appeared there would be a payoff from one attorney to another. We couldn't be sure but it pointed to that direction.

We waited for the next chess move. As the months flew by in 2014, we continued to look for more clues about the cheat in the game. It would be May 14, 2014, before we would hear from the notorious Harold P. Bulan. It would be the first paperwork we would get from Harold Bulan since we had filed bankruptcy in 2004. It was reaching almost ten years.

As we opened the letter, it appeared to be a Notice of the Trustee's final report and applications and the deadline to object. It was the long awaited Certificate of Service. Harold Bulan had submitted the paperwork stating the contents of the certificate was true for both Peter and myself. Both of the certificates were absolute lies and filled with confusing disbursements except for Harold Bulans. Also with the certificate was a date for us to show up in Judge Bucki's court on June 2, 2014, then Judge Kaplan's court two days later.

Peter's Certificate stated he owed Elaine L. Chao, the Secretary of Labor, $8,014.54 according to the case number #000001a, and $39,960.58 under case number #000001b. It also stated he owed and Susan Buranich of Orchard Park $448.87. The other side of the certificate was the proposed payment to Harold Bulan for his trustee fee. It would be $8,250.00, with another $576.00 for himself, then $260.00 to the Clerk of the Bankruptcy Court, and a cost of $51.77 to International Sureties. There was no mention of the previous $700.00 Harold Bulan had collected in 2003 from us. t was for Advanced Massage the company that was not involved in this scheme of dollar signs.

 We were missing a significant amount of money and this little group knew it.

Harold Bulan had cleaned up a sweet deal for himself. We wondered if he was trying to close it again because by the following August of 2014, ten years would have run out and he could not continue or collect. Then the deal he made with Dan would be defunct. By then we were the only ones with the paperwork.

There was no mention of Dan in the Certificate of Service. That was kept in the background for future use.

It didn't matter. What did matter was the fact we were entitled by law to be heard in a courtroom, to defend ourselves. We would go in and fly by the seat of our pants, while the audio and the transcriber were ready to capture it all.

Hastily, we made plane reservations with Southwest Airlines to arrive in Buffalo on May 31, 2014, Memorial Weekend. It was the cheapest flight with the longest hotel stay.

We would challenge the matter of the labor fine, since we had paid the fine down to $33,623.57 from the original $50,000 in less than a year way back in 2000. It was not the amount Harold Bulan had recorded, and it looked like there was money missing in Judge Bucki's court. Perhaps we would find it in Judge Kaplan's. Harold Bulan's paperwork was a nightmare, inaccurate and sloppy. As if he had done it so many times he did it without a thought.

Arriving in Buffalo, we checked into the same hotel as before. After unpacking, we went to the local office retailer to make copies of the proper paperwork to be handed to Judge Bucki and Harold Bulan, or whomever he sent in.

The next day was a Sunday. We got up and headed for Leroy, a small town known for the discovery of the versatile product Jell-O. We would meet with Buffalo Snoop and get some details of the workings of Federal Court while we enjoyed the weather and some lunch. We knew things were being stretched for Snoop in Buffalo. We needed to get our side as tight as Harold Bulan kept his. After lunch, we walked the sidewalks of the small town of Leroy. If anyone was following us, we would know it. Out of the blue Snoop said, "They want you gone and will do anything to make it happen and get rid of you." I laughed at the thought of the "they" still in my life.

Peter, on the other hand, shifted his weight back and forth concentrating on the information. "Federal Court does not like anyone to come in and represent themselves, they are above it, especially in Buffalo." Snoop said.

Looking at Peter, Snoop continued, "You might be OK with Bucki." Then looking at me, "You on the other hand, with Kaplan, will have a tough time of it. He is known for his attitude, and he sides with Bulan almost all the time." Continuing Snoop injected "Here is one of his attorneys on Facebook. Probably uses it for stalking the ligigants in the courtrooms of Buffalo. I'm thinking if you look around the room tomorrow he will be close to the Judge." "What do you mean?" I asked as I gazed at the man with the side profile. "Just look and observe."

As we wrapped up the social gathering we parted ways, not sure when or if we would ever see each other again and probably not in Buffalo.

Driving back to the city, we turned in for the night at the hotel knowing we were going to get our butts kicked. We had a plan of our own and it would be recorded on the transcripts during the following week of escapades.

Arriving the next day at the Bankruptcy Court House, we entered the doorway to sit down at the small deli located in the lobby of the Federal Court building. We ordered a coffee to sip on while we did some people watching as they mingled around the open courtyard. By now I was also makings entries in a small spiral notebook that I carried in my purse. Sitting down at the small table before going through security, I wrote on the activities in the piazza and of my feeling hopes and fears of us now representing ourselves in Federal Court. Tampa Snoop had given the warning of representing ourselves in court but we had to. Besides, Harold Bulan had been one of the worst attorneys I had even seen. He had filed his paperwork with the wrong information without as much as a phone call to get it right. It would be worth it to show his careless mistakes ruining people's lives would be shared in an open courtroom. I had a feeling we were not the worst either, we had just been the fortunate people who had caught it and chosen to run with it.

Within minutes, we got up from the small table to go through the security located within a few feet away. The same guards, probably retired police officers, were at the area that had been there August of

2013, when we copied and picked up the paperwork from the Federal Court House and shipped it out of Buffalo.

As we entered the security entrance, the guards told us where the courtrooms were located. "Go to the elevator and when you arrive at the correct floor you go right, then turn left, to Judge Bucki's courtroom."

We sat down on a bench and waited outside of the court for the session to begin. I noticed paperwork that had been enclosed in glass along the opposite wall of where we were sitting. Approaching the encasement, it appeared to be the schedule of the day's events in Judge Bucki's courtroom. I looked through the listings starting at the bottom. Peter was the up first, before the hostile firing squad.

I sat down to give him the great news that he would be able to speak first before the Judge Bucki, as he was first-up when things were still fresh. As we sat on the bench, we were aware of more people shuffling about. We noticed a short heavy-set man that walked past us four times. Looking at Peter, I smiled and told him I thought it was one of the law clerks for either Judge Bucki or Judge Kaplan. We continued to make small conversation until the doors to the courtroom opened. We entered the room, staying to the left and sitting in the second row back from the gates.

As the courtroom filled with the newly bankrupt claimants, I kept thinking "we have to be the oldest bankruptcy case in the Eighth District of New York and the most unethical." The chatter continued between the attorneys and their now broke clients. Fortunately, the attorneys had collected a tidy sum beforehand from their clients so they could even claim bankruptcy. As did Harold Bulan for us.

It was depressing to see so many people from a fairly small city without the means to pay their bills.

Soon the courtroom became quiet and the chant began: "All rise." Federal Judge Carl Bucki entered the room sitting in his high backed chair. He appeared to be reading the list of petitions set before him flanked by his law clerk and the court stenographer.

This was the first time in fourteen years we had seen a Judge other than the Honorable Magistrate Hugh Scott. He had listened to us, representing ourselves in his court, shortly after Peter had major surgery, when we had gotten thrown under the bus by Michael who told us he could not go to Federal Court because he was not qualified. Another lie.

Surely this Judge would listen to the truth and reason backed up by the original and copies of the documents Peter had in his possession and had copied the day before.

Peter looked to the right of the courtroom. Whispering to me he said, "Who is that guy with the receding hairline and the glasses?"

I looked over for a second. "That's Morris Horwitz. He is on Facebook remember ? Snoopy showed us his picture." Snoopy had also showed us a picture of him from when he left the courtroom in January of 2013.

We were walking the sidewalk in the Village of Leroy after lunch. Snoop had mentioned "They were not sure we would be at the courthouse so had not done much to prepare." Then he said, "Here is Harold's picture on Facebook,"

Laughing I told Peter, "He is probably here to observe, stay cool, he thinks he is being unnoticed." I wanted to cackle like Buffalo Snoop always did when finding more interesting news.

CHAPTER 42: CHESS GAME TIME CLOCK

June 2, 2014, 10:05 A.M.

BEFORE FEDERAL JUDGE CARL L. BUCKI

PETER'S TRANSCRIPT

Page 2, Line 1: A voice called out "Peter Kirisits." Peter got up and moved his way through the gates, turning him into an attorney representing himself. Before another moment passed, a woman with shoes loudly clomping on the carpet between the separations of the rows of pews came down the center of the courtroom aisle pushing the gates open and plopped at a conference table before Judge Bucki and his law clerk.

Page 2, Line 2: Judge Bucki then stopped the proceedings before they began, saying "Who are you?"

"Jill Zubler I'm appearing on behalf of Mr. Bulan. He called our office last week and advised our office that he had a long standing appointment that he did not want to reschedule. And he has nothing further to add."

As the scenario continued this was my chance, I eye balled Morris Horwitz. He appeared to be smiling to himself with the prospect of upsetting the proceedings and making Peter and I nervous. Too nervous to continue with our chess game. So far, the only attorney for the trustee was Jill Zubler with Morris Horwitz keeping his eye on her. He was hiding behind her skirts and remained in his seat, observing the antics before the courtroom of the day's visitors. Daniel Schoenborn was also mysteriously missing from Judge Bucki's courtroom.

The Judge appeared unaffected by the antics occurring first thing in his court.

Page 2, Line 7: "We have an appearance. Sir, please state your name." Peter, standing at the podium, said his name.

Page 2, Line 10: Judge Bucki asked, "What do you want to say?"

Page 2, Line 11: Peter starts. "Well, we were never invited to the first hearing. Our attorney told us to—that even if we did come from Florida, that we wouldn't be allowed in the courtroom, or we wouldn't be able to speak. So I filed for some transcripts of that meeting and they're not accurate. So I mean I've got a lot of new evidence here, Your Honor."

Page 2, Line 18: Judge Bucki asked Peter "What is it---I hear what you're saying but I don't know what you mean. You reference a first hearing what was the first hearing about?"

Page 2, Line 21: "When they made the first transcripts ---I'm not---this is my first time in court, so bear with me."

Page 2, Line 23: Judge Bucki continues "That's all right. This is the first hearing you are talking about?"

Page 2, Lines 24 to Page 3, Line 3: Peter, "We were told not to come, and if we did come, we wouldn't be allowed in the courtroom, and if we were allowed in the courtroom---I have plane reservations that have been canceled at that time."

Page 3, Line 4: Judge Bucki ignores the first set of documents and states "I'm not sure the basis---I mean, everyone, these are open court hearings, so anyone who wants to come, certainly has a right to."

Page 3, Line 7: Peter tells the Judge "Well I didn't know that."

Page 3, Line 9: "We cancelled the flight."

Page 3, Lines 10 to 14: Judge Bucki says, "It was a hearing of a Motion of Settlement of a dispute. All right. And that settlement was approved, I believe in January. And what is it that you have new evidence on, that you're troubled about now?"

Page 3, Lines 14 to Page 4, Line 6: Peter told the Judge "I was not satisfied with the settlement, I turned it down and was told not to come to the first hearing. I turned the settlement down. And they came into court and approved it without me being here. This has been going on for fourteen years, I lost everything, it broke me, and I did not have personal debt. We had a fire in a business, there was never an arson investigation. It says, [meaning the transcripts] there an arson investigation, Peerless sent in their people Gary Gable and Stauffer, we were never accused of anything, I lost my business, my home, everything. I was not given the opportunity to come to the first hearing."

Page 4, Line 14: Judge Bucki jumps in, "Well that's not quite correct. Because if you---First of all, I don't know who told you that the hearings were closed. These hearings are always open."

I looked across the courtroom at Jill Zubler and Morris Horwitz. I almost burst out cackling like Buffalo Snoop, having been in a perfect spot to watch Morris Horwitz without him knowing it. He was starting to shift his movements as Jill Zubler turned to look at him. He was the one who had made the lying libelous statement, of an arson investigation of the corporation business in January 2013 to this very same Judge. He had slowly started to change his attitude from amusement to interest.

Page 4, Lines 14 to Page 5, Line 14: Judge Bucki fills the rest of page 4 of the transcript covering Dan Schoenborn's and Harold Bulan's butts. He mentions Harold Bulan reopening the case in 2012 and then states the date isn't significant for the reopening of the case. He apparently does not know or care about the truth of the whole case coming out in Supreme Court. The date is significant; it was less than a month before our second Judge Deborah Chimes supposedly left Buffalo for Chautauqua, New York to fill in as a judge there

Page 5, Lines 15 to 20: Peter makes a statement to Judge Bucki, "Daniel Schoenborn was the attorney in the corporation case against Peerless Insurance, then he had himself appointed administrator of the personal bankruptcy. He was the one Your Honor who told us not to come to the so called meeting, he showed in front of Kaplan, not you, Your Honor."

Page 5, Line 25: Judge Bucki ignores Peter "We have the docket, bear with me for a moment." After a short stop in the proceedings, he states "We sent a notice." He fails to say where the notice was sent. It was sent to the wrong address and both Harold Bulan and Daniel Schoenborn knew it. The notice was not sent to our home in Tampa, Florida.

Page 6, Lines 2 to 6: Once again Peter stated as he held up the cancelled plane tickets that were for the Supreme Court trial. "Here are the cancelled plane tickets." Scheduled the same time the attorneys went into the bankruptcy court to stop the Supreme Court case. They had mixed the two totally different cases and thought they were so sure of themselves by having a court date and preventing our civil liberties. The very people that are responsible for keeping our liberties free.

Page 6, Line 7: Judge Bucki said once again, "Well now who told you not to come?" Peter countered "Daniel Schoenborn."

Page 6, Line 10: Judge Bucki says, "he does not represent you. He represents----"

Exasperated, but keeping his cool, Peter then noticed the Judge seemed to be working with smoke and mirrors or he was not even close to knowing what was going on in this case.

Page 6, Line 12: Peter then stated, "Yeah he represented us in the fire case."

Page 6, Line 14: Judge Bucki says, "Well, by the time that this matter came on, he was representing the trustee, not you, you were represented by Dennis Gaughan." He had not listened to his own statement, stating anyone could come to his courtroom. He had not listened to Peter telling him he had been refused into his courtroom by an attorney that had jumped ship in Supreme Court to get a better deal in his Federal court. Apparently, he could not get it through his head. It popped into my head the rumor of him being a 'Boy Scout.'

We were then convinced the Judge was either clueless or would not listen. Dan Schoenborn had been appointed to represent Harold Bulan two weeks before we were to go to trial before either Judge Chimes or Judge Dillon.

There was a sustained silence in the courtroom. Once again, I looked at Morris Horwitz, who shifted his posture to once again look Jill Zubler, the woman who had burst through the gates and sat at the conference table to the right in front of the Judge Bucki. She must have known something; Judge Bucki now was ignoring everyone except he was looking at his law clerk. He was not paying attention including to the written evidence.

Page 7, Lines 2 to 4: Jill Zubler states, "Your Honor I'm in a difficult position. I just received a phone call and was asked to appear and say nothing further. I don't know anything about this case." I looked at Morris Horwitz who now was looking at his old pal the Judge.

Dumbfounded by the antics of the cast of characters in this courtroom, I knew Peter had it handled. They were playing with him - dancing as if he was a dog ready for the bullet. Not quite, he was more like a dog with a steak bone and they could not shake him off the meaty piece of evidence.

Page 7, Lines 5 to 25: Judge Bucki now chimes in again, oblivious to everything around him. "I don't see where there was a notice given to the creditors, or creditors had an opportunity to challenge the paperwork." He then added "Daniel Schoenborn is getting a substantial amount too." Continuing, "There was an opportunity to challenge this." He was looking through the paperwork for Dan Schoenborn to get his payment of $30,000. Apparently Daniel Schoenborn had forgotten to put through the paperwork. If he did not do this, he would get nothing, not a dime. That would make him mad since he no longer had any paperwork to defend his actions.

Page 8, Line 1: Judge Bucki repeated, "The settlement was approved in January 2013."

Page 8, Line 3: Peter replies, "I never got notice that there was approved, Your Honor."

Page 8, Line 5: Judge Bucki states, "The notice was sent to you at 3 Pine Terrace in Orchard Park."

Page 8, Line 7: Peter tells the Judge, "Well I lived in Florida for the last eight years."

Page 8, Line 8, Judge Bucki states "Well the rules-----and it also went to Mr. Gaughan who was your attorney.

Page 9, Lines 11 to 13: Peter thought to himself as he stood before the Judge, thinking of the craziness of it all. It was insane, not only had we lost our house in 2005, we changed the address to a post office box in Tampa. Then everyone knew where we were and we had saved everything. Peter the packrat had made me. Instead he said, "And he and Mr. Schoenborn knew where I lived. I mean we lost that house because of this."

Page 9, Lines 14 to 18: Judge Bucki rattles on that it is not obvious to him that there is any basis to avoid settling the matter. He ignores the facts of the case, that many letters had been sent from the Federal Courthouse to fictitious addresses and he knew it. He had to, he was the Judge for God's sake.

Judge Bucki continued on as I looked once again at Morris Horwitz, who was looking at his watch then and at Ms. Zubler sitting at the conference table. Something was up and he needed to get out of the courtroom. Here he was, representing us January of 2013, stating downright lies, now he is in this courtroom as an observer, with nothing to say. Certainly the other bankruptcy attorneys located in this room had to be watching this fiasco also.

As the Judge fumbled through his paperwork, suddenly he turned to his law clerk and threw up his hands as if to indicate he was in fact lost in the incorrect paperwork and he did not know what to do. Reclaiming his composure, he then stated, "Not sure if I can reverse this, Harold Bulan is not here, and he wanted to close this case and make a distribution."

I almost laughed out loud. Yeah, a distribution to himself and Dan Schoenborn with illegal funds from the Peerless Insurance and Katherine Fijal.

Page 8, Lines 22 to Page 9, Line 20: The following statement was unbelievable to me. "Creditors are getting more than they usually get, in a bankruptcy proceeding, because they are getting paid on the claim in full." He had just finished saying he did not see where the creditors were given notice to challenge the paperwork.

Judge Bucki continued, "I'm not satisfied with it, because there is no application, no notice given to anyone as to the approval of the legal fees for the special counsel that handled the… that handled the insurance dispute."

"I'm going to adjourn this for a month. I'll adjourn it to July 7th."

Judge Bucki had just adjourned our case so Daniel Schoenborn could submit for his legal fees of his payoff. Keeping the secret intact and us out of the loop.

I laughed to myself. Snoop, over the weekend, had told us they had forgotten to pay Daniel Schoenborn to abandon the Supreme Court case and join the gang in Bankruptcy Court. He had forgotten to do his paperwork to get his unfounded, illegal money moves done. Judge Bucki had now given him time to get his act together. It didn't seem to impartial for a Federal Judge to me.

Judge Bucki then added a bunch of nonsense, such as bankruptcy court is about moving on, getting our past behind us. A. I wondered if he knew we had been in Judge Glownia's courtroom for over ten years, then bounced around throughout the court system for another four years into Judge Chimes and then Judge Dillon. All with false statements made by the attorneys. I did not matter too much. Judge Bucki had already made up his mind and he was sticking to it.

Page 11, Line 14: Peter told him that Dennis Gaughan had filed the case for $490.000.00 as assets in his bankruptcy case, when in reality the amount had been filed in Supreme Court on September 12, 2001. "They put the cart before the horse your honor. $490,000.00 and they settle it for a total of $200,000.00? You are looking at nine percent a year that the State says that they got to pay on the.... on the court fees on the lawsuit. If they had paid the darn thing."

Judge Bucki responds, disassociating himself, "Um-hum."

Page 12, Lines 11 to 14: Judge Bucki interrupts, ignoring the math problem. "All I can tell you is this. The settlement is not insubstantial. It was $200,000 divided between the corporation and your individual case. It was considered by the Court, there was an opportunity to argue it."

Page 12, Line 15: Peter said "There was no opposition here right?"

Page 12, Line 17: The Judge answered, "I don't recall."

Page 12, Line 19: Peter said, "I understand that." Trying to show the Judge something fishy was going on adding "The circumstances were that I was told by my attorney, don't come."

Page 12, Line 20: After more crap, Judge Bucki states "there are other defects with this application. I have to give that…. I have to delay it till July 7th in any event. If you think, there's grounds…."

He then explains what to do to get the opposition going, he continues repeating himself with the wrong information, the incorrect information, and the brutal tactics of the trustee Harold Bulan was catching up with him. Peter continued to explain to Judge Bucki we did not have money problems before Peerless Insurance nailed us to the wall.

The Judge continues the procedures of the court. The correct way, not the Bulan, Goldstein & Illecki way.

Page 13, Line 9: Judge Bucki added, "The trustee did not get notice of today's events, and he needed to be heard." Clearly the Judge was confused. Harold Bulan had sent the Certificate of Service himself. In front of Judge Bucki were two people from Harold Bulan's firm of Bulan, Illecki & Goldstein. They were attorneys Jill Zubler and Morris Horwitz. Attorney Horwitz had said nothing while Attorney Zubler had said Harold Bulan was busy with an appointment.

It was as if the corruption going on in the Judges courtrooms in Buffalo was normal. I laughed to myself. Well, well, the trustee did not get notice but he was the one that sent it and had canceled the appearance sending in Jill Zubler.

Page 14, Lines 2 to 24: Judge Bucki continues to rattle on while intermittently looking into the audience of the court then at his law clerk. As he continues, the recorder is running. He mentions that Harold Bulan has a right to be heard, ignoring the fact that Harold Bulan along with his henchmen Morris Horwitz and his new friend Daniel Schoenborn, had tried to close the case without telling us in January of 2013.

The Judge wished Peter "Good Luck."

I had been watching the proceedings and the staff of the Judge. I could have sworn a member of the Judge's staff looked at Morris Horwitz then at Judge Carl Bucki. Still not sure, there was a weird silence that had fallen over the courtroom. As if we were gathered in an area and the first man to say anything would be shot. The attorneys sitting to the right of me, their eyes fixed on their own thoughts looking everywhere but at us, or their clients. It appeared their clients were looking around the room and at us, wondering what had just happened, and would they be involved in the same arrangement.

Peter walked through the gates once again turning him into a regular person. As we got up to leave, Morris Horwitz jumped up from his seat to make a beeline to get out of the courtroom first. I stepped in front of him indicating we would be the first, not you. Smiling at him, I let him know with my eyes I knew who he was throughout the morning events and I had been watching him. He looked at Judge Bucki, who was reading a document, then eyeballed the full courtroom then let us through. We then passed through the courtroom doors into the hallway, careful not to say anything other than casual conversation of what we were going to do with the rest of the day, all the way to the car.

The chess game was now getting some serious action. We were on our way from the first detectable attack to checkmate in a game that would take three more months to complete.

Arriving at the car, we remained uncommitted in our thoughts until we got out of the range of the city. "What do you want to do?" Peter asked. I indicated we should go to a park and get some air. "The weather is beautiful we should enjoy it." Knowing full well we could not say anything in the rented car also. The chess game was getting harder and all the pawns were at risk. The transcripts would be our lifeline to the truth.

We headed over to the Green Lake area in the center of Orchard Park, enjoying the fresh air. I laughed. "What do you think the massage therapists would think if they knew we were so close to their office?"

Peter looks at me and said, "It never stops around here, I just want to know who really is running the show in Buffalo, and does anyone care."

We looked towards Green Lake and pondered the thought. "Apparently not." I answered remembering Snoop telling me even some of the Judges could not wait to retire and get out of Buffalo for good. What a shame for such a great city with so much potential for so many years to be denied the right to some respect, all because of just a few really bad people, running the city.

That afternoon we again stopped to have lunch at the Globe Restaurant in East Aurora. We both devoured a fish fry that we missed so much. True happiness. Discussing the events of the morning, we wondered who had started the problems in 1999. Apparently they had no shame, seemingly without a conscience. The damage they had done in the name of greed, jealousy and hate had followed us ever since. We felt sorry for them to be loaded with such an evil burden. Apparently, they had no idea what life was about and probably never would until they hit the locked pearly gates.

The problems in life are not due to God's revenge on us, it is due to the devil, and evil. To be consumed by the devil is to be living a lost life. Better to avoid such people as they will spread their ways to your soul. Follow the other path, let the Good Lord help you solve your problems of the evil people. He has more power.

As we left the Globe, we started across the street. Suddenly, I swore I saw Daniel Schoenborn's car pass us only to stop at the traffic light at the intersection. Looking at Peter, I told him, "Do not walk in front of that car, let's head over to Vidler's."

"Why?" Peter asked.

I responded "I think we just saw one of the henchmen for Bulan and Michael Drumm. Your old buddy Dan, he must live around here or he is watching us."

We messed around the old-time 5 and 10 Cent store, picking up a few things to take back to Tampa. Thankfully, we had parked the car next to the store before we had headed over to the Globe. We finished what we had come for and now could leave the store and head back to the car parked on the main street of East Aurora. If we saw his car, we would know he was looking for us.

That night we relaxed, went to the local mall, walking the hallways, it appeared the winter clothes were set out already for the next season. How odd, I thought, I have no use for any of that stuff. The only thing I needed was an occasional sweater and some jeans. Mentally, we were pulling out of Buffalo, just a little left to go and we would be out of the quagmire of the courthouse. Let someone else put up with the garbage from Buffalo, we were done.

The next day was Tuesday. Getting up early it was a busy day before us. As Peter had gone before Judge Bucki, I would do before Judge Kaplan. We had gone to the office store, copying the paperwork for both Judge Kaplan and Harold Bulan as a courtesy. Maybe Judge Kaplan would notice the opposition and would read it and follow Judge Bucki's same move. Push it off to the future giving us time to get yet another attorney. Hanging low for the rest of the evening, I was curious to know what would lay before me the next day. Peter had done pretty good representing himself in court the previous day, I could only hope I would do as well.

Late that afternoon, we stopped at Wegmans near my old office on Sheridan Road. I loved the Wegmans brand honey mustard, grabbed a bunch and bought a few other things I could not buy in Florida. As we started down the condiment aisle to pick up the mustard, Snoopy buzzed by us at the end of the aisle. Startled, we walked around to the end of the aisle. There was Snoop, finger held to lips, a wink then a point to meet at the front end of the store outside. We knew what to do now after so many meetings on the sly. I pulled the throw away phone out of my purse and turned it on. Continuing throughout the amazing store, we knew the phone would not ring yet. We meandered through the store, looking at the delicious cheeses, breads, meats, and various other items. Everything precise in the presentation, so unlike the workings of the city itself. Paying for my goodies, they would have to be put in the check in luggage. Darkness had fallen as we entered the parking lot of the store. I was ready for our next project.

The phone rang and we would now drive to the back of Advanced Massage Therapy office. After all, it was almost across the street. Peter steered the rental car into the back parking lot of the building, the light filtering from above bounced shadows across the parking lot as we sat in the car and waited.

As usual, Buffalo Snoop popped up from nowhere and peered into the driver's side of the window. Looking directly at Peter, the snort came. "You will never win."

Peter snapped back, "We know that, we got forced out of Buffalo, we didn't leave by choice. Peerless Insurance and the attorneys made sure of that! One mistake covered up over and over, you tell one lie, then you have to cover it up with another, pretty soon the attorneys will get caught in the web so deep, they will probably turn on each other."

Snoop grunted, "They will get their money first, then turn on each other, that's how they operate. You are in so deep and so close you have to keep going, do not let these people and Peerless Insurance ruin you."

Peter leaned out the window paused and got into Snoop's face. "They already did, now it is beyond Peerless Insurance and the attorneys, we have been dragged through the mud and quicksand for no apparent reason. I'm sick of it and we are taking it as far as we can through the bankruptcy court. The attorneys, their greed, and cover-up turned us from plaintiffs to defendants and we have the right to continue this and get a trial. It's in the Constitution!" Now seething, Peter continued, "Something is missing and we are going to find out what it is."

Snoop, with narrowed eyes and a tenseness that had never been present before, smirked. "Good, go for it, things will be helped as much on this end as possible. I'm going to call our friend in Tampa tonight, it's time you guys caught up. It's going to be a very hot summer. Watch out for tomorrow. He is not pleasant and I may get you some news."

Continuing, Snoop said "Judge Bucki is confusing the Motion with the Certificate of Service. Usually a Motion has to do with discovery, for just motions you usually use only the Certificate of Service."

Not quite understanding the last comment. I turned to look Snoop, who had sunk below the level of the car window. We knew not to search, it would prove of no use.

Turning the car around in the parking lot, we headed to the hotel to get ready for the court date the following day. As we entered the hotel lobby, we were greeted by the staff who were becoming familiar with our periodic visits from Florida. They had just finished making cookies for the guests and had placed them on a nearby table. Greeting them, I grabbed a couple to keep me occupied while we went to the room to finish the paperwork we had copied earlier.

We made three piles, just as we had made before, as a courtesy to the Judge Michael Kaplan and Harold Bulan. A courtesy that had not been provided for us.

Judge Bucki had refused to look at the correct paperwork it but perhaps this Federal Judge would be different. I had brought the original copies of the paperwork, for all the bills that Dennis Gaughan and Harold Bulan had said I owed. It was all exempt and had to do with the business.

It was the receipts for the machinery for Pro-Pak and Pilate's equipment. Peerless Insurance had to be stopped. What did everyone have to gain in Buffalo by doing this? Money? Or a false sense of power.

The answer would come in the next three months, a secret so vile, so illegal, so disgusting, it would prove to be at best a reason to lose your attorney's license for the rest of your life in every state, It was also jail-time material. If I had the wish to fulfill, the participating attorneys would have to live as we did for the last fourteen years, living in cramped quarters with boxes up to the ceilings that were filled with black mold.

CHAPTER 43: 5,028 DAYS

The next morning, we started our now familiar ritual. This time we packed our luggage. We would be leaving the courthouse right after our hearing and go to the airport to fly back to Tampa. It was now our home, surrounded with friends that were more like family. We had support there, very different than Buffalo.

Once again, we entered the Federal Courthouse to go through security, up the elevator to Judge Kaplan's court. Walking up to the glass enclosed frame it appeared I would be the first one up, as Peter had been two days before. Sitting back down at a bench outside the Judge's courtroom, we spotted the same familiar personal as Monday passing before us as if they were looking for something without looking at Peter or I in the face. At one time, a short pudgy man coming from an inner office glanced at us, looked away, then took a sneak peek again.

Soon, the courtroom doors were unlocked by another staff member. We entered through the doorway and once again sat on the left hand side of the courtroom. The new bankruptcy defendants were once again filling up the room, speaking quietly to their attorneys who were holding their future in their hands. I spent some time with a defendant who could not pay off his college loan, we exchanged ideas as his attorney looked on. I asked his attorney for his card, he said he didn't have one. Strange.

Suddenly, a loud noise from the back of the courtroom door sounded with the door being thrown open. I could hear boisterous, loud laughing comments being made to each other. They boisterously proceeded along the center aisle of the courtroom only to sit in front of us. There were two rather tall men and one short portly one. It appeared they were having the time of their lives.

One of the tall attorneys had another case and appeared to be just snuggling up to the other two. The other tall one? Morris Horwitz. Peter leaned into me. "Is that Morris Horwitz from Judge Bucki's court on Monday?"

"Yep."

I was busy looking at the short one. I hadn't seen Harold Bulan in almost ten years and the immensely tall Harold Bulan had either shrunk or he had been sitting on a huge pillow ten years ago. At 5'4" I was even taller than him, by a few inches. I was amused by this scenario. What was going to happen in my case to warrant two attorneys for my case with a standby to nestle in? Suddenly the chant began. "All Rise."

JUNE 4, 2014 10:00 A.M.

BEFORE FEDERAL JUDGE MICHAEL KAPLAN

Judge Kaplan entered the room, and sitting down he announced, "The first person up is Jo Anne Gleason; we will meet in my chambers at the end of the proceedings." This was a surprise to hear. And a good thing for sure. We finally had a judge that had taken the time to look at the paperwork and to want to talk to me in his chambers. My imagination filled with the excitement of it all. Hallowed ground. I imagined the layers of wood walls with pictures of previous Federal Judges. The book cases would have loaded with law books to use as reference. His desk covered with various paperwork dealing with his position and, last but not the least, perhaps a patterned maroon carpet to keep everything calm but serious enough for the Judge to study the civil liberties of the citizens under the Eighth District of United States Federal Court.

As I settled back in my seat to view the process before me, it was a sad sight. One by one the defendants were called. Some were businesses, others college loans or medical bills. I was intrigued by the process of coming before the Judge in the courtroom. As time went on, it appeared the three men in front of Peter and myself were not busy with other cases, apparently they had just one, mine. I wasn't worried or upset about the case, just butterflies because we were appearing in Federal Court acting as our own attorneys in both cases.

Looking at Peter's watch, almost an hour had gone by. People had come and gone, their lives now back on the right track. I didn't know how many were behind me or see if the courtroom was empty. Suddenly, I heard the Judge say:

JO ANNE'S TRANSCRIPT

Page 2, Line 1: "Jo Anne Gleason final report and account."

The time registered on the transcripts as 10:53 a.m.

Caught off guard, my mind raced. "Hey Judge, wait a minute you said I was to come to your chambers after the proceedings!" My stomach flipped and I stood up cool as a cucumber on a hot summer day walking through the gates. Harold Bulan calmly came to the front of the courtroom to stand next to me. I looked down at him and smiled as a gesture of good faith. Morris Horwitz, the wizard from Judge Bucki's courtroom, stood next to him on his other side. Just in case he needed protection.

Page 2, Lines 3 to 5: "Harold Bulan, Trustee your honor." The Judge looked him and said "Thank you Mr. Bulan. Are you Miss Gleason?" "I am Your Honor."

He answers "OK."

Page 2, Line 6: Morris Horwitz tells the Judge he wanted to appear with Harold Bulan. This is the same Morris Horwitz who lied his way through the "Meetings," as Daniel Schoenborn had called them, during January of 2013. Then he states "I just want to note my appearance, if Mr. Bulan." [Inaudible.]

Page 2, Line 12: Judge Michael Kaplan thanks Morris Horwitz and continues "Mr. Bulan final report and account receipts of $100,000 payment to the unsecured creditors, with interest from the date of the filing of the petition, will be about 27---about 31,000 or thereabouts altogether?"

Page 2, Line 17: Mr. Bulan answers the Judge. "I didn't look at it this morning." I'm looking at him with bewilderment of the figures of the claim and the false numbers, thinking, and you didn't look at the paperwork today. You have never looked at the paperwork in the past ten years, the only thing you wanted was 20% off the top of the lawsuit against Peerless Insurance in 2003. What a vile smelly slime bag I thought.

Page 2, Line 18: Judge Kaplan continues, "Well, I think it----So he intends to pay the unsecured creditors who filed timely claims, 23,700 plus post position interest, that is estimated to be about 4,800, and the balance would go to you."

Page 2, Line 22: I then looked at Judge Kaplan and said "I disagree with that Your Honor, I disagree with that as far back as January 9, 2013."

Page 2, Line 24: The Judge asked me "What do you disagree with?"

Page 3, Line 1: "I disagree with the transcripts of Morris Horwitz."

Page 3, Line 3: The Judge then says "No, just----please. What aspect of this do you disagree with?

"Is it that the trustee got more than $100,000?" I thought to myself why that greedy little piggy instead,

I looked at the Judge and then at Harold Bulan. How did anyone know that Harold Bulan got $100,000 when we didn't even know it? I cruised through that comment letting it go. I had other things I had to get forward in this courtroom.

Page 3, Line 8: I inserted, "I disagree with the taxes of it. We do have the taxes that were paid."

Page 3, Line 10: Judge Kaplan looks at me "Which taxes?"

"Thirty-three thousand, nine hundred and seventy-nine dollars and sixty-four cents." I said.

Attorney Kaplan then inserted, "What was the-----Where did the hundred thousand come from?"

Page 3, Line 12: Harold Bulan chirped in at this point. "Came from a settlement from a fire loss case, Your Honor."

Page 3, Line 14: The Judge asked, "A fire loss case?" totally out of the loop. Attorney Bulan showing respect true or not for the Judge, answered "Yes Sir." He forgot to tell the Judge that he, Harold Bulan, had closed the case years before and that he had another motive. One of the Bishops was in trouble at the courthouse, and he was almost ready to get caught.

Page 3, Line 19: The Judge looked at me. "The trustees not proposing to pay any taxes." I then shuffled my feet, not sure which way to fly with this, I was blowing it "Okay then I also---"

Page 3, Line 22: Judge Kaplan looks at Harold Bulan "So by not paying any taxes---he has to pay the Chapter 7 estate taxes, right? Is that correct?" As I look at Harold Bulan, he is looking at the Judge and he looks smaller to me. He says, "I'm sorry I didn't hear you."

Page 4, Line 1 to 3: The Judge asked Attorney Bulan, "Does the Chapter 7 has any tax liability?" Harold Bulan answers "No, sir." The Judge then says: "Okay. So by not paying out anything to the taxing entities, because they are secured claims, not unsecured claims, that increases the money that goes to you."

Page 4, Line 15: I make the statement, "Okay, Your Honor, but it says New York State Department of Taxation and Finance, I owe 33,000. I have paperwork, not only-----"

The Judge looked at me and said "He's not paying it. I don't care what it is." I looked at him with disbelief and said "OK."

The Judge continues "See the proposed payment, zero?"

I answered him "Yes I do."

He says, "Last column? Ok."

I then try and introduce the correct information "Okay. Then I'm referring to---"

Page 4, Lines 14 to 23: Judge Kaplan then states, "I'm not sure why. Why are you not paying it? Did they file a priority claim? Apparently not."

Harold Bulan innocently peeps up in again. "I don't remember Your Honor." Convenient I thought.

Judge Kaplan looks at him. "You don't remember, okay. But---"

Harold Bulan looks at the Judge again. "I'd have to cull through all this."

Out of the corner of my left eye I saw Morris Horwitz moving closer to Harold Bulan. A subtle move was being made, as they closed in to each other with their physiques. Now flying by the seat of my pants through the stifling air of the courtroom. I was going on pure instinct, the knowledge of the case over the last fourteen years, still not sure what going on, it felt as if all the tax authorizations that had been asked for by Michael Drumm, Daniel Schoenborn, Maurice Sykes, David Sleight and Katherine Fijal had been unnecessary, and they knew it. Probably the only person that did not know it was Judge Kaplan. Hopefully.

Page 5, Line 19: Judge Kaplan then states, "Okay. Well, he's not proposing to pay New York State Department of Taxation and Finance or Erie County. I don't know whether that's because they filed secured claims or what. But--because this money would not go to any secured claims."

Once again, I'm pondering about the eight or nine tax authorizations we have stored with the paperwork in Tampa. What had been the point of the last fourteen years? My question remained unanswered for the next few moments. I had to move on, this court moved quickly and you better keep up with it. The chessmen were in danger, it looked like the knights were going through a move and would perhaps delay or end the game. Skipping through that thought at that precise minute I had to move on.

Page 4, Line 24: I raised my next object. "The next one is Pamela Ashmall."

The Judge answered "Yup."

I said, "Pamela Ashmall was---I owned a massage therapy, Your Honor-"

Page 5 Lines 3 to 10: Judge Kaplan asked, "Did you ever object to her proof of claim?"

I answered "Yes."

The Judge asks, "When."

I respond, "In a letter to ---we discussed it with Mike Drumm from [inaudible] at the time, in 2002. September 20th. And the only thing I have with me Your Honor is a letter to Mr. Drumm---"

I thought immediately of the Judge in Orchard Park who had decided the stolen names and addresses of the clients did not fall under the HIPAA Act in his mind. Buffalo has become a constant battlefield on the chessboard. Standing before the Federal Judge, I wished I had turned her into the State of New York for violating the HIPAA. Surely they would turn her into the Feds.

Page 5, Lines 11 to 17: The Judge once looks at his paperwork then at me "Did you file a claim in this [this being the key word] court?"

I answered "No."

"Okay" the Judge said.

I continued "I was not aware of it until we got the final report." Two weeks ago.

Judge Kaplan starts to speak "Well" as I continue telling him, "It is very confusing and there's----"

He then interrupts me as I'm getting ready to tell him what has been going on for the last fourteen years.

Page 5, Lines 19 to 23: He does not want to hear it, ignoring my input he then says, "Well, I'm sorry ma'am, but it was your obligation to monitor the claims that were filed, especially once it became an asset case, once there was money for the payment of collection, and to object to any claim that you disagreed with."

Sorry about that Judge Kaplan. You see, your buddy Harold Bulan refused to have contact with me and he is lying in his paperwork to you! So if you want to believe this greedy little man, go right ahead.

Now I'm getting my dander up. To many attorneys were lying to this Federal Judge? What the hell was going on? I find out fourteen years later again there were no taxes, no reason for authorizations, who the hell was lying? It had to be the attorneys from the Supreme Court and Harold Bulan.

Page 6, Lines 1 to 14: Instead I said, "We never received notice of any hearings or anything until we called last June to Lisa Beaser and asked him if there were any transcripts from the meeting of January 9, in 2013 regarding our case before----"

The Judge cut me off. "The only address we had for you was 3 Pine Terrace, Orchard Park."

Trying to be patient with the Judge I answered "Right." I was going to tell him someone had gotten into the federal court records at the courthouse and changed our address without our knowledge. I wanted to tell him the paperwork from the Federal Court itself had been sending documents to us all over the United States except for Tampa, Florida, where we lived. I could not say a word, protection mode of my own set in for the Snoop.

Page 6, Lines 3 to 14: The Judge then states, "It's not our fault that you didn't change your address with us."

Rather than fight with the Judge over Harold Bulan's refusal to answer our letters or the missing Dennis Gaughan I said, "I know it was our mistake. However, the attorneys all did have my address." I was dying to tell him about the documents showing someone had gotten into the records and changed our address to Orchard Park, six months after we gave the Court our correct address in Florida. I kept my mouth shut.

Page 6, Lines 15 to 21: Judge Kaplan continues ignoring the fact that I was not notified of Harold Bulan's moves. "If there is no proof of claim, you want to come in at the end and say, well that claim shouldn't be paid."

Again I did not want to get into a pissing match with the Judge over Harold Bulan's refusal to cooperate with us. I just looked at him and said "Alright."

He then asked me, "What else? What's next?

I answered, "The CITIBANK and MBNA were charges used for the tools of trade." This is an important issue if a contractor lost his tools in a fire they should be replaced under the insurance laws, or exempt under the bankruptcy laws so you can re build your business.

He wanted none of it. What he stated next was so unbelievable to me it appeared he needed to communicate with the trustee.

Page 6, Lines 17 to 24: Judge Kaplan stated, "Tools of trade is a term that refers to being able to claim an exemption for property. It is not a term where you do not have to pay a debt."

I countered, "I agree, but I never got to pay the debt, Your Honor." Meaning in the rules of the court they machinery was an exception.

Page 7, Line 1: The judge now makes the next comment as a statement rather than a question "You never got to pay the debt."

"No, I filed bankruptcy."

He then says, "The trustee is going to pay the debt for you."

I then countered, "But, in truth I had to file bankruptcy, I lost my house, I lost my business, Evans Services. I lost, I lost Advanced Massage Therapy."

He did not want to hear about the Tools of Trade that were exempt from bankruptcy for both Evans Services, Pro-Pak and Advanced Massage.

Page 7, Lines 5 to 13: Judge Kaplan did not want to hear it. "That's what bankruptcy is about. You turn over your nonexempt assets to the trustee."

I wanted to scream! But, Judge they were exempt under not only insurance law but, bankruptcy law as well! I kept quiet and let him go at it.

He continues, "Who turns them into cash and pays your creditors, to the extent that the assets are there to pay them. That's what the process is."

I try and ignore the fact he is not listening to me, he is listening to Harold Bulan and himself. I respond, "Okay, but there was a lack of communication definitely." Meaning Harold Bulan never answered our messages or letters, I was grateful that I still had the proof.

The Judge then remarked "But the lack of communication was because you moved to Florida and didn't give us the address, it's not the fault of the Court or the Trustee." Not true, Your Honor and Harold Bulan knew it, I could see him sweating from inches away. I was disgusted with this smoke and mirrors technique, I couldn't resist, I eyeballed to my left. Morris Horwitz was now attached to Harold Bulan's hip. Disgusted with all of it, my mind filled with the facts.

If I had had a meeting with Harold Bulan to discuss what was exempt and what was not exempt, we never would be standing here today. I would have both businesses and the machinery. Judge Kaplan should have realized that we filed personal bankruptcy, it had nothing to do with the business of Evans Services or Pro-Pak. They were both exempt. The trustee Harold Bulan had mixed the corporation and the equipment with the personal bankruptcy of Peter and myself.

In 2004, if Harold Bulan had in fact had a true 341 Hearing, instead of the façade that showed in the paperwork he would have known what was exempt. From August 10, 2004, until this day he had botched the whole case handed to him by Dennis Gaughan. If everyone had been doing their job instead of looking for the quick buck and doing a cover up, we would be living in Buffalo. It was that simple. I would be watching my children grow older and my grandchildren grow up. I would be continuing to donate to the community, I would be a viable member of the Western New York area enjoying my life along with Peter. Instead, we were left to flounder while the cast of the chess board continued to cover up. I would not stand for it one more minute. I felt as if we had been loaded to a camp with electric fences and towers around it so we could not get out. I was sick of these so called professionals not listening to their own laws that were passed. And last of all, the "they" who wanted us gone and would do anything to get it done.

Page 7, Line 14: I blurted it out. "I never had a 341." The courtroom suddenly filled with noise, rumblings, increasing with a din as if I said something unusual. Judge Kaplan looked at me and made the statement rather than a question.

Page 7, Line 15: "Never had a 341." The noise in the back of the courtroom got louder, right before my eyes Harold P. Bulan went into a swan dive. I looked at the drama of the situation. Morris Horwitz was helping him to his seat, Harold Bulan was holding his chest as if something terrible had been said. Sitting down, he leaned forward in his seat appearing to be in trouble or it was an act. In my opinion the latter, it was that funny or sad depending how you looked at the judicial system in this country.

Page 7, Lines 16 to 22: I continued, "If I got notice of it, it wasn't sent to me. I would like to know who sent out those notices." Leaving out the fact we already had in our possession documents from the court itself with many different addresses for us. That I wanted to keep for myself at the moment.

Judge Kaplan answered my question. "The Bankruptcy Noticing Center. It's a national governmental entity. And the certificates of servicer are all on file."

"Was that presented by an attorney?" I asked.

Page 7, Line 22: Judge Kaplan answered, "They're automatic, based on the things that happen. Many of the events are computer generated, and the notices go out from the BNC, the Bankruptcy Noticing Center."

Page 8, Lines 2 to 12: I look at him somewhat amused that he still did not answer my question. Judge Kaplan shifts his weight in his chair to look at something. "Hold on I want to look at this, 341 situations."

[Brief interruption in proceedings.]

The Judge looks up from whatever he had been studying and says, "The notice of hearing of a 341 meeting was sent to you by the Bankruptcy Noticing Center at-----JoAnne Gleason at 3 Pine Terrace Orchard Park, by first class mail, sent on July 15, 2004. It advised you that the 341 meeting would be held on August 10, 2004 at 11:30." He continues "Now let me see what happened on that date. August 10, meeting of creditors held, debtor appeared and examined. You were there."

Page 8, Lines 14 to 17: I replied "I was not there, Your Honor. I was not there. The only time-----"

He interrupts me again.

"Okay, we're going to get the tape of it."

"Okay." I replied knowing what the paperwork said and what Harold Bulan said to me almost ten years before were totally different.

Suddenly a voice yelled from the back of the court

Page 8, Line 19 "We don't have that, Your Honor, I apologize, but we're only obligated to keep records for five years. We won't have something-----"

I was more than astounded at this new information. Everyone knows a bankruptcy lasts ten years.

Page 8, Lines 20 to 25: Judge Kaplan, acting as if this was an everyday event, states, "Oh, its 2004, isn't it? Well here's what I'm going to do. I'm not going to sit and argue with you.

"I'm going to put this over for three months. You're not going to get any money."

I was amazed to hear a Federal Court Judge would allow the court to destroy documents of an open case. The second bothersome thing was that a Federal Judge went along with destroying evidence. The third comment of Judge Kaplan sewed up the rumors. Harold Bulan needed time to get his act together. It was not me. Rumor had this particular Judge always sided with Harold Bulan no matter how bad he messed things up.

Page 9, Lines 6 to 25: Judge Kaplan states in essence that it does not matter if there are transcripts or not, and sided with his good friend Harold Bulan.

I looked at Harold Bulan. His companion Morris Horwitz had his arm around him. Thankfully Attorney Horowitz was there to capture the fall. Poor sweetie, I hoped he felt alright, I really did. I wasn't finished with my court business yet, the last thing I needed was for Harold Bulan not to be recorded that day or in the foreseeable future.

Page 10, Line 5: Looking back to Judge Kaplan, I said "Okay," I had a couple of attorneys I could call in Buffalo. I had inserted an unknown piece in the chess game, creating a block ... for now.

Page 10, Line 25, through Page 11, Line 20: I asked Judge Kaplan to combine the two bankruptcy cases since they had combined the two corporate cases in 2001. It would mean one flight, one hotel, one case. Judge Kaplan refuses, instead he gave me budget tips. The case was adjourned at 11:07 a.m.

The fiasco in Judge Michael Kaplan's court was over in fourteen minutes. As we got up to leave the courtroom, Harold Bulan started to push ahead of us to get out of the courtroom first. Morris Horwitz had also continued the performance, holding on to Harold Bulan's shoulders in case he needed help. He pulled him back, close to the front of his body, apparently showing the courtroom he needed protection from me. Finding this to be more drama in the theater of justice, it was probably intentional to the spectators of the court. I chuckled to myself, thinking what a false self of importance this little man had.

I stepped in front of them and opened the space for Peter to leave his courtroom bench. As I followed Peter through the room, I scanned the courtroom once again, almost as if I was looking for an attorney that had some balls to challenge this little bully in the Eighth District. If all the 341 Hearing had gone like both Peter's and mine had, it meant there was a long standing set of illegal activities going on in the bankruptcy court under the helm of both Judge Carl Bucki and Judge Michael Kaplan.

Morris Horwitz and Harold Bulan stayed behind. I did not wait to see or turn around to see if Harold Bulan did another swan dive to his devoted audience or if he was unsteady on his feet and needed help getting out of the courtroom. If I did I would have cackled like hell, just like Snoop.

Without saying a word, we continued out of the paper-filled corrupt bankruptcy court, walking to the elevator, out the doors of the Federal Court building, and into the rental car. Peter looked at me with surprise. "I thought you were going to lose it in front of Judge Kaplan until you pulled out the 341 meeting, where did that come from?"

Looking back into his face I said, "Now, you do not really believe you have a 341 meeting for your case do you?"

The whole thing in the Bankruptcy Court is a sham and it is my belief that Harold Bulan has been pulling this crap for a very long time. Looking at him I stated, "Why don't you see if you have an audio and transcripts of your 341 meeting?" Peter replied, "You know we don't, why bring any notice to it, remember we are here to collect the current audio and transcripts."

Harold Bulan had botched the bankruptcy case, mixing in Evans Services and Pro-Pak both civil lawsuits, including the tools of trade exemption, along with numerous false accusations written in a court documents. His newly appointed administrator Daniel Schoenborn knew it and had helped keep it in the background.

Apparently, it did not matter if the audio and transcripts had been destroyed by the court because they did not exist to begin with. I wondered how long Harold Bulan, his Majesty the King of the Bankruptcy Court, had been pulling off this fiasco. Was he digging for his take on the proceeds of any case before him or was he more selective, picking and choosing the cases that would mean more money for him to collect to put in his bank or some other account.

It was then that I speculated on Judge Kaplan's take of the destroyed documents in his courtroom, his lack of concern over a legal document being wiped out by someone in the courthouse of an open case. He seemed to be siding with the trustee with no questions asked. If the transcripts were destroyed, the case should have been too. Harold Bulan had corrupted the paperwork so he could squeeze the most for himself. He had me paying for the losses of the machinery that belonged to the corporations. Not answering our phone calls or letters made him into a suspect even more. He needed to be investigated, along with a few other attorneys in the Eighth District.

We headed for the airport to get away from the corruption going on in Buffalo as fast as possible. There were evil things going on in this town and we needed to get back to Tampa to take a hot shower get the crud off. We also needed to get ready for Peter's case scheduled for July 7, 2014.

As we boarded the plane, I pulled out my notebook to make notations of the statements and actions in Judge Kaplan's courtroom that day. While Peter had less than a month to get his paperwork together for Judge Bucki. I had until September 3, 2014, so I had some time to spare. We would once again be looking for a needle in a haystack. At least Harold Bulan and his "Bullies from Buffalo," whoops, attorneys, would be stopped for the moment. They now had to notify us of any court action coming up. No more sneak meetings, hearings or any other court proceedings without our knowledge.

Once arriving in Tampa, we took a shower to scrub off the dirt and the vile mechanisms of the attorneys working for Harold Bulan. They had been observed all week lying in the courtroom to the Judges without a care in the world. With the audio running.

The next day we ordered the transcripts from both Judge Carl Bucki's and Judge Michael Kaplan's court. No more lost audios, no more lost transcripts. The chess game had moved into a new genre.

Peter once again booked another flight into Buffalo, while also looking for a new attorney to be hired in the Eighth District. The word had gotten out to the community. To be represented it had gone from a standard of $15,000 to reopen the case with no guarantees to "Sorry I'm booked with cases right now, I don't have time to prepare your case."

Calling Buffalo Snoop, it was once again verified that "Harold Bulan is not your friend and he will do anything to keep his end of the case out of the mud pile. Watch your back, the "they" know where you live and have for a very long time, since your car blew up." Trust me, we wanted the "they" to stay out of Tampa also.

It was time to get ahold of Tampa Snoop to see what could be done from this end. Tampa Snoop and Peter met in a restaurant to discuss the future of the corrupt bankruptcy case. Once again, Pacer the public access to the court electronic records in Federal Court came up.

What also came up was how many times Judge Kaplan sided with the Harold Bulan and how many times Harold Bulan had been challenged for improper documentation in the Federal courthouse in the Eighth District. We could not get into Pacer and we could not hire an attorney to get us back into Supreme Court. We were held in the legal vice of the system in Buffalo.

Peter, talking with Snoop, decided to once again go into the courtroom, tell the truth, and hope for more than a one-sided statement from Judge Carl Bucki.

Snoop said, "Don't forget to get the Certificate of Service out to Harold Bulan along with the Labor Department and Susan Buranich, along with the courthouse, at least ten days before the hearing. That is your objection, and it is within the laws of the land." Laughing, he added, "Not that they pay attention to it."

Peter knew the labor fine would have to be paid. Plus, Peerless Insurance had stalled so many times during the Supreme Court trial,

Peter was sure there would be a certain amount of interest tagged on to the document.

A fender bender with Peter and an Orchard Park policeman's wife, Susan Buranich, had been another issue. While we had reported the accident to our insurance company, her husband had come into the office and tried to extract $440.00 from me so he would not have to report it to his insurance company.

Apparently, he had looked into the files of the Orchard Park Police Department and discovered I owned the car Peter was using when he backed out of the parking space in front of the massage office. His wife was driving from another area in the parking lot. Instead of reporting it to the insurance company as we had, he wanted us to pay for his damages. When I reminded him that he also had insurance, he put a lien against us for the damages to his car. We hadn't been informed until Harold Bulan had been forced by our input of the correct address into the court system into sending the Certificates of Service to our address in Tampa.

What had been a fender bender in a parking lot had made its way to Federal Court under Judge Bucki's control. Peter called Buffalo Snoop to try and figure out the Susan Buranich claim. "What the hell is she doing on the claim now? She was never on any claim at any time when you filed your bankruptcy in 2004. It is an insurance case to be settle by an insurance company, not you."

Continuing, Snoop said, "You show me where she is on the claim from 2004 and, along with that, you show me where the exemption for the equipment for Pro-Pak Evans of Advanced Massage is on the paperwork from the claim in 2004. This whole case is tainted, what the hell, let's see what Judge Bucki says in the courtroom when you go in."

"What about the lost audio and transcripts from 2004 do you think they tossed mine too?" Peter asked. "Then it came out of his mouth. "Why would a courthouse throw out an open case that would continue until this year."

"Never mind, the record will be running, wait and see what comes out on July 7," was the reply.

When Peter relayed the phone call to me I agreed with Buffalo Snoop. There was weird stuff going on in the courthouses in Buffalo. Not only with our case but periodically things would pop up in the news relating to members of the legal field. I also agreed with the suggestion of letting the record run to see how Judge Bucki acted in the courtroom. Did he side with Harold Bulan as consistently as Judge Kaplan or did he have his own opinion?

Within minutes I was on a role, my filibuster would continue, "I highly doubt Judge Bucki will let you go on and continue this case, we have gone through three Supreme Court judges and two Federal Court judges, with the illustrious attorneys in Supreme Court. They are going to close us down. Buffalo is a city run by a certain few and you better be in the group. They are like mean girls in high school.

"Do you honestly think they will turn on their own and follow the rules of the Federal Court? If they get caught in the web, they might get indicted for withholding information of the Federal courthouse and how is that going to look for the Eighth District of Western New York?

"You forget, Peter, we now have all the paperwork from all the attorneys, both plaintiff and defendant, Supreme Court and Federal Court. If they want it, they will have to file a lawsuit against us and file a subpoena to get it, you don't really think they want to open that can of worms do you?

"If you think the horse abuse case was bad, wait until we show all the paperwork between the attorneys, law clerks and Judges of the Eighth District. This District needs a complete overhaul, it is without a doubt the most corrupt district in the United States and they are running with a free hand over people's lives, no one is sitting up and taking notice not, even with their own, everyone is afraid to make a move in case they get singled out in the courthouse as being a troublemaker.

"You just saw that in the courtroom with me remember?"

As I continued my outburst, I realized there were so many problems related to our case and the intertwining throughout the courthouses it was possible it had been a plan put on by the participating attorneys with intention years ago. We just did not have the proof.

Why did we have to continue to fight for our lives every time we stepped into the city of Buffalo, with its worn out tattered courthouses?

Instead of dwelling on the situation, Peter needed to get to work and get the Certificates of Service out to all the parties, including Harold Bulan, Susan Buranich and the U.S. Department of Labor. This would all be sent as usual by certified mail to ensure the right party would have to sign for it.

During the July 4, 2014, holiday, Peter flew to Buffalo to meet in Judge Bucki's courtroom on July 7, 2014 for yet another court hearing. The flight via Southwest, hotel, and rental of the car came to just under a thousand dollars. Peter had to eat, so it actually would hit over the thousand dollar mark. I laughed as I drove him to the airport. "Did you notice the Federal Judges schedule you during every holiday and then I have to listen to Kaplan's budgeting tips?"

As we entered the Tampa International Airport, I would go with him to get a bite to eat at Friday's. It's the same chain we had scheduled our lunch for the day of the fire so many years before. Having a quiet meal, we reflected on the cast of characters in Buffalo and marveled at the narcissistic attitude of Peerless Insurance and the attorneys, the blasé efforts of the Supreme Court Judges, and lastly the Federal Judges themselves. "Who the hell is running Buffalo?" I asked. "I mean why do they even bother having elections? Oh wait the Supreme Court Judges do run for election and promise you, the voter, justice for all."

Peter shook his head as he replied, "This whole thing is just crazy, Peerless has spent more money in attorney's fees than if they just paid me. It is an insult they offered the same amount the fire was assessed of fourteen years ago, and the judges and courts went along with it, something is wrong."

As he continued with his meal, I asked him if he was going to meet with Snoopy while he was in New York. "Not if I don't have too, Snoop always knows when we are there, it will be taken care of."

We moved on to another conversation, one that had nothing to do with Buffalo. I was concerned about some people from Buffalo that had taken up part time residence in the St. Petersburg area. Peter, stone-faced as he gazed at his watch, said, "I took care of it, they are being watched when they are here. We have to go; I have to get to the plane."

Good. Looking at Peter I thought, not bad for a victim of five strokes. He was going to take care of business on his own. Get the freedom of speech thing out. Michael Drumm and his cronies should be ashamed of their comments.

While Peter was going to be in Buffalo I had some business to take care of. I needed to start getting ready to validate everything I would be putting in the book. Luckily it was hot, humid and rainy in Tampa so there would be nothing to interfere with my undertaking of writing more notes for the book.

On July 7, 2014, Peter drove to the courthouse. He called to tell me he was in the parking lot near the Federal Building. I reminded him to leave his cell phone in the car and leave it turned off with the battery removed and placed in the trunk. "Ok." Peter commented, "This will be the last conversation until I get out of the courthouse and back to the car."

"Have fun, and don't forget everything will be recorded in the courtroom and on the transcripts!"

Peter walked through the now familiar courthouse, though security, up the elevator, turning right, then left. He then walked up the enclosed appointments encased in glass, observing he was once again first up. He then turned to sit on the bench to wait for the courtroom's doors to open and the proceedings to begin.

Peter heard the elevator door open. He could hear Daniel Schoenborn's footsteps shuffling as he said, "Mr. Bulan, I'm Daniel Schoenborn." Apparently this was their first meeting. Together they walked from the elevator to the bench, perhaps in their own minds thinking of the future money they had negotiated for stopping the Supreme Court trial.

The huge doors opened and they all filed into the soon to be crowded area. Peter, once again sitting on the left side of the aisle. Daniel Schoenborn and Harold Bulan chose to sit together on the right side of the courtroom. Brand new buddies with something in common ... a secret ... about the defendant Peter Kirisits.

Suddenly the familiar voice rang out. "All Rise." It was 10:04 a.m.

Judge Bucki called out "Peter Kirisits, let's have appearances." Peter walked through the gates to represent himself. Harold Bulan and Daniel Schoenborn flung in from the right.

Harold Bulan rose to his brief height "Harold Bulan, Trustee." Daniel Schoenborn, hands dangling by his side, with his fingers contracting, then lengthening and stood as far away from Peter as he could. "Daniel Schoenborn, Special Counsel for the trustee."

Judge Bucki looks at Harold Bulan stating, "All right Mr. Bulan, this is your application." Attorney Bulan puffs up his chest with a false sense of importance, and states "Yes." The Judge, holding some paperwork, then says "Anything to add to the papers?"

"No Sir." he states.

Judge Bucki turns to Peter. "All right, Mr. Kirisits, you have an objection?"

Peter answers "Yes."

Judge Bucki then stated, "This is your opportunity to expound."

He answered the Judge, "Okay on which issue? On---"

Judge Bucki interrupts and states, "On any issue you want."

Peter says, "The first issue I have is Susan Buranich, her $400.00 or so. I mean, I didn't— I never owned the car. I don't know why she sued me. She came into a building, maybe two days after she said the car hit her. And----"

Judge Bucki interrupts Peter. "I gather she is a creditor of yours? Or listed as a creditor?" Peter answers, "No she wasn't on their main list. And now she's on the list to collect $400, $480 or whatever it is."

Judge Bucki says, "What is her name?"

Peter answers, "Susan Buranich."

Judge Bucki then tells Peter, "Four hundred and forty-eight dollars and eighty-seven cents."

Peter looks at the Judge, trying to capture his attention as the Judge shuffles a paper from one place to another. Amazed that a fender bender of an accident in a parking lot had been brought into a bankruptcy case, Peter started to rev up for his objection.

"I mean, I said if we hit her car, to put it through the insurance company. Her husband's an Orchard Park policeman, and he says he don't want to put it through the insurance company. So we put it through our insurance company, and I---"

Judge Bucki interrupts him again astoundingly he says, "All right, and what are your other objections?" ignoring the fact of a police officer put a judgment against him for a fender bender in the parking lot instead of going through the insurance company.

Peter answered, "The other objection is the Department of Labor. I know I owe a fine. I owe—they had a lien against me—against the company, for $50,000, I think there is $32,000 left over. But I mean, I didn't own the building and I didn't own the business. And JoAnne Gleason owned the business and the building but she wasn't included in the fine, and she wasn't a corporation. She got a meeting later on this month or next month with Judge Kaplan."

Judge Bucki leans forward slightly, "So your claiming that there no money owing."

Peter watching the Judge states, "Well, there's money owed. I mean, I won't get out of---I won't back out of paying my debt. But I mean, I think that since we were both---I was just an officer of the corporation; she owned the corporation and she owned the business and the building; I think she would have been liable for some of the debt too."

Judge Bucki then explains the issues of counter claiming the claims of the trustee, Harold Bulan. There is no mention how the case came to bankruptcy court. No mention of Daniel Schoenborn, no mention of a Supreme Court trial, and lastly no mention of Harold Bulan abandoning the bankruptcy in 2005. The only thing the Judge states is the fact Peter should have filed a claim. Which is pretty hard to do when you don't have any means of commutations with the trustee.

Judge Bucki brings up how old the case is, and claims the trustee is trying to wrap the case up. The Judge apparently ignores the abandonment of the case by Harold Bulan years before. He does state that he could defer the trustee claim for thirty days and Peter would then file another claim to defer it again. He then turns to the trustee. "Mr. Bulan?"

Attorney Bulan states, "Your Honor, if I may, in his wife's case, which is in front of Judge Kaplan, the claim----she's going to get money back. She is going to get money back. I think 25,000 some odd dollars. The claim was filed in both cases. And in going over, it seemed that it's one case to pay it and the other would get away without paying it."

Peter interjects "She not my wife."

Attorney Bulan answers, "Okay whatever it is. I think her name is Gleason. She's going to get money back."

Judge Bucki looks at Harold Bulan and says, "All right. So---but it's your assessment that one or the other is responsible for this Department of Labor claim." Harold Bulan puffs his chest up again and answered "Correct."

Harold Bulan had botched the case so bad by this time he would tell the either Judge anything to keep the heat off himself. He was the king after all of this chess game. Or so he thought.

Judge Bucki once again says, "All right. I understand you don't believe you owe the money; that doesn't mean you don't owe it. They filed a claim, the Government filed it, there's no----you're not giving me..."

Still concentrating on the Judge, Peter tries to counter, "Well I didn't say— "

Judge Bucki finishes, "... adequate basis to challenge it."

Peter declares, "I didn't owe the money. I mean, if---because I was an officer of the cooperation. I didn't say that I didn't owe it. But I think that the debt should be shared. I mean, there's two of us, we both filed bankruptcy at the same time. And it wasn't for—it wasn't because we were careless with our spending. We had a fire. And the---in 2008."

Peter continues. "And for fourteen years I've been arguing with Peerless Insurance over the fire. I mean I lost a house, lost two businesses, lost everything because of a fire. My debts were paid they forced me into bankruptcy.

"I had to move to Florida because I had to live. It was---it's just a case where I don't think it's fair and equitable that one gets charged and the other doesn't get charged.

"I mean we paid all our bills on time. I mean we weren't in debt. I mean an attorney says you owe $240,000 and it wasn't, it was only $50,000 and I paid $15,000 of that off. I was paying it off at $500 a month. I probably would have paid it off, you know, within the next year that I---- you know. I had more time. I probably would have paid it off. But they took away my building. And I had extra insurance policy just on the equipment, because it was leased, with a dollar buy back after two or three years. And they wouldn't even pay for the extra----the extra policy that I had for the equipment."

Peter is on a roll and he is going to get as much in as possible, particularly in front of the podgy bungling Harold Bulan, and the newly hired Daniel Schoenborn who already knew the true story.

Peter continues as if he is Atticus Finch defending a victim against false charges, the evils of the courthouse and the cast of characters coming to light.

Continuing Peter states, "I mean we weren't ever accused of arson or anything, I mean, and we were out of the country the next day, and the attorney told us, go on vacation, your building will be ready when you come back. Fourteen years later, never was ready. I mean, I've been fighting this thing for fourteen years."

Judge Bucki blows Peter saying, "All right. We also have before us the application by Mr. Schoenborn to approve his legal fees." Peter jumps on that, loudly protesting. "Well, I disagree with that, too."

Judge Bucki asks "Any basis to object to that?"

Peter continued on to refresh the Federal Judges memory. "Yes, I disagree with that. I feel that Mr. Schoenborn withdrew from the case [in Supreme Court] according to the contract that he and I had, and JoAnne had, and I have papers here that indicates that he withdrew from the case."
The Judge turns to Harold Bulan "Did you retain Mr. Schoenborn independently?"

Harold Bulan outright lies to Judge Bucki and replies "Yes."

The Judge asks, "And that was by appropriate application?"

Harold Bulan lies again. "Correct"

The Judge answers, "All right."

Peter interjects. "There was no corporation involved in this."

Judge Bucki blows him off again "Mr. Schoenborn was hired by Mr. Bulan, the trustee."

Peter knew Daniel Schoenborn had lied to us, his clients. He probably was not capable of handling the case in Supreme Court. He had other interests rather than the personal bankruptcy with now three attorneys, four counting Jill Luber who plopped down in the courtroom conference table the previous June 2 in Judge Bucki's courtroom. Who and what made this case so special? It would be a whopper when we found out.

As Peter continued to battle for his civil rights, Judge Bucki still does not have a handle on the bankruptcy case. He responds, "All right. And so--- and he may have represented you in the past, and you may have discharged him. Then Mr. Bulan as trustee, evaluated the case and decided he wanted Mr. Schoenborn to handle the matter for him. And it is that representation that results in a recovery of the insurance."

Peter once again attempts to inform the Judge he has false information "Yes but, I did not discharge him; he withdrew. I have a letter here that says that."

Judge Bucki asks, "Do you have any other basis to go and challenge the legitimacy of this claim?"

Peter asks "Other than the letter saying that he withdrew?"

Judge Bucki replies "Other than that."

Peter once more continues his stance on the chessboard. "Well, I mean I got letters here going back to 2004, where I tried to get ahold of Mr. Bulan, I called his office numerous times, I got it on my phone. You can't bring your phone in here or I would show you. Wrote letters as far back as September 2004. And the in April 2004. Then I wrote you a letter, I wrote him recently, wrote Dennis Gaughan, called Dennis Gaughan called Mr. Schoenborn I mean every time I turn around, I'm running into a blank wall. Where am I going to go? Who am I going to talk too? Before you in June, you gave me till today, but I couldn't hire---I mean I talked to four lawyers. They couldn't take it because of the short amount of time; was probably my fault when I came before you last month. But---a, they put me out of business. I mean I have no retirement, and I worked all of my life for a retirement. But--and they---even if I wanted I'd have to have a retainer of----one almost $30,000, the other was $15,000 I'm 75 years old. I mean they put me out of business. I have no retirement, and I worked all my life for a retirement. But I have none. So what I read is this, after Mr. Schoenborn gets his [payoff] Department of Labor gets theirs, Susan Buranich gets hers, I end up with $8000. After 14 years, I end up with $8000. I don't think that fair and equitable. If the Court does, so be it."

Judge Bucki appearing bored, then asks "Anything else?"

Guess who answers that question with the biggest rambling long winded tedious lies I would imagine were ever put before a Federal Court in front of a Federal Judge with a full courtroom full of other attorneys, paralegals, federal court house staff, and the transcripts running so not to miss a word. It was a disgrace to the Constitution of the United States and an embarrassment to the legal profession including the very fibers of the courts themselves.

It would be Daniel Schoenborn, he had the secret intact for now but, soon it would be out of his hands. These transcripts would not be thrown out or destroyed as the 341 Hearing transcripts had been in 2005. We had made some friends who knew what was going on behind the scenes of the courtrooms in Buffalo.

The courtroom fell to an awkward silence for a moment. It was at this time Daniel Schoenborn decided to make his move. Bringing himself up to his full height, his hands folding, contracting and lengthening ever so slightly in front of him as he shifted his stature side to side. He was so close to getting found out and he had to do something. Dan should have paid attention to the first transcript from January of 2013, when he told us not to come to the "meeting." His statement to Judge Carl Bucki had been different. Anything to take the heat off Harold Bulan, his Majesty.

The following statement is from Daniel Schoenborn on July 7, 2013:

"Well I suppose I ought to know when to shut up but, that's never been a problem I had. Just briefly, I'd like the court to realize I didn't meet Mr. Kirisits until-----I believe 2008. [It was January of 2009] So that point in time, there were other attorneys involved. And whatever happened to me at the time of the fire, until that point in time, there were other attorneys involved. And I thought there were some issues of that, looking at it from my standpoint, there were a lot of issues that Mr. Kirisits had regarding that insurance loss that I didn't think we could prove. And there were also issues of liens."

Daniel Schoenborn continues and is lying through his teeth, to a Federal Court Judge. He knew in January of 2009 we had to file bankruptcy, and mentions a letter to Bulan. He either foolishly destroyed the letter to Harold Bulan or he is lying again to the Judge. We never found any letter in Daniel Schoenborn's file to indicate in his diary, or his files a letter to Harold Bulan. We did find something else in his files that would come to the surface shortly. We just had to get to September 3, 2014. He forgot to purge his file and he was lying. Why did we have all of his files and the only thing missing was the above so called letter.

The lies and cover-up continue. Daniel Schoenborn states, "So I think I did everything under the circumstances. I mean, sure, it's easy for us to say, okay, Peerless really was not nice to Mr. Kirisits or Miss Gleason in this whole proceeding, going back to 2000. But come today, were faced with what were faced with. And that gets us to today. And I would only submit that I've put a lot of work into this case, and I wish it would have a better outcome, given all the circumstances."

He contradicts himself when he made this statement. In a previous transcript, and in Judge Deborah Chimes office to meet with the Peerless representative, he admitted he didn't do that much with the case when he was begging us to take the offer. It was embarrassing to see in in the transcripts from January of 2013, then today July of 2014.

Judge Bucki chirps up "Anything to add?" once again looking at his Law Clerk.

Harold Bulan takes his next big step and informs the Judge, "Your Honor, before Mr. Schoenborn was involved in the case, Brown & Chiari were involved in the case, and they apparently washed their hands of it and I closed this case, and then reopened it when Mr. Schoenborn got in touch with me, that there was a possibility of a settlement with the insurance carrier. This case goes back to 2004. It's a voluntary petition, no one forced Mr. Kirisits to file bankruptcy he chose it." Judge Buck looks at his law clerk with his eyes wide open and arms up in the air.

Harold Bulan is lying to the Judge. It is inconceivable that he does so with such blatancy. Brown & Chiari did not pull out of the case until we filed a grievance in 2008. Harold Bulan knew Brown & Chiari had pulled a fast one, of practicing out of their specialty. Harold Busan lied about the bankruptcy being voluntary. Harold Bulan is also lying to Judge Bucki.

The Judge now brings up the famous line, "All right. Any other argument before I give you my decision?"

Peter says, "No Your Honor." In his opinion, Judge Bucki did not want to hear the truth, he wanted the case gone for good, he had listened to Harold Bulan, not the truth backed by documents.

Judge Bucki continues. "All right. Bankruptcy Court often deals with tragic and difficult circumstances. Because people are frustrated---this is not just this case, this is many cases---parties are frustrated, they can't liquidate or get the results they want, sometimes it's because of high expectations, sometimes it's because of opponents that are being obstreperous or difficult and sometimes things just don't work out. And when that happens people file chapter 7 bankruptcy."

The Judge continues. "The effect of Chapter 7 bankruptcy is to take whatever resources are available, put them into the control of a trustee, a trustee with experience, hopefully with experience, a trustee that will look independently at the questions that are at issue.

"If the trustee fulfills those obligations, exercises appropriate diligence and acts responsibly, the trustee will then make a final report, which the Court will approve, as long as it's demonstrated to the Court's satisfaction that this appropriate discretion was exercised. And that brings us to the case we have right here. This case was filed in 2004. There had been a fire loss; apparently an inability to recover on that fire loss. The trustee made an initial attempt to recover on the fire loss, determined that it was not to be had, and, therefore, closed the case. He then found out that there was a potential that perhaps he hadn't---

there were facts that were not brought to his attention, and therefore reopened the case."

The Judge has done everything to continue the haphazard antics of the attorneys and he was not done. Out of the blue he continues. "He hired counsel. And counsel, Mr. Schoenborn, was representing the trustee. I've been provided with an application to justify the fees and I'm satisfied with them."

The Judge had mentioned in June that Dan had forgotten to get his application in, or he would get nothing. We had gotten that information from the courthouse itself.

Outrageously Judge Bucki states, about Schoenborn "I think he is entitled to the fees that are requested. Especially in this case, where many years had already passed, and there was no recovery. It's like finding money that no one else could find. Even the trustee in his best efforts couldn't find the money in the beginning." What a crock and what did the beginning have to do with anything, it was a lawsuit against Peerless in Supreme Court a corporate lawsuit.

The craziness continued as Judge Bucki then states, "And so an effort was made, a recovery was had of $100,000 in this case. I know there's a separate recovery over before Judge Kaplan. But the matter was settled. Notice went out on that settlement." Not so Judge Bucki, if a notice was sent out it was a phony and it was sent to the gang of attorneys not us.

Now it was hard to decipher who was lying to whom, or was the paperwork in the courthouse being tampered with. In other words, Judge Bucki had misinformation, whether generated by his staff, Attorney Bulan or the paperwork. In any case it was not true. My case had not been settled. Where was the judge getting this constant flow of wrong information? It would have to come out soon, possibly by my hearing.

Judge Carl Bucki continues, "The Court [who in the court? Not the Judge] evaluated any objections that were raised at that time, and was satisfied with the trustee's recommendation that it was in the best interests of everyone to take the $100,000 in this case. And there was money in front—in the case of Judge Kaplan---to take the money and then make a distribution. Particularly since all available creditors would be paid in full and there would be some surplus for the debtor; Mr. Kirisits, that's you. And I approved that application. There was no appeal from that application. So it became final. And now the trustee is making his recommendation."

He continues, "I hear your----and the matter came before me more than a month ago, at which time I adjourned it to this date. I adjourned it through one reason primarily, because I found that there was no notice given of Mr. Schoenborn's fee application and the creditors needed an opportunity to review it. I'm not persuaded with any objection that you've raised as to the legitimacy of Mr. Schoenborn's application. I'm satisfied with the reasonableness, and so, therefore, I'm going to approve it."

The Judge stopped, turning to look at his staff, content he had made the right judgment. He had given Dan almost a month to steal the deal. Judge Bucki wasn't quite finished. He had to complete the smoke and mirrors for the courtroom.

Looking at Peter he stated "At that time I also gave you, and you were present in the Court, an opportunity to today hire counsel and pursue any other issues that you may wish. We are essentially distributing money to two creditors." He then added "If more creditors had filed, you would not be getting the $8000 that is available for distribution."

"But we have two creditors that filed claims the Department of Labor and Susan Burnish [sic]." As he continues, he states "Claims have a presumption of validity. Unless somebody can come here and challenge it, we presume it to be valid. This matter was before us before. I delayed it once, with an opportunity to file any objections, and I have no further objections being presented. Now the Buranich case is $448.87. I would not be shocked by anyone saying it's not worth my trouble to hire a lawyer to go and challenge a claim of that size. You can, but I'm not surprised that there has been no objection on that." Judge Bucki had not only heard the objection of the claim against Susan Buranich, it was in the transcripts.

Judge Bucki then continues, "The Department of Labor is a much larger claim. Altogether were looking at almost $49,000. And---a very significant amount of money. But there's an acknowledgment of liability. The money is owed to the Department of Labor and I think they're entitled to get paid."

He continues, "Now they're entitled to collect whatever the money is available, whether it be in this case or across the way with Judge Kaplan. When is Judge Kaplan's case coming on for hearing?"

Peter answers, "The first week in September."

The Judge says, "All right. In the first week of September, if you feel that you're entitled to some form of contribution from their estate you should file a proof of claim, get----Mr. Bulan are you trustee for that case?" already knowing the answer.

Peter looks calmly at Harold Bulan. He is nervous and with good reason, the paperwork is messed up and he knows it. He answers, "Yes Sir."

Judge Bucki then asks Harold Bulan, "If you feel---Is there a surplus in that case as well?" Harold Bulan answers, "Yes Sir."

Judge Bucki looks at Peter. "If you feel you're entitled to some form of contribution, file a claim in that case. And if there's a basis for honoring that, then it will have to be honored. But right now the only question I have is whether the money is owed in this case. And I'm satisfied that it is owed in this case. The State of New York, through its Department of Labor has filed a claim."

A red flag went up. New York State and the Federal Labor Department were two totally different entities. Was the Judge given false information? Only he could answer that.

Judge Bucki continues, "No one has shown me any reason to believe the claim is not legitimate. And so therefore, I'm going to approve it. If you want to get contribution from the other case [Susan Burnaich] then you have to file a claim, and then Mr. Bulan will evaluate that claim as to whether or not it feels it's a legitimate claim for contribution."

This statement was almost funny, stating if you want to make a claim, do so, but you have to make a claim to the guy that screwed up the whole bankruptcy case to begin with.

Judge Bucki then goes off on a tangent regarding the labor fine. The Department of Labor was the least of our issues and it did not take a judge, attorney, or a citizen to figure it out.

He continues, denying all the paperwork and objections made by Peter. He had to get the case out of his courtroom.

Judge Carl Bucki continues the sham and had given Schoenborn to get his paperwork in" Mr. Schoenborn has presented his case in terms of why he feels his fees are owing, and I'm persuaded that they are. So I'm going to approve these fees." Peter looked at Schoenborn, he appeared to be almost giddy with the excitement, that he had almost pulled it off. Just one more hearing to go in September and he would be good to go.

Then the most bizarre statement came up, Judge Carl Bucki looked at Peter and said, "You need to file a proof of claim, and then take that matter up in the Donnelly case, which is before Judge Kaplan. But I'm going to approve the fees in the final report as presented."

Who the hell is Donnelly? Peter wondered. He didn't say anything he had to get his licks in for the courtroom and the transcripts. The transcripts don't lie, as long as they didn't get destroyed. We would first get out of Buffalo and order the transcripts the next day.

Once again Judge Bucki is rambling on about the Labor Fine. He states "So I'm going to approve the final report. I think the claims are legitimate." Wow, unbelievable he fell for these lies to him. He lived up to his name "The Boy Scout."

Judge Carl Bucki then switches back to Attorney Schoenborn and the real reason they had adjourned the case the previous month. "I think that the work done by Mr. Schoenborn; because of course he has a very substantial claim for his legal services. I think the report, as presented by Mr. Bulan is consistent with the requirements of the law."

He continues, "This case when it came before us a little more than a month ago, and that's why I adjourned it." The case had appeared before him over a year ago in January of 2013, he was not paying attention in his courtroom and his law clerk wasn't either.

The Judge continues, "But think he's corrected his deficiencies; the notice has been given." Attorney Schoenborn has presented his case in terms of why he feels that his fees are owing, and I'm persuaded they are. So I'm going to approve those fees."

We did not have access to the previous conversation with Daniel Schoenborn and Judge Bucki.

Whether it was a private meeting with the judge done orally, or it was paperwork submitted, we would not be notified, or have the ability to counter claim. It was done under the covers perhaps in the Judge's Chambers or with Harold Bulan, who perhaps had submitted once again false information to the Judge.

With that said Judge Bucki asks, "Any questions?" This was Peter's chance to get it into the transcripts, he no longer trusted any of the courthouse staff, and with good reason.

Instead Peter answered, "I have lots of them, but there's no sense in--- as long as you approve it, there's no sense in me arguing the case."

The Judge answers, "All right."

Peter continues "I mean, originally they said that this case was---the fire claim was for $300,000, so they settled it for $200,000. Originally, it was for $980,000 not $300,000. And I got the paperwork when they filed the claim. So after $980,000, not $300,000, it's come down to 14 years later, an $8000. Wow. A kick in the butt."

Judge Bucki unbelievably states, "I fully understand that you feel that it's worth more. But if it was collectible more---"

Peter interjects, "Well there's attorneys and I live in Tampa. They can't correct a flaw in New York, I mean, they don't have New York licenses, you know, the district license or anything that they can practice law here."

Peter means a Florida attorney can't just fly up to New York and handle a case. Not only does he have to have a New York license, he has to be admitted to practice in Federal court too, since that is where our bankruptcy case is being heard.

Peter continues, "But I've had a couple of attorneys look at it, and they say, keep fighting it Peter, because you've got a good case. I mean, and you know, there's so many stories told that I owed all these tax liens and all liens $240,000—I mean, they read Judge Curtains decision, and they get to the fine that says $240,000, they did not bother to read any further."

Judge Bucki does not want to hear this in his court. He is in protection mode and states, "The bottom line though is you weren't able to collect this money before bankruptcy, and now it's taken the trustee more than---almost ten years to recover this case. I think we have to be

Plaintiff to Defendant

realistic. The trustee has made---has presented to the Court the rationale for why he recommended settlement."

Peter answered, "As long as you agree Your Honor."

Judge Bucki continues, "And I had no opposition in that proposal when it was originally made. I'm persuaded that this is money that could easily have just been overlooked and never recovered at all. If you have a claim for contribution from the Donnelly case, you need to file a claim."

Peter, amazed at the Judge, tries to correct him. "Gleason." Which was then corroborated by the Judge's law clerk.

The Judge answers, "Or the Gleason case. I'm mixing up names. I only have the name of Kirisits in front of me because the other case is not mine. In the Gleason case you need to file a claim. And I urge you to get counsel so that you maximize your ability to recover that."

Peter then added, "Yeah, I got---probably got till September now before she goes in, but, I mean, you've got to—you've got to realize that, like I say, I haven't worked in ten years, money's short. And when counsel looks at you and says I need 15,000, $30,000 retainers, I got to eat."

The Judge answered. "I understand. The application is approved. Thank you."

The time was 10:32 a.m. It was over, or so they thought. The secret had been kept for the moment. It was hard to tell if the Judge was involved or not. It appeared through the paperwork involved he gave Harold Bulan a little too much rope. Harold Bulan had been pulling so much crap for so long he was getting lazy. He needed this case closed for himself and it would show up within a few weeks in September when I would go to my hearing in front of Judge Kaplan.

Peter started to leave with Harold Bulan following him. Harold Bulan looked at Peter and said, "Wait a minute, I need your address." Peter shocked by this pint-sized man's behavior replied, "If you would answer my letters for all these years you would know my address. You never answered my phone calls or letters not once and you botched this whole case. Why?" Harold Bulan shifted from one foot to another looking off into space as if he was in another world.

Peter aghast with loathing, continued, "Not only do I find you greedy, but you worked the law to your favor and yours alone. You took money that belonged to me, and kept it for yourself, you ruined my life with intention, I lost my retirement because you are so greedy, so self-absorbed, and it had nothing to do with the law. You let me sit for one month less than ten years, who else have you done this too?"

Bulan ignored the question, a slight shift in his eyes. That pretty much settled it, not one person had challenged the king of the chess board before.

At exactly the same time, Daniel Schoenborn came through the doors of the courtroom. He walked towards Peter, as if he was going to say something. Thinking better of it, he slowly slinked behind Harold Bulan and Peter having their chat, getting on the elevator without saying a word. He had just made $33,333.66

The cover up job had been done, Dan Schoenborn, Morris Horwitz and Harold Bulan had lied to a Federal Judge and it had been recorded on the transcripts. They thought they had gotten away with it. Peter smiled to himself thinking all the hearings had transcripts, and it now was on file. He would call for the transcripts as soon as he got back to Florida.

The trustee squirmed in his ill-fitting suit. "I just need your address that's all."

Continuing, this abrasive little man said, "I only park on Pearl Street for this court, too much money, it's cheaper and I've never paid a ticket." Harold Bulan adding, "my time is running out and I need to get back to the car."
Amazed at this man's self-love, Peter shook his head and gave his address to him as Harold Bulan wrote it down on a piece of paper. He then started to walk away before turning back to look at Peter.

"I thought this case would be easy, it turned out it isn't." Then he said the most outrageous of all statements, "By the way you will not get any money, it was eaten up in interest." Peter now so wanted to take this little jerk out. It had just been recorded on the transcripts to Judge Bucki five minutes ago that Harold Bulan had money for Peter. He lied to a Federal Judge and it was in the transcripts.

Peter disgusted with the demeanor or this little man and at the same time thinking he should be investigated with his behavior in a Federal Court "The case would have been easy if you had done your job you were hired to do, how long have you been doing this to people in Buffalo? By the way, you have had my address for years, we sent everything to you certified. It's called 'proof' for future use! You lied to the Federal Judge about my settlement, you ass. You lied to a Federal Judge with the transcripts going." Peter was angry.

Harold Bulan scurried through the hallway, perhaps to join Dan for lunch, after all they were newly formed friends and they had performed an assignment together. Perhaps they were giggling like teenage girls over a lunch date thinking of the claimed funds. To say the least, it was shameful professionalism right in the face of Judge Bucki and his staff. Peter wondered how far up the chain it went in the courthouses of Buffalo. It was scary, very scary indeed to witness this firsthand. Peter then wondered if Buffalo Snoop had been aware of this and how far had the plans gone to protect an local attorney and his firm.

As he left the courthouse to go to the airport, going through security, Peter stopped at a concession stand for water. He wondered if Peerless Insurance had been involved in this also. Certainly the Cast of Characters had been growing at a steady pace over the last two years. Getting in the car he left for the airport to get back to Tampa.

Retrieving his cell phone, inserting the battery, Peter called me with the results. As we were talking, apparently Harold Bulan had lied to him about getting back to his car parked in the street. He was walking out of the courthouse and heading down the street to his parked car Pearl Street. He had stopped for something before he left the Federal Courthouse. As he crept down the street, Peter talked with me while he followed him to his car. Passing him, Harold Bulan was fumbling for something in his pocket. Maybe it was the check for over $33,000. Or his car keys.

Peter continued to Buffalo Airport to get away from the toxic waste. Dropping off the car, he headed across the small walkway to check in for the flight. He would study the set of circumstances in his mind for the next hour waiting for his plane ride back to Tampa. Sitting at the gate he spent the time envisioning the set of state of affairs, starting from the beginning. What had started out as a mid-day fire on August

28, 2000 had turned into one of the strangest court cases we had ever heard about, let alone been involved in.

As it started to fall into place, everything over the years became more evident. The years of strange phone calls, the banging on the house, the strokes attributed to stress, the greed jealousy and hate the first hearing in Judge Bucki's courtroom when Daniel Schoenborn had told us not to come. The refusal of Judge Bucki to look at the original paperwork. Then there was Judge Kaplan who always sided with his very good friend Harold Bulan, or was it more than that, and why?

Peter recalled part of the conversation with Buffalo Snoop and Tampa Snoop in the cemetery in St. Petersburg. The statement had been made while the two Snoops were conversing about the case. "Their civil liberties had been violated they were not being able to be heard by the courts in Buffalo, it didn't matter. It was if they had a different agenda." Peter getting ready to enter the doorway of the Southwest Airline, recalling that moment he was told Judge Bucki thought Peter was lying. Buffalo Snoop had mentioned it after Peter's hearing on June 2, 2013. Within minutes the plane had arrived, it fully loaded with passengers for the nonstop flight to Tampa. Peter walked through the aisles of the plane, content there was no one he recognized, he could go over the events of the morning and take notes on his way home. As the plane lifted off, he pulled a pen and paper out of his suit pocket. Writing down the events of the day, he knew the transcripts from the hearing would hold the true events of the court scene to complete the set-up by the attorneys in Buffalo starting with the first.

Once in Tampa, for the next few days he would once more go over the files to try and find the missing chess piece. Whoever the King was in Buffalo had to be protected at all costs or the whole bankruptcy case would fall in their faces, perhaps embarrassing the Judges themselves. Peter knew something was amiss in the courtrooms of Judge Glownia, Judge Chimes, Judge Dillon, and all of Supreme Court. It appeared the same thing was happening in Judge Carl Bucki and Judge Kaplan's as they pulled up the rear in Federal Court.

The clues and the evidence had to be in the files of the attorneys, and it appeared that we were the only ones that did not know what it was. We had all the attorney's files in our possession since the trip to Buffalo in 2013. What was in those files that had been overlooked? Exhausted from the antics in the Federal Courthouse, the chess game had been blocked for now and the circle had been contained.

Peter arrived home that night grateful to be back with our Tampa group. The ties to Buffalo were almost completely cut, and it would be doubtful we would ever recover or return to the area. We had been forced out of the city by the corrupt attorneys and we had made a new life.

We would just make one more trip and it would be over. We were scheduled to be back in Buffalo September 3, 2014, and I was ready to stand up to Judge Kaplan, the judge who seemed to think it was normal to throw out evidence of an open federal case. As usual, the schedule made by both Judge Bucki and Judge Kaplan would be over every holiday weekend that summer of 2014. The first being Memorial weekend, the second July 4th, the third Labor Day weekend. I needed to call Judge Kaplan or his staff for budgeting tips on this one. The judges scheduled the court date and we had to listen to Judge Kaplan's flack about spending money in his courtroom.

The next day, Peter would go through the files looking for the missing pieces. It would not be a one-day event. First, he would have to go to the storage unit, pick the files of Daniel Schoenborn, Harold Bulan and Michael Drumm. It would take days to go through just these three immense files to look for the missing paperwork.

Within the next few days, he would also call various attorneys who could practice within the Eighth District of New York. It would prove to be a tedious project because he would have to go over the whole lawsuit against Peerless Insurance since the fire in 2000, continuing with how and why he had ended up in bankruptcy court. He would hear the same reply when he mentioned Brown & Chiari as representing us. "How in the hell did they represent you they are personal injury. They should have told you." Of course it would be followed by "Daniel Schoenborn? Never heard of him, and he knew about Brown & Chiari right?" Followed by, "and Peerless Insurance refused to pay you right? Why?"

It would be a tiresome conversation for both Peter and the various attorneys in the Western New York area. It had been made so confusing and difficult to understand, the only thing to do was write it down from the beginning to see if the smoke and mirrors would clear enough to show the whole set of bungling by the ever growing number of attorneys, starting with Michael Drumm and Daniel Schoenborn. It was the summer of 2014 and we still did not have the answer to how they tied in together. Peter would then go back to the storage area and pull more files to unravel the missing chessmen.

Other weird things were happening. We hadn't heard from Buffalo Snoop lately and we wondered why our Nickel City Snoop wasn't peeping as in the past. Buffalo Snoop hadn't told us about the collusion of the cast of characters either. Perhaps now too close to the scene of the corruption to make a move. We would sit and wait.

As the summer breezed away without too much thought about Buffalo, we spent time with friends and I continued my work with Morris Chiropractic. It was good to get away from the cramped quarters and the endless paperwork Peter was filing through. As July passed into August, Peter would continue to call attorneys in Buffalo to have someone clear up the mess. "You need to pay me $15,000 up front to clear up this mess, it is a tough case and will take a lot of work." adding there are no guarantees followed by, "This case is one of the worst I have ever heard about, it is a real mess," adding, "the Judges had probably already made up their minds before you even went in."

One day, Peter called the courts in Buffalo to get some advice from a volunteer group of attorneys who help you represent yourself. "They have disbanded for the summer," He heard on the other end. We would have to do it ourselves.

It would prove fruitless to hire an attorney to get us out of this mess. It was as if the attorneys involved in our case had formed a circle that would not be penetrated by anyone outside of their field, and certainly not by the clients that paid them. We started to wonder how far this case had stretched from one attorney to the other. Did it in fact include the various Judges and why?

We were at the point of no return. We had told the truth throughout the years and would continue to do so verbally and in the written word. "Freedom of Speech," the First Amendment of the Constitution, backed by the paperwork of all the courts, all the attorneys, and Judges in the Eighth District of Buffalo, New York. Not libel or slander, just the facts. The libel and slander had been made by the attorneys from Katherine

Fijal to Daniel Schoenborn to Michael Drumm in order to protect their actions of cheating in the chess game. There was blood all over the chess board and it had to stop, and stop now.

While our paperwork was growing, the attorney's correspondence and notes was dwindling. We now had the whole case sitting in our hands looking very suspicious but nothing we could put together. Peter continued to make runs to the storage space, to look for the missing pieces to get ready for my next court date.

On August 21, 2014, I started to make out the Certificates of Service. Now the next chess move would be mine. I looked at Peter's certificate and would copy it along with the Motion to Dispute the actions of the trustee Harold Bulan. I knew what to write, I would copy his and submit my objections with the motion. I filled it out the same way, the same title, the same everything. As I finished making them out, I then putting them in an envelope to mail that same day. I had to time it right since the postal deliveries would be interfered with the Labor Day holiday coming up. If it did not get there at the proper time it would be null and void.

There would be six Certificates of Service going out with the Motion to Dispute. One by one I counted them off: the Clerk of the Court, Harold Bulan, KeyBank, MBNA, Citibank/Choice, and of course Pamela Ashmall, the massage therapist, the least important one of all.

Finally, I was done. Grabbing the certificates, I sprung into my Volkswagen, driving the few miles to the Post Office in Tampa. There were many concerns to be accounted for. Would everyone get the notice in time and within the ten-day period? Would they be represented in court? I hoped they were. Harold Bulan had made a mess of this stuff, his agenda was to grab the money and retire at all costs, he was the most important in his mind, he was the King of the chess game.

Arriving at the Post Office, I entered the building to stand in line to wait for my turn. I felt nervous getting ready to push out the letters. My mind drifted back to the beginning of the summer of 2001, Peerless Insurance had a plan since day one not to pay. They had continued to ignore the Insurance Codes of New York State while collecting premiums from their customers. My mind drifted to the hang up phone calls, the banging on the house, followed by the lazy attorneys in

Buffalo, Peter's strokes, the move, followed by the blast of flames coming out of my Volkswagen a few years before.

One by one, the postal employees waited on the customers. Finally, it was my turn, explaining the situation to the woman, she assumed the role of the stamper, writer of the Certified Mail, putting the letters on a shelf, slowly and methodically going through the stack. Suddenly everything stopped.

The clerk next to her had just acquired a hundred-dollar bill from the customer next to me. He asked her for change. As my eyes darted to the Volkswagen that held the first chapters of this book, my mind went into high gear. What was taking minutes to get the change seemed like hours.

I looked at the neighboring clerk, and half kidding said "Please we are busy here, she need to do her job perfect, these people I'm sending it too will find any excuse to throw my butt out of town. "

The clerk stepped over, looking at the addresses and laughing, he said, "Yeah I left there twenty years ago."

"Good move." I said.

Finally, my time was done with the clerk who had made sure everything was pristine. "That will be $95.95 please." More money thrown into the ever growing money basket of bankruptcy court.

Buffalo, the "Nickel City," named after the back of the Indian Head nickel, was nickel and diming us to death. Living under this crushing mess for over fifteen years, we were led into some very dark lives of some very dark people. It hadn't stopped since the labor fine, with the outrageous fees of the outrageous attorney's way back then. Starting with the $15,000 up front Cashier's check to attorney Ginger Schroder. I was glad we had kept all of that paperwork over the years also. Jumping into the car, I made a mental note to go over her paperwork, it had never been done and the box she had sent us right after the fire had never been opened.

Driving back to the house before leaving for work, I gathered the duplicate Certificates of Service, the Motions, and the receipts for the certified mail. Handing them to Peter, I asked him to file it in the storage unit, adding it to the ever growing collection of paperwork.

During the last days of August, Peter made one more phone call to an attorney in Buffalo.

"Who is your Judge?" the attorney asked Peter.

"Judge Bucki was mine, he finished my case, I got nothing from the lawsuit after thirteen years in the courtrooms as a plaintiff, Harold Bulan continued to keep me in and out, then back in Bankruptcy Court he also tried to close the case without our knowledge"

A long pause followed, before the attorney asked, "Who is Jo Anne's Judge?"

"Judge Kaplan."

He laughed, "We have a special name for him, he always settles with the trustee and all the attorneys know it, she will have it tough."

Peter hung up the phone and told me the news of Judge Kaplan. "To bad we can't get into the Pacer files on the internet, it would show everything about him." A challenge, I thought to myself. I started to get more clothes and paperwork ready for Buffalo, still feeling in my bones things were not quite right. I would wait until my instincts told me what to do.

There were other things on my plate, the cost of going to Buffalo to fight our way in Supreme Court had cost thousands, then to get out of Bankruptcy Court had reached again into the thousands. We were on a limited income and if I lost my ability to work it could only get worse.

The Labor Day weekend came, we had everything ready to go. That Friday heading to Circles, we were to meet with some friends. The conversation touched lightly on Buffalo and the continued problems. One of our friends had lived in the suburbs of the city years ago. Commenting, "No wonder everyone leaves that place, glad I got out when I did." Adding "Buffalo is a great town to be from." Moving on from the uncomfortable conversation, we ordered the food and enjoyed overlooking the vistas of Tampa Bay.

The next day was Saturday. As I gathered up the paperwork for Buffalo, I put it in a suitcase. Making mental notes in my head I thought of Daniel Schoenborn. For some reason a thought occurred to me about Daniel Schoenborn and the copies of the original invoices we had given him relating to the damages to the equipment of Pro-Pak and Evans Services. They were exempt according to the bankruptcy laws and Dan Schoenborn and Harold Bulan knew it. I wanted them to make amends on this issue before Federal Judge Kaplan. It was time he found out the truth about his cronies and the audio would be tallying up every word for the transcripts.

CHAPTER 44: CHESS CHEATS AMONG FRIENDS

Peter was sitting in the living room looking defeated while I was getting my paperwork together.

"Where is the rest of the paperwork we had shipped back from Dan Schoenborn's office last September?" He told me it was in the shed next door with the Labor Fine and Ginger Schroder's paperwork from 1999. The hairs on my neck rose as I felt an immense surge of significance of finding it.

"I want to see it right now!"

Looking at me with a quizzical look, he pulled the keys from his pocket as we went out to the shed to get it. As we pulled it from the storage area into the house, Peter reminded me we had been the ones who had filled the missing files of Michael Drumm ourselves and had sent them to Daniel Schoenborn.

"The only thing you will find are the files we sent to Dan, nothing else," Peter said.

Bringing Daniel Schoenborn's file into the house, we opened the box, beginning to pour through the files we had not looked at in a year. This file was different, very different than the file we had found in the carryon suitcase that had spilled open in 2013.

Suddenly we came upon Katherine Fijal's defense file for the court trial. It was neatly stacked with two punched holes in the top of the stack. It was her file for the trial. As we looked through the file it held various compartments. In one of the compartments we found our taxes. Shocked I pulled them out from her file.

I exclaimed, "Look! Peerless' attorneys had the taxes all along, all of them dating back to 1996! Peerless Insurance and their attorneys, Maurice Sykes, David Sleight, and finally Katherine Fijal had continued to ask us for the taxes until 2012."

They were lining to Supreme Court Judge Joseph Glownia's court. They had them all along since the first tax authorization we had signed way back in 2001 it was right in front of both of us. Who had lied along with the Peerless Insurance attorneys? Always asking for our authorizations? It centered on Michael Drumm, Peerless Insurance attorneys Maurice Sykes, David Slieght and Katherine Fijaland, Dan Schoenborn.

I was furious. Continuing to pour through the paperwork we found Dan's file right next to Katherine Fijal's. It was beyond belief what we found in Dan's file. It was far worse and further proved the suspect actions of not only the attorneys, but the judges as well. This was serious stuff and it proved my instincts had been right again.

The first item we found was a letter dated May 20, 2008, written to Michael Drumm by the Town of Hamburg Police, indicating the fire report he was looking for did not exist with their files. Eight years after the fire, Michael was looking for the fire report of our business fire. Along the bottom of the letter from Hamburg Police was handwriting. I looked through the rest of his file and saw the old note in his diary when Mr. Drumm had referred to me as clueless. The handwriting matched perfectly. It looked like he had inquired to the Hamburg Police after I wrote him the letter that same month, then to top the cake he had requested the fire report from the wrong people and from the wrong place.

Michael apparently had a vendetta against his own clients and had lied to us for many years. We had never seen this bit of information and Dan had never mentioned it to us in the four years he handled the case for Supreme Court.

The next set of astounding paperwork was worse. There were three pieces of original paperwork stapled together as if it had been a plan to hide something. The first page was a fax with our address at the top. The date and time registered October 24, 2011, 1:08 p.m. It was sent by Peter with our fax address to Dan. He had called Peter that day asking him if he had a copy of a Supreme Court paper that was a Notice of

Motion to Preclude filed in Judge Glownias courtroom. It was signed by Michael Drumm dated December 11, 2003.

Peters memory took him back to October 24, 2011 when he was on the phone with Dan. Peter had told Dan he should have this copy, there was a long pause on the other end in Buffalo, then Dan had said. "If you have it just send it to me." Peter had him wait on the phone that day while he pulled the paperwork from the files of Mr. Michael Drumm.

"Here it comes and I don't think Michael Drumm did anything about it "Adding" We have a copy signed by Judge Glownia in January of 2004. Do you want that also?"

"No just send the copy." Then he changed the subject, telling Peter he was working on other aspects the case.

Looking at the three copies of paperwork, it was a Notice of Motion to Preclude. Peerless Insurance had ignored the discovery demands and violated the CPLR Insurance Code Sec. 3126. It had been filled out by Michael on December 11. 2003 and signed by him.

Flipping to the next page. We noticed what appeared to be a nervous scribble written in blue ink in Michael's handwriting of the address of Dan's office located at the Brisbane Building in Buffalo.

More hand scribble in Michael's almost illegible handwriting, he wrote seven attorneys names in Buffalo, including one close to Buffalo Snoop. As we poured through the three pages of the paperwork the there is a number written, it is hard to decipher if it meant 26 miles or 26 minutes. As we continued to look at the paperwork, Peter checked his phone on MapQuest. "It look like it is also 26 minutes to go from Brown & Chiairi to Dan's office".

Michael Drumm's handwriting contained more notes, names of people including seven or eight attorneys written in a row, as if they were coming up in a conversation relating to possible charges against Mr. Drumm. Flipping to the next page, I found more attorney's names barely readable in the sloppy handwriting of the usually impeccable attorney. It was followed by a coarse piece of small paperwork measuring about 2 inches by 4 inches, with more scribbling of attorney's names.

Looking at the coarse piece of paper it appeared to be a check reorder form for M&T Bank. The bank had Michael's name embossed along with a family member, inscribed in the upper left hand corner with his home address in Eden, New York. I peered back into the box that contained the original check reorder stub found stapled in Daniel Schoenborn's file.

Giving it to Peter I said, "What the hell is this between Michael and Dan?"

Peter replied, "It looks like they had a meeting."

I replied, "Why would they have a meeting? Dan was hired to sue Michael for malpractice not, become his friend."

Handing the paperwork to Peter I asked, "Do you remember sending this fax to Dan?"

"Yes I remember it vividly. Dan had denied that Michael had made this Motion to Preclude and I told him we had it in the paperwork from Supreme Court and the files of Brown & Chiari."

"Do you realize this paperwork was sent by you to Dan Schoenborn right after they delayed our trial of 2011 and kicked us from Judge Glownia to Judge Chimes?"

Looking at me Peter stated, "Well all the pieces finally are starting to fit aren't they?"

"Yup," I said.

The whole thing has been a cover-up to protect the attorneys themselves and prevent us as citizens of this country from going to Supreme Court for a fair trial. I exploded, "Why were Michael and Dan so intent on keeping us out of a Supreme Court as a trial?"

I then asked if he thought the Supreme Court Judges were involved in the delaying of our case for over thirteen years. Holding the letter and the order signed by Judge Glownia, Peter looked at me. "I asked Dan way back in 2011 when I faxed this to him if the order signed by Judge Glownia had anything to do with a violation of his court."
"What did he say?"

"He said he would look into if after I sent the Motion filled out by Michael to him."

"And why did Harold Bulan legally stop the case from continuing in Supreme Court?" I asked.

"They all would have made more money." was Peter's reply. "Harold Bulan himself stood to make over $400,000 from both our cases, remember he wanted 20% from both of us and we had two not one corporation lawsuits. Someone in Supreme Court took it upon themselves to combine both our separate cases into one."

"Who do you think did that, who would have the most to gain, not financially but, with a false sense of importance and power?" "Would it be one of the Confidential Law Clerks to the Judges or Michael Drumm?" Once again my frustration with the court system over flowed.

I continued, "The fact that Michael had all the correct paperwork back to 2000, including all the reports from the various fire, and police departments. It also indicates that he and Dan joined forces. What were all these attorney's names written down in Mike Drumm's handwriting after I wrote him indicating he needed to keep open communication the same month in May of 2008, right before we filed the ethics complaint in September?" Peter looked at me asking, "Do you think he wrote the names the same month in May of 2008, you wrote him?"

"I'm not sure but, he mentions the same attorney in a letter he sent you that very same month. Why would his name also be on the stapled paperwork, with his own check order stub we found in Dan's file today?"

Peter replied, "I don't know but, we used Magic Jack to get the files from Brown & Chiari and this paperwork was not included, a deal had to be made between Daniel, Michael and possibly Harold Bulan."

My first thought was, what a crowd of thieves we had run across in Buffalo. Apparently, they had no shame. My second thought was that the paperwork had to be given to Judge Kaplan on September 3, the day after Labor Day. He was being made a fool of by Harold Bulan and Daniel Schoenborn. It was shameful.

We didn't know what to do, there was no time to connect with the courts. It was Sunday and Monday was the Labor Day holiday. We were flying into Buffalo late on Tuesday, and the court date was Wednesday. We had followed Judge Kaplan's budgeting tips and made the plane reservation as late in the day as possible, arriving after the court closed on Tuesday afternoon.

I would have to introduce the evidence into his courtroom that morning along with the original receipts for the tools of trade that were exempt from the bankruptcy and should have been paid by Peerless Insurance.

Judge Bucki had let Peter have his say on July 7, surely I would get to have mine. As the participant within the legal system of the courthouse I had the right to freedom of speech under the First Amendment to the Constitution. I had to be able to state my case and at least show the Judge he had made a mistake about the tools of trade issue. The other paperwork was a different matter and a serious one. I was not sure what to do with it. I knew I had to give Judge Kaplan the respect he deserved to know the real story about the attorneys that came before him in his courtroom.

CHAPTER 45: THE QUEEN

The Queen moves in a straight line, but cannot jump over other pieces. Which pretty much describes my personality when I know a wrong has been done.

Tuesday morning came quickly enough. The flight out of Tampa was crowded and the Southwest plane was completely full. Thinking it was a good time to write in my tablet, I picked an aisle seat with Peter across the way. I could write in the tablet my ideas for the book that was now outlined in a rough form ready to be filled in with the events and the cast of characters.

A young man came up to my seat before we took off. He looked as if he worked for the airline and was hitching a ride to start his day out of Chicago or Buffalo. As I wrote furiously, he sat down in the middle seat. He was quiet and ready for his day. As the plane lifted up into the sky, I continued to write with a passion newly founded, having the time and the energy to continue until we got to Buffalo, New York.

Within an hour, the man sitting next to me needed to get by me to visit the crew clustered in the back of the plane. As he passed over my, seat he turned looking at the tablet he said, "You are writing intensely on your tablet."

Stopping for the moment I answered, "Yes I'm writing a book."

"Fiction or nonfiction?"

'Non-fiction." I replied.

He laughed and stated, "Good there is too much fiction in this world." I laughed with him, thinking if you only knew what was going on you would be very curious indeed.

Twenty minutes later he returned. I was still writing at a furious pace. He sat down and commented, "How is the book coming?"

Looking at him, I told him it was my first book and it was tedious work but it had to be done. The conversation continued with me giving him the finer details of our long expedition through the court system in Buffalo.

"What do you do for a living?" he asked.

Telling him I had been a massage therapist for years, he yelped "Me too, over in Clearwater!"

I squealed back, "This is great news, someone to talk to about something else other than the courtrooms of Buffalo."

We yakked away for the rest of the trip about the massage business, the different techniques, the classes we had taken after graduation what we thought of the different instructors. It was a blessing; he had broken the spell of feeling constantly on the defense. All to soon the plane landed in Chicago, it was time for him to start his shift and the woman next to him by the window had probably endured the worst flight in her life. Nothing worse than listening to two massage therapists talking the talk. Knowing we would probably never see each other again we wished each other well in our adventures.

Soon the plane landed in Buffalo. We rented a car and we checked the time to see if the courts were still open. Apparently they had closed for the day and we would not be able to talk to Judge Kaplan, or anyone else. We then drove to the hotel to check in. Then, getting back into the car driving once again to the Globe restaurant in East Aurora. We chatted with the staff as if we still lived there. The winter of 2014 had been especially brutal, the summer cold, and winter they had been warned of was fast approaching. It would be one of the worst on record for the Western New York area.

Finishing dinner, I called Buffalo Snoop on my throw-away cell phone. During the conversation I mentioned the newly found evidence, "It's too late to call the courthouse, so you will have to introduce it to Judge Kaplan tomorrow in the courtroom. After you leave his hearing meet me on Sheridan Drive towards Delaware Avenue." Click.

As we edged back to our hotel, Peter commented, "We can't ever come back here again. If we had known when we lived here what had been going on we could have prevented it. But we didn't, so let's call this our last trip, the City of Good Neighbors is not the town for us, they treated us like yesterday's garbage while we were here, it's time to turn the page."

I looked at him. "Why yes, and don't forget the attorneys have been using the Buffalo wooden nickel to nickel and dime us, and probably others to death for years while, they used the money we paid them to cover their own asses. The asses that they are."

We pulled into the hotel and spent the night in the front lobby copying the paperwork to be given to Judge Kaplan and Harold Bulan, the nightmare attorney who had control over our lives over the last ten years. Compiling the original invoices from Key Bank for the machinery, the original invoices for the Pilates and massage equipment, Michael's letter to the Hamburg Police inquiring about the fire eight years after the fact, and last but not least the deal that had been made between Michael and Dan to continue the violation of our civil liberties and civil rights including Katherine Fijal lying about the first deposition in 2001 and, the constant tax authorizations that the Peerless Insurance and the rest of the attorneys had since the beginning of the lawsuit.

These people made me sick to my stomach.

The missing piece to the chess board had finally been found. So much hatred, attorneys covering up and then charging their clients for their intentional mistakes to keep themselves above the law. It was disgusting and gluttonous. To have attorneys and possibly law clerks to the various judges covering for each other under the name of "justice for all" and "do no harm" was a joke. They would protect each other first, apparently even if a Judge got in the way.

September 2, 2014, had been a long day. Finishing the paperwork, we turned in early for the best night's sleep in over a decade.

The next day, feeling refreshed and ready to go fight the next battle, we headed for the courthouse. Reaching the entrance, I felt a little queasy remembering Judge Kaplan had a history of always siding with Harold Bulan. Walking toward the security area, one of the guards appeared to be either new or was filling in for the now familiar one. As I pulled my license out of the billfold my gun permit fell on the floor. He looked at my license, and asked if I was related to anyone in Hamburg.

"Used to be ages ago." I said.

"Who is your Judge?" he asked.

"Kaplan. He is going to beat me into the ground and take me down."

"Who is representing you?"

"Myself."

"Ahh. You are doing it the right way." was the reply.

It was a bizarre conversation but it reminded me of a quote about courage in the book To Kill a Mockingbird. "It's when you know you have been licked before you begin but you begin anyway and you see it through no matter what. You rarely win but, sometimes you do."

The guard then added "Are you carrying?" Referring to my gun permit in Florida.

"No, but I do in Florida, just to protect myself."

"From what?" he asked.

Ignoring the question, laughing to myself, I picked my identification along with my gun permit, smiling at the men as we continued through the gate. Turning to them I smiled, "So you used to be New York State Police?"

"Yes, we are retired."

"Nice gig, see you later!"

As we headed up the elevator, I was surprisingly at ease. Soon we arrived in front of the courtroom of Judge Kaplan to wait for the courtroom doors to open. Within a few minutes the elevator door opened. Harold Bulan without his protectors, shuffled his feet to the area as if it was just another case.

Starting with the usual pleasantries he seemed uneasy sitting with us. I didn't want him to have a clue of what the years of torment he had done to us. I let him ramble on about himself. He had grown up outside of Manhattan coming to Buffalo to secure a license to practice in the Eighth District of New York.

On and on he went about his life and career. Hearing about his family and the enjoyment he got from them. Sitting there, looking at him with amazement I, could not believe what was coming out of his foul mouth. "I need to retire, and do it now, I need to visit with my grandchildren." I almost lost it right then and there. This little man had now gone on for more than twenty minutes about himself, nothing about anything other subject than him.

Not only had he bungled the bankruptcy, he never answered phone calls or letters, certified or not. Almost in a rage, I was thinking, "so you stopped me from seeing my grandchildren, forced me out of Buffalo with probably Michael and his boss's blessing, you dropped the bankruptcy only to open it again, then tried to close it again without our knowledge in January of 2013."

I laughed and pretended he was my buddy just like Buffalo Snoop had told me, "He is not your friend, play along with him."

The elevator door opened once again. Dan Schoenborn entered the lobby and sat on the bench the farthest away from not only us but Harold Bulan as well. "Hello Jo Anne." I looked at him with revulsion then almost laughed. His appearance was hardly professional in a rumpled wrinkled suit as if he had been out all night long. Eyeballing him, I wanted him to know what I had in my briefcase. Harold Bulan was still rambling on about West Palm Beach while I kept my eyes on Dan. He was nervous, frumped up and wrinkled. Purposely I shifted my eyes to Harold Bulan still yakking away. As I did, I got what I wanted, Dan was looking at my briefcase and possibly realizing what it contained. He was wringing his hands, shifting his weight in his chair and sweating profusely.

The new round of the chess game was on my shoulders and I had to keep it going in Federal Judge Kaplan's courtroom. My moves had to be precise and accurate. I was the defendant with no money, all I had was my right to free speech in the courtroom of Federal Judge Michael Kaplan. I felt confident the Judge would give me that entitlement and see the case for what it was, a sham.

The doors to the courtroom opened. We entered the room, filing to our normal spot: second row from the front on the left. Harold Bulan and Daniel Schoenborn sat as far away as they could on the right side of the dirty, corrupt courtroom.

TRANSCRIPT FROM JO ANNE GLEASON'S HEARING

SEPTEMBER 3, 2014   10:04 A.M.

BEFORE FEDERAL JUDGE MICHAEL KAPLAN

The chime rang "All Rise."

Page 2, Line 1: Judge Kaplan, states "Jo Anne Gleason is here. Mr. Bulan is the trustee and the other appearance-------"

Page 2, Line 6: "Daniel Schoenborn, special counsel for the trustee."

Page 2, Line 9: Judge Kaplan starts admonishing me, claiming I did not do as he told me, that I did not hire an attorney. It was not true - I had an attorney and Harold Bulan pulled him from my Supreme Court case and hired him for your courtroom Judge, you see he got a better deal. Judge Kaplan starts to raise his voice with agitation as if I had created the mess, adding my Certificate of Service states I oppose everything that Harold Bulan had done with my case.

Page 2, Line 15: On the record that was being recorded, I agreed with the Judge stating I did oppose everything that Harold Bulan had done as trustee. He had made a mess deliberately with no regard to the people he was representing. He was making me pay for the tools of trade.

Page 2, Line 16L: Judge Kaplan was getting angrier, the veins on the side of his right neck were starting to protrude through his collar of his robe, again overrules me. He tells me my objections are not sufficient and will he not let me speak to say why I oppose it. His face is turning a bright red as he continues to raise his voice louder defending Harold Bulan. He states the United States Trustee has audited Harold Bulan's report and has approved it.

I wanted to protest and tell Judge Kaplan I had never seen the United States Trustee's report and if it did exist, both Peter and I should have had it made available for us for review. We had never seen any paperwork from Harold Bulan for over ten years. I wanted to scream back at Judge Michael Kaplan. "Hey, Judge, who the hell was sending out stuff from this courthouse to phony addresses across the country?

Instead I let it go.

The Judge, with his voice rising to almost a high pitch scream, with the right side of his jugular neck veins pulsating even more, goes on to say the commissions, attorney's fees and the calculation of the distributions to creditors had been examined by the paralegals or the accountants in the Office of the United States Trustee. His face was now contorted in a visible weirdness. I let him continue. He said, you have said nothing over the years about why you object to every payment in this case. I had a feeling he knew we were never in contact with Harold Bulan after his bizarre 341 Hearing. His rage was showing because we were perhaps the first to ever object to Harold Bulan or the Federal Court under Judge Michael Kaplan or Judge Carl Bucki's helm.

Page 2, Line 25: Judge Kaplan continues, "One of them is a sizable one to the New York Department of Taxation and Finance, another one for Erie County." This was the exact opposite of the previous June 7, 2014, transcripts where Judge Kaplan said I did not owe taxes. He was not reading his own paperwork or Harold Bulan had steered him the wrong way.

I was amused by his lack of knowledge of the case or his concern for the mistakes that had taken place over the last ten years in his courtroom. It looked like the gossip I heard over the summer had been right, he always sided with the trustee Harold Bulan. It seemed almost unreal what he came out with next.

Page 3, Lines 1 to 7: "There is a Lord and Taylor for $182.00, GE Capital consumer card for $483.00, Kaufman's for $48.70 Pamela Ashmall for $1125.80. Citibank----must be a credit card---Citibank Choice---for $7548.48 and Key Bank for $7548.48 and Key Bank for $9337.62."

I had gone bankrupt with supposedly $488,000.00 in assets and owed less than $800.00 to department stores and another $1,125.80 to Pamela Ashmall, who had copied the personal files of our clients at Advanced Massage Therapy for her own use. Thankfully I have kept her address book until this day, let her work for it. HIPAA Law or not, she had done it, over ten years ago. Harold Bulan had let us go into bankruptcy over this amount and made sure we stayed there. I wondered how he had managed to keep the information away from us for over ten years. Did it have to do with Brown & Chiari? Since Harold Bulan's law partner is a Chiari brother?

It was then I heard a bankruptcy claimant say directly behind my back, within the range of the Judge the attorneys and myself to hear. She apparently turned to her lawyer stating, "Do you believe the money she spent?" I almost cackled like Buffalo Snoop. What a dope she was and a great fit right into the frame of gossip mongers forming their own opinion without the facts. I laughed to myself. She did not have a clue what was going on in Judge Kaplan's courtroom. I wanted to turn around and ask her why she was in bankruptcy court that day. I didn't. I would wait and get a good view of her and her attorney when I left this fiasco.

Page 3, Line 8: I icontinued to ignore the stupid comment made by this woman as I carried on and answered the charges, I was against "All of them." I had gone bankrupt over a total bill of under $800. Everything else was exempt under the tools of trade. They were business related, and they knew it. Unbelievably, the Judge and Harold Bulan did not realize this or he thought he would not be trapped. This court was an embarrassment to the Eighth District of Western New York. As I concentrated on this ridiculous court scene, it crossed my mind to investigate how close this Judge was to Harold Bulan and what made him so angry with me.

Page 3, Lines 9 to 17: Judge Kaplan is now in a full-fledged rant screaming at me, his head, bobbing, as if a circuit breaker was going to pop any minute in his head. I was amazed he had gotten this far out of control in the courtroom, apparently my little case had confused him to the point where he did not know what had gone on over the years. I was not sure if he was aware of it or I was getting to close or something else. He first states my objections are not entered right, which they were according to the paperwork and my contacts in Tampa. He states, my objection is overruled. The allowances are approved.

Page 3, Line 18: I state, "May I enter something I found Sunday night Your Honor?"

As soon I asked to be heard by the court, Daniel started to pass behind me, he violently pushed through the gates turning him from an attorney in a court case to a court room observer. He was running up the center of the courtroom aisle heading towards the exit doors to get out as fast as he could, while the fellow participants in the courtroom watched.

Surprised at his sudden departure, it was my turn with the judge. Daniel had his chance in January of 2013, when he had been a no show. He had let Morris Horwitz, the new partner to Harold Bulan's office, handle the case before Judge Kaplan with totally inaccurate information either given to him by Attorney Schoenborn or made up in his head. Whatever it was, it was the first set of lies we had become aware of after being in Harold Bulan's clutches.

Dan had ditched Harold Bulan, leaving him alone with me in front of the Judge. Harold Bulan was in danger of doing another swan dive, with no one to save him. Remarkably he held up well under the stress of standing before the Judge. I had a number of things to speak about I and it was time Harold Bulan sat up and took notice of the damage he had done to other people's lives, before he retired or died.

Feeling unbelievably calm and distant, I continued my objections of the bungled mess made by Harold Bulan, of now trying to enter the original receipts from the very corporations that indicated the machinery, and the equipment that was exempt tools of trade. The Judge would not have any part of it. Then I explained the deal between Michael and Dan, written in Michael's handwriting. Suddenly I knew I had to protect the paperwork. There would be fingerprints of both of the participants on it. I wanted to make a statement to the court.

Page 3, Line 20: Judge Kaplan screams "No, I gave you three months to."

Page 3, Line 21: I ask, "May I make a statement to the court?"

It was at this point I realized that a number of amendments to the Constitution had been violated by the courtrooms in Buffalo. This latest was the First Amendment and the freedom of speech. This Judge would not let me enter my plea as a participant.

Page 3, Line 22: Judge Kaplan continued, "No it's overruled." As he continued screaming, a refreshed Daniel Schoenborn turned from the half opened exit door at the back of the courtroom and came back through the gates, once again making himself the attorney representing Harold Bulan as his most trusted attorney and, the Administrator of our bankruptcy case.

Page 3, Lines 24 to 25: Judge Kaplan is now coming down from his rant and suggests "You can appeal the case after the distribution is made." Then the oddest of all statements, "Let me see. No, I don't sign the final order of distribution. So you can appeal the order approving the trustee's fees, and you can say what you want to the District Court, but---" inaudible.

I found it very strange Judge Kaplan had gone into a tirade, as Daniel had made his way back and forth through the gates representing Harold Bulan. The secret had been kept.

Page 4, Line 1: Judge Kaplan then laid the biggest bomb I could hope for. Snoop Tampa had said, "Just get him to say the words 'appeal.'"

"You can appeal the order approving the trustee's fees, and you can say what you what to the District Court, but---" inaudible.

I had to look like the biggest idiot in the room that day, I had gotten my job done with the words flowing out of the Judges mouth with a venom, "Appeal." I almost yelled out to Judge Kaplan, "Not in this Eighth District, Judge. Sorry, I don't live here, I live in Tampa and you, Sir, are representing a Federal District Court that crosses all states of this country, not just New York."

I let it ride.

Page 4, Line 4: I again ask the Judge to allow me to state my case of the tools of trade with the various loans, including Key Bank. He shut me down with another scolding, I was happy about it, participating in this ridiculous drama in a Federal courtroom in Buffalo. It was so amazing to go through the corruption and realize the whole district was a mess and it needed to be looked into.

I let the record roll.

Page 4, Line 6: Judge Kaplan once again states I had not done the paperwork right and goes along with Harold Bulan, once again giving me tips of how to live in bankruptcy world.

Page 4, Line 11: I'm still trying to get my say in the courthouse under the First Amendment and Judge Kaplan is shutting me down again.

Page 4, Lines 12 to 14: Judge Kaplan says, "You are trying to take the easy cheap road out." More than slightly offended by his opinion, which in no way was neutral for the Judge, I replied, "No, Your Honor, I did not."

Page 4, Line 15: "Yes you are." The beginnings of a pissing match are once again started by Judge Kaplan. I felt as if I was back in the grammar school yard defending myself against a bully.

Page 4, Lines 19 to 22: The insults continued as he now turned into a parent, "Don't argue with me. You've had ten years to object to these claims, and I gave you three additional months and you didn't. Your objections are overruled. I will not give you leave to say anything further."

Page 4, Line 23: "Fine with me." Smiling to the Judge and Harold Bulan, who looked as if he had missed the whole thing or was so used to winning with this judge, he did not pay attention.

Daniel Schoenborn looked as if he had just swallowed a toad, wringing his hands, he was bent over in his cheap wrinkled beige suit. No worries, he would be buying another one. He had just collected another $33,333 to put in his pocket, for a total of over $66,666.67 from both Peter and me to keep us out of Supreme Court. Funny thing about the numbers he had just gotten in his paycheck, you know, all those 6's and everything.

Court adjourned at 10:08 a.m

My case took four minutes. I felt sorry for those claimants following me. The Judge started with a bad day and he was not happy.

I turned around to face the courtroom straight on. Glancing at the stupid woman sitting right behind me who, had made the irresponsible remark behind my back, both she and her attorney were looking at my two opposing attorneys Harold Bulan and Daniel Schoenborn.

I wondered if Judge Kaplan knew and he was covering up for Harold Bulan. My First Amendment right had been denied both as a plaintiff and in Supreme Court and again as a defendant or debtor in Federal Court. Whatever it was it felt like a violation of my civil rights.

My case had taken four minutes, with a screaming Federal Judge who had the wrong information in front of him. How he could not realize this was overwhelming, was beyond me. All he had to do was his homework and view the previous transcripts he was part of to see the big picture.

I then turned to Peter, who was sitting to the right of the judgmental woman. He was looking at me with surprise at what he had just witnessed, the antics of Judge Kaplan, Harold Bulan, and Dan Schoenborn had been observed by the filled courtroom.

Smiling to myself, I had accomplished what Tampa Snoop had told me get the Judge to say the word "appeal." Turning to the courtroom and Peter, I said, "The Goose just laid the golden egg." Loud enough for the two rows behind the woman with the bad attitude to hear and her attorney, who was now looking the other way to avoid any eye contact with me. I scanned the courtroom to see what the reaction was. Not one person looked at me straight on, perhaps afraid the Federal Judge would catch them looking the wrong way. It was then I saw Snoop slinking down on the pew in the back of the room surrounded by attorneys and their clients.

Harold Bulan bounced up from his bench and rushed up once again to be the first out of the courtroom. Standing before him holding my hand to his face, I said, "Wait a minute you and your new Administrator Dan Schoenborn need to show a little respect for me, back off." Dan sat back down on the bench looking sweaty and frumpy as if he had just run a marathon. Looking at him for the last time I muttered low enough for him to hear me. "You need some sleep boy, you look like you have been out all night." If this last comment would not resonate with the observers in this courtroom, I did not care. I was done with the corrupt behavior of this town and the courthouses. It was loaded with corruption of a double- edged sword.

Harold Bulan who was practically crawling up my backside to let me through the gates, that changed me from an attorney to just another victim of a hustle job. I walked up the center aisle looking at the people filled benches, pushed open the huge wood door and out of the courtroom. The Queen had just taken over the deadly chess moves going on in the chess game. "His Majesty" was following me like a duck his feet flapping on the carpet as if he was following his Mama to water.

Outside of the courtroom, Harold Bulan waddled up to me "I need your address." Laughing at him, I directed him to the nearby bench we had sat on less than an hour before. As we sat down to enjoy our second conversation in the last ten years, Daniel came rushing out of the courtroom in a panic hustling his in his cheap beige suit towards the elevator. Casually, I looked up at Dan Schoenborn as he made a beeline for the elevator, he knew had been caught, along with the rest of the corrupt attorneys all one hot weekend in Florida.

I laughed at his stupidity and lack of professionalism, following the stupidity of the apparent y deceitful Brown & Chiari and their attorney Michael Drumm.

As we continued to sit at the bench while Dan was running the emotional marathon to the elevator, Harold made a major faux pas and it was too late for him to change it. He was nervously fishing for his pen and a piece of paper out of his pocket.

"Look at him." I chided to Peter who was standing nearby. "Don't you have a notebook for your paperwork Harold?"

Ignoring my question, "I need your address." he repeated.

Putting my arm around him as if we were good old cronies locked into the same deal, I answered. "Harold, you have it, and have had it for years, we both know you messed up the bankruptcy with the 'tools of trade' and you helped put us out of business, why Harold did you wait so long to reopen the case?"

Squirming, he said, "I need your address."

"No, wait Harold I have something for you."

"What?"

"Just wait a minute Harold I have to find it in my file." "Oh here it is, the letter Dan Schoenborn sent to you last year with our address on it. Oh wait, look see? Here are the certified receipts for the letters we sent you. Sorry I'm keeping these but you can have the letter."

Handing the letter to him, he watched me replace the receipts. He then stated. "I never saw this letter." Digging into my file again I pulled out more Certified receipts from the Post Office. "Have you seen these Harold?" He shifted his weight from one foot to the other. I decided if he started to do another swan dive, I would let him go slamming into the worn out carpet of the Federal Courthouse.

"Oh come on Harold you have certainly seen all the letters we sent you, I mean we have these certified copies of it." I continued. "Oh wait let me get this paperwork out, sorry this is our paperwork not yours. You probably have your own copy at your office of Bulan, Illecki, Goldstein & Chiari." I again pulled out all the certified letters and receipts that his office had signed for.

Harold Bulan protested, "My name is not on the partnership."

I laughed, "That's right you are retiring aren't you?"

He was trying to get away from me. I pulled myself closer to him. "Harold look at me." He sat looking down at his shoes. Taking my two fingers I pointed them from my eyes to the side of his then back again, to mine. "Harold look at me right now meet me in the eye Harold."

He turned his lowered head towards me and looked at me with no shame.

"Guess what Harold, you have been... had!"

He replied, "I don't think so, I got to go now."

Standing up and bustling towards the elevator door he disappeared. Probably to meet up with Dan in the nearby restaurant for an early contaminated lunch.

Peter had been standing out of hearing distance came up. "What was that all about?"

"Nothing I just gave Harold some of his own medicine."

Peter moving on to the next topic spoke of Judge Kaplan and Daniel Schoenborn. "I have never seen a Judge scream at anyone in a courtroom like Kaplan did to you?" " Did you see Dan start to run out of the courtroom?"

"Yep, I felt him sweep by, and everyone else in the courtroom saw it." "Doesn't take a genius to figure out that something was going on under the of suit jacket pockets of the two attorneys. Looking at Peter I stated "I wonder about the Judge don't you? Why all the screaming?"

Peter then continued, "Well we got our wish. Judge Kaplan said we could appeal it, maybe we can take it to Federal Court in Tampa." He continued, "Tampa is not a district court like Buffalo, it is the real deal adding they will have to fly to Tampa to defend themselves."

I added, "Bulan could drive, he spends his time in West Palm remember?"

Leaving the courthouse, we got into the rental car anxious to meet Buffalo Snoop who we had not seen before this day, since meeting in Florida. Driving to the restaurant, it would be the last time we would meet, and the first time in a restaurant. Snoop had served us right and was the only one in Buffalo that had stepped up to the plate to help us out saying since the beginning in 1999, that "things are not right."

We entered the restaurant, going to the back room. Fortunately, it was not crowded and we would be able to have a quiet conversation. As we sat down a waitress came to our table. "Anything to drink?"

"Yes a double vodka please, and an appetizer."

It was delivered within minutes and we savored the last meal we ever had in Buffalo.

Having made good time from the courthouse, Snoopy arrived walking through the aisles of the restaurant plopping down next to Peter. "Have a drink Snoop, we have to celebrate, Buffalo has kicked us out of town and we are happy about it."

Another order for a double went into the waitress.

"We have to wait for the transcripts from today until the end of the week, but, I can show you this."

Handing over the packet of the deal made between Dan and Michael. "Look here is where Michael presented the Motion. And here is the signature of Judge Glownia," adding, "here are the handwritten notes written by Michael and the fax from our address on October 11, 2011 to Dan."

"Do they know you have this?"

"I think Schoenborn figured it out today that he had forgotten to purge his files before we picked them up. Isn't it a federal offense to withhold information in a Supreme Court or Federal Court?"

"What do you mean?"

"Well they used the phone lines and the internet to commit deceitful actions involving two courtrooms of the Eighth District. Schoenborn withheld information of the Supreme Court and Judges Glownia, Chimes, and Dillon. I would think that would be a crime for an attorney to lie to a Judge. Then they did it again in Federal Court."

"What!" Snoop exclaimed.

I continued, saying to Snoop and Peter, "We just got our first notification of any paperwork from Harold Bulan in May of this year. Before that, there were letters made out to a huge amount of phony addresses. When we got the Certificates of Service it was our first notice in ten years of what was noted in the bankruptcy case, and everything Bulan entered with court, everything we owed, had to do with the tools of trade. I went bankrupt in Buffalo for $713 and some change. Kaplan would not let me introduce it today, you saw him he was totally out of control, it was ridiculous way for any judge to act in public or even worse in a courtroom."

I asked Buffalo Snoop "Do you think he knew?"

Buffalo Snoop looked back at me with shock. "What the hell. Is this a cover up with the attorneys? How much do you have, and do they know it?"

I replied, "We have everything, all the Supreme Court paperwork from the courthouse. All of Michael Drumm's paperwork, all of Peerless Insurance paperwork from the four attorneys they had hired, all of Dan Schoenborn's paperwork,. all the statements from Gary Gable to the depositions. The Federal Courthouse letters sent to phony addresses. We have all the transcripts, we have the whole case from Supreme Court and for Federal Court. The only thing we are missing is the stuff from Pacer."

"You had to see Schoenborn run out of the courtroom only to come back when Kaplan refused to let me have my say. Kaplan refused my right under the First Amendment to the Constitution. Plus the

Certificate of Service was not good enough for him from me but it was good enough from his buddy Harold Bulan, who had done it wrong."

Snoop said, "Get this case out of Buffalo and put it where it belongs in Federal Court in Tampa. Buffalo is a district court, these guys have violated every rule within the two courthouses and used the postal service and internet to do it."

I laughed again. "These guys in Buffalo have screwed up the case so bad, how do I make it known to an attorney in Tampa without writing it down and enforcing it with paperwork collected from the files in our possession?"

"Yeah you are right, what do you think you should do?"

I said, "Well I started a diary of the chain of events a number of years ago when Michael Drumm started the case."

Snoop interrupted, "Yeah that was wild, personal injury attorneys taking your case, not even their specialty."

"Let me finish, I would sporadically take notes, then as the years passed without any results from Judge Glownia's courtroom, the notes intensified after we put a grievance against Brown & Chiari and Michael Drumm in 2008.

"I think the best way to get it out to the general public is to write a book about our experience and the corruption in the Eighth District in Buffalo. Any attorney we would try and obtain would not be able to get through the massive amount of paperwork we have in the storage unit, and make it worth his while. If I write it down because we know the chain of events and had lived it, it would be easier to understand. Let's just say, I was forced into it and we will see how it turns out," adding my parent's adage, "If we know the true facts and do nothing about it is a bad as if we also committed the crimes."

"They might sue you." Buffalo Snoop stated.

Peter retorted smiling as only he can to Snoop, "It would be good for book sales wouldn't it? And we could get the facts out to any attorney who might enjoy representing our case. After all we were called 'an attorney's dream' by some lawyers in Tampa."

We laughed knowing this was the end of it for both of us in Buffalo. Having been friends for so many years we had seen a lot of bad things going on around us. Greed, hate, and jealousy, followed by gossip. We were denied the main things that kept you from living as a human being and made it through.

Finally, free to make my own choices, our tough time had been served in this town.

We had gotten what we came for in Buffalo New York, the transcripts that would hold the untold story of how far people will go to hide the truth, to fulfill their own self-importance.

It would be another year of fighting in Buffalo court system before we were set free. Peter would call for the paperwork from the Office of the United States Trustee in Buffalo to send us the final paperwork. It would take a few months and then repeated phone calls by Peter, who finally threatened them with a choice: "Either send the documents or we will prosecute in Federal Court here in Tampa for withholding our paperwork from us"

"Why?" the female would say at the other end of the phone in Buffalo.

Peter continued, "I need it for my files."

It was followed by a another "why?" Then by a "We don't do that, we send files to no one, angain asking the ever present "Why?"

He answered, "Because I do, it's a public document, if you don't send it I will take you to Federal Court here in Tampa."

On August 7, 2015, short by twenty-one days to being a full fifteen years since that fateful day on August 28, 2000, the paperwork was sent from Buffalo. It was filled with the same false statements Harold Bulan had set forth before. We were told by one of the staff, "we are sending it as a courtesy," as if we were not allowed under the law to have it in our possession. Evidently no one had ever asked for it before.

Looking through the paperwork It was signed by a Jill Zubler. "Looking a Peter I said "That name is familiar to me and I don't know why." He replied "That is the woman that showed up in court in June when I was before Judge Bucki." " Remember? she pushed through the gates and sat down at the conference table." "The one that told Judge Bucki that

Harold Bulan had called her?" I asked. "Yes the very same one." It was totally insane. All over greed, jealousy and hate."

"Was she the one you talked to when you called the Office of the United States Trustee in Buffalo?"

"That I couldn't tell you but, I did speak with a woman." "Interesting I replied, as I wrote a note to myself on my tablet.

It was time to sit down with all the proof of our statements and finish the book we had started so long ago.

Good or bad, the punctuation sometimes not correct, it was our story, we had lived it, breathed it, been tortured by it, suffered sickness through it, we spent tens of thousands of dollars in attorney's fees, we had been subject to lies and cheating and some serious issues with the court system in Buffalo, New York.

We took no prisoners, using the names of the Cast of Characters placed in the front of the book.

We had heard, "They're going to come after you."

"They will probably kill you."

"You better watch it, carry your gun."

I really did not care if they came after us or not. We will make sure everything is kept mum until the book comes out.

This is a book written by our own hands letting people know to investigate in case something happens to us. Until it is published, it will be held for in a safe place.

It was that easy….

ABOUT THE AUTHORS

Peter Kirisits and Jo Anne Gleason had met twice before during their lives in Buffalo, New York. They had found each other again in the early 90's. Peter having been a causality of a large steel company closing. It was then he was hired by Roblin Steel as an electrical foreman. The opportunity came before him to start a outsourcing company in Buffalo, New York which he took. Jo Anne following her divorce about the same time went to nursing school. Finding this to be incompatible she followed her instinct to be a Massage Therapist when a school opened in Buffalo. Twenty plus years later she is still enjoying her profession working for a Doctor in Tampa Bay.

Plaintiff to Defendant

www.ingramcontent.com/pod-product-compliance
Lightning Source LLC
Chambersburg PA
CBHW072003150426
43194CB00008B/979